CW00670245

Other Books by James DeMeo

* *The Dynamic Ether of Cosmic Space: Correcting a Major Error in Modern Science*, 2019.

* *Saharasia: The 4000 BCE Origins of Child Abuse, Sex-Repression, Warfare and Social Violence In the Deserts of the Old World*, Revised Second Edition, 2006.

* *In Defense of Wilhelm Reich: Opposing the 80-Years' War of Mainstream Defamatory Slander Against One of the 20th Century's Most Brilliant Physicians and Natural Scientists*, 2013.

* *Preliminary Analysis of Changes in Kansas Weather Coincidental to Experimental Operations with a Reich Cloudbuster: From a 1979 Research Project*, 2010.

* *Marx Engels Lenin Trotsky: Genocide Quotes. The Hidden History of Communism's Founding Tyrants, in their own words*, 2016.

* (Editor) *Heretic's Notebook: Emotions, Protocells, Ether-Drift and Cosmic Life-Energy, with New Research Supporting Wilhelm Reich*, 2002

* (Co-Editor with Bernd Senf) *Nach Reich: Neue Forschungen zur Orgonomie: Sexualökonomie, Die Entdeckung der Orgonenergie*, 1997

* (Editor) *On Wilhelm Reich and Orgonomy*, 1993

For Additional Information on the Orgone Accumulator adding to what is found in this *Handbook*, see:
www.orgonelab.org/orgoneaccumulator.htm

The Orgone Accumulator Handbook

Wilhelm Reich's Life-Energy Discoveries and Healing Tools for the 21st Century, with Construction Plans

James DeMeo, PhD

Third Revised and Expanded Edition with New Sections on *Living Water* and the *Cosmic Ether of Space*, plus Many Weblinks for Additional Information.

Natural Energy Works
OBRL Greensprings Center
Ashland, Oregon, USA
www.naturalenergyworks.net

Publication and worldwide distribution rights:

Natural Energy Works
PO Box 1148
Ashland, Oregon 97520
United States of America
http://www.naturalenergyworks.net
Email: info@naturalenergyworks.net

ISBN: 978-0980231632   0980231639
Third Revised and Expanded Edition, 2010

200410

Library of Congress Catalog Card No. 89-90975

Front Cover: NASA photo of Apollo 12 astronaut walking on the surface of the moon (see Life Magazine, 12 Dec. 1969). His body orgone energy field is softly glowing a blue color in the lunar vacuum, possibly due to excitation by his high-frequency radio communications equipment. This blue coloration of the energy field in the photo, which has been seen in a few other lunar astronaut images (but often deleted in published versions) has been systematically ignored or explained away as an effect of "lunar dust", "water vapor" or "camera lens smudges". In fact, it is a visible expression of the human orgone (life) energy field. For more information, see:
        http://www.orgonelab.org/astronautblues.htm

Rear Cover: Orgone accumulator stimulation of sprouting mung beans, experiment by author, see page 153.

Acknowledgments

This book is the product of many years of experimental investigation and study of the prior research findings of Dr. Wilhelm Reich, and other dedicated physicians, healers and scientists, without whose efforts it would not have been possible. The reader will find their names and publications listed in the Reference section of this book. I have corresponded with, and learned from many of these researchers over the years. In particular, I thank Dr. Eva Reich and Jutta Espanca for their constructive criticisms of the first edition of this *Handbook*. Additionally, I thank my own mentors, Robert Morris, Prof. Robert Nunley, and Dr. Richard Blasband, from each of whom I learned different things about life energy. I thank Theirrie Cook and Don Bill, loyal friends who have helped with the progress of my research in many ways, and also James Martin for the initial ideas and encouragement to revise my original small *Handbook* into a more detailed edition. James also prepared the typesetting and graphics in the early editions, providing many helpful points along the way. Thanks also go to the various researchers and doctors in Germany, who today are openly working with the accumulator in a manner presently difficult in the USA. From them I learned about the possibilities and limitations of physical orgone accumulator therapy. Also thanks to Vince Wiberg, for the simple and inexpensive methods for detecting electromagnetic disturbances, presented here. A big appreciation also to my wife Daniela-Sabina, for her valuable proofreading and translating of many documents from German into English. And finally, *Thank You Wilhelm Reich*, for the discovery of the orgone energy and the orgone accumulator.

James DeMeo, PhD
Greensprings, Oregon
1989 (Revised 2013)

"We consider the discovery of the orgone energy among the greatest events in human history."– from a letter to the American Medical Association, signed by 17 medical doctors in 1949.

"THE ORGONE ACCUMULATOR IS THE MOST IMPORTANT SINGLE DISCOVERY IN THE HISTORY OF MEDICINE, BAR NONE" – Theodore P. Wolfe, M.D., from *Emotional Plague Versus Orgone Biophysics*, 1948.

"It is justifiable that the discovery of orgone energy and its medical applications by means of the orgone accumulator, the orgone shooter, bionous earth, and orgone water have opened up an abundance of new and, it appears, amazingly good prospects." – Wilhelm Reich, M.D. from *The Cancer Biopathy (Discovery of the Orgone, Volume 2)*, 1948.

"What would you say of the leading philosophers here to whom I have offered a thousand times of my own accord to show my studies, but who with the lazy obstinacy of a serpent who has eaten his full have never consented to look at the planets, the moon, or telescope? To such people philosophy is a kind of book... where the truth is to be sought not in the Universe or in nature, but (I use their own words) by comparing texts." – Galileo Galilei, Italian astronomer of the 1600s who proved that the Earth moved in the heavens, shortly before being prosecuted and threatened with torture by the Catholic Church. From a letter to Kepler, 19 August 1610.

"...the orgone energy does not exist."– Judge John D. Clifford, from a 1954 U.S. court ruling in which all of Dr. Reich's books and research journals were banned, and ordered burned in incinerators; Reich was later sent to a Federal Penitentiary, where he died

CONTENTS

Part III:
Construction Plans for
Orgone Accumulating Devices

Author's Preface

In the years following the 1989 publication of the English-language edition of *The Orgone Accumulator Handbook*, there has been a slow but steady growth of interest in the discoveries of Wilhelm Reich. Orgone accumulator therapy has spread around the world, from humble beginnings by Dr. Reich and a small circle of his students, and is now applied by every kind and form of health practitioner, as well as for self-treatment by ordinary people. Additionally, modern research undertaken on the issue of forest death adjacent to nuclear facilities, and the toxic nature of low-level atomic and electromagnetic poweline fields, cell-tower microwaves and radiofrequencies, has powerfully confirmed Reich's findings discussed under the term *oranur effect* (see Chapters 8 & 9). This book is not the place for a complete discussion of those related issues, but it underscores the need for anyone studying orgone energy functions in nature to become more aware of environmental factors. Nonetheless, one criticism of the early English editions which may hold some validity, is a too-cautious emphasis upon possible dangers from using the accumulator in polluted environments.

For example, in the text the reader is informed that it is unwise to use an accumulator within 30 to 50 miles of a nuclear power facility, or within "a few miles" of very high voltage power lines and large radio broadcasting towers. If people are already a bit anxious about the accumulator, I am told, these warnings may serve to dissuade them completely from ever trying it out. Such hesitancy might not be warranted. In Germany, for example, clinicians are treating patients with accumulators located in environments I previously might have considered "too polluted", such as within rooms or basements of structures located in large cities. Living on the West Coast of the USA, in a relatively clean and natural forested environment, one clearly has a different perspective from those who live in the hearts of cities, who do not wish to be excluded from the benefits of an accumulator, in spite of their surroundings. From those constructive critics I have learned the accumulator can be beneficially used, even in those more difficult environments. On the other hand, in recent years we have also seen an explosion in the use of microwave radiation as from cell phones and towers, wi-fi networks, "smart" meters and 5G systems, and every kind of "wireless" technology, the long-term life-energetic and toxic health consequences of which are increasingly being documented. When in doubt, it is best to obtain electromagnetic field meters and nuclear radiation detectors* for personal evaluations of the place where you will use and store your orgone accumulator – and where you live, sleep and work, for that matter, as we also are composed of life-energy – or to consult with someone who has that kind of expertise. I have also observed, some of the more sensitive orgone energy experiments definitely produce better results when the more stringent environmental guidelines are followed. In retrospect, if I do err, it clearly is on the side of caution.

While I have not changed the original text on these issues, and still view *moderate or strong* electromagnetic fields or nuclear contamination as a constraint against accumulator usage, the reader should view my cautions as an invitation to evaluate one's local environment. There are numerous possibilities for personal use and experimentation, and even in somewhat polluted environments an orgone accumulator can be water-cleaned, sheltered under a porch or in a ventilated room or garage location, and yield a healthy, strong energy charge (see Chapter 9).

I've expanded the Introduction to include *New Information on Reich's Persecution and Death*, identifying the central-most perpetrators which most people will not know about. Chapter 9 now includes a *Spectral Comparison of Different Light Bulbs with Natural Sunlight*, from an evaluation carried out at my institute, the Orgone Biophysical Research Lab (OBRL). This will literally be "eye-opening", especially if you've been suffering under the new and ugly compact fluorescent light bulbs, which are life-negative in character. Chapter 10 has been revised so as to emphasize the question of *Living Water,* which is an

---

* For example, see: www.naturalenergyworks.net

important adjunct to human use of the orgone accumulator. A new Appendix also provides additional details and findings on the *Cosmic Ether of Space*. I've also included an annotated review of cancer-mice experiments with the orgone accumulator, in Chapter 11. Some additional discussion is also given in the Questions section, on what orgone energy *is not*, to address a growing trend of destructive mystification of Reich's discoveries by various internet hawkers. The Question section also gives a bit of discussion on *psychic healing*, or "laying of hands" which itself requires some kind of energy exchange, similar or identical to the orgone energy. Many new graphics and images are added, to reflect newer research findings from OBRL, though for full scientific and experimental details, the reader must consult the original publications as given in the References. Overall, the scientific, historical and therapeutic discussions have been fleshed out considerably, given the abundance of newer findings. In most cases, however, I anticipate the reader will be hungry for even more details. For this, I have given many internet weblinks and published references.

This update was overdue and necessary. I believe it makes for a better and more helpful, accurate book.

James DeMeo, PhD
Greensprings, Oregon, USA
April 2010

1. Foreword

At last, thirty two years after the 1957 death of Wilhelm Reich, human beings can begin to study orgonomy like any other body of knowledge, helped by the *Orgone Accumulator Handbook*. This concise and informative book contains in a nutshell a condensed, clear account of the discovery, made usable by all who are interested in the cosmic life energy. Herein is printed: the scientific definition of the orgone energy; the history of how the steps of observation, experimentation, and theoretical insight led Reich to practical applications; the principles for construction and experimental uses of the orgone energy accumulator, with detailed suggestions for needed material, layering, and dimensions; and finally a very useful reference list. Professor J. DeMeo shows his thorough knowledge of the subject, which as yet is banned and omitted from the 20th Century academic curriculum, except for a few pioneering lecture courses (in New York and West Berlin).

Wilhelm Reich said that even though the life energy had been known for thousands of years, he managed to make it concretely usable, and that the era of its applications has just started. However, this *Handbook* is the first printed material in recent years on specifically how to concentrate the energy from the Earth's atmosphere. It is usable for a laboratory course on the subject of cosmic life energy. This material could be comprehended by intelligent high school or college students. It answers my almost fifty year old hope, for the inclusion of life energy facts in the body of knowledge that all educated people on Earth should learn in their schooling.

Thank you James DeMeo.

Eva Reich, MD
Berlin (West), March 1989

Wilhelm Reich, MD 1897-1957

2. Author's Introduction

When I was 12 years old, a favorite uncle of mine died a suffering death from lung cancer. The doctors had removed one of his lungs, and for a few months he lingered, being incapable of talking or moving very much, and in a great deal of pain. My aunts would not allow the children to see him in such sorry shape, except for one time, when he was dressed up for the entire family, which had gathered to quietly say good-bye. I was very sad when he died. When I was 15, my mother was diagnosed as having breast cancer. I was by her bed in the hospital when she recovered from surgery, and when she was told that her breast had been amputated in a radical mastectomy. I will never forget the look on her face. She survived the surgery, but the sexual stasis and emotional resignation which she carried, and which preceded her cancer by several decades, was never diagnosed or discussed. Friends of our family had urged us to look into some alternative treatments for cancer, but everybody believed the doctors in the hospital knew best. Listed as a "survivor" in the cancer statistics, my mother progressively declined after the surgery, and died about eight years later, having refused to undergo additional surgery.

My experience with relatives dying of cancer is not unusual, as degenerative disease is now at epidemic levels. The statistics today demonstrate the "war on cancer" has been lost, and that in spite of all the radical surgeries, drugs and radiation treatments, patients today survive no longer or more frequently than they did in the 1950s. Indeed, degenerative disorders have today spread into youthful age groups and populations where they once were rare. Scientific evidence does not exist to support the assertion that surgery, radiation, and chemotherapy are effective forms of treatment for cancer, and conventional medicine today gives hardly more than lip service to preventive considerations. These troubling facts become all the more disturbing when one begins to study the various alternative, non-invasive and non-toxic cancer therapies.

3

Dismissed for decades as "quackery" by organized medicine, most of these therapies appear to be reasonably or even remarkably effective. Their advocates and practitioners have often taken great risks to bring what they believe are safe and effective treatments to sick people. And the same methods also frequently serve the function to prevent degenerative illness. The organized medical community, with financial links to the pharmaceutical industry, has not cared to seriously look into these techniques. Instead, the techniques have been unwarrantedly attacked, and pseudo investigations have been launched, with predictable outcomes: the treatments are denounced, clinics are shut by brute police force, through court orders; medical records and research protocols are seized to prevent positive evidence from getting out into the public, and jail sentences have been handed out. Books have also been burned. In this context, a great fraud has been perpetrated upon the American people, and upon our courts and legal system, by the larger organized medical associations, and related government bureaucracies.

In this short *Handbook*, I cannot give a history of these anti-scientific and unethical abuses, but a few articles and books on the question are listed in the Reference section. Clearly, a major reason for the impotence of modern medicine in dealing with degenerative diseases lies in the fact that the organized medical community has used police-state tactics to suppress important new findings, and the unorthodox practitioner, irrespective of any scientific evidence that exists. In fact, the most well documented and effective unorthodox therapies have been the most hotly attacked.

We also today see a new phenomenon, of old liberal social-reform groups which once stood in opposition to government authoritarian trends, now joining with and supporting overbearing medical bureaucracies. In this, they get much help from the mainstream media, which leans left and also is beholden to the pharmacy industry for expensive, and frequently insane advertisements about new drugs – where the side-effects take twice as long to recite as the claimed benefits. The mainstream media, like mainstream science, will support and boast about every new pharmacy drug or surgical procedure – no matter how toxic or ghoulish – while predictably hammering down with contempt every kind of natural healing method people may wish to try out, but which does not require an MD's prescription.

The motivation in these cases seems more aimed to build up an even more massive government bureaucracy, by which to "regulate our lives down into the underwear" (a common complaint of East Germans living as prisoners in the Communist utopia) and build up government power for its own sake. It is not just about medicine and health-care anymore. In this process, the truth has been trampled badly, and the methods of science, discarded.

The most clear and telling example of how these social forces combine to kill a new discovery, and its discoverer, is the case of Dr. Wilhelm Reich and his orgone energy accumulator. Reich had been one of Freud's younger co-workers, and was a prime mover in the early psychoanalytic movement in Vienna and Berlin. However, his ideas were more revolutionary than those of the older psychoanalysts. He forcefully argued that human misery and mental illness were the result of *real traumas* from repressive social and family conditions, which could be changed to prevent neurosis.

Reich wrote extensively about these matters in the 1920s and 1930s, exposing the roots of *both* the National Socialist (Nazi) and International Socialist (Communist) movements (which he called *Black Fascist* and *Red Fascist,* respectively) in the obedience-demanding, patriarchal, child-abusive and sex-negative German and Russian family structures.[1] For his anti-fascist writings and lectures, which addressed both human sexuality and the natural need for freedom and self-regulation, Reich was branded as something of a "troublemaker" by nearly every powerful group and organization. While admiring of some aspects of Marxist thought (whose most violent and inhumane writings came to Reich's attention only much later[2]), and for a few years, using the Communist Party as a platform to spread his own sexual-reform agendas, working with the Communists against Hitlerism, Reich later emphasized,

---

1. See for example, his books: *The Mass Psychology of Fascism, People in Trouble, The Sexual Revolution*, and *Reich Speaks of Freud.* Full citations are given in the Reference section.
2. See my books: *In Defense of Wilhelm Reich*, and *Marx Engels Lenin Trotsky: Genocide Quotes.*

repeatedly, that he had never been a political Marxist or a Communist.[3] True enough, the German Communists soon expelled Reich for being insufficiently obedient or committed to Party doctrine. He was also expelled from Freud's inner circle and also from the International Psychoanalytic Association (IPA), for his vocal criticisms of Freud's own social compromising. German psychoanalysis was at that time leaning towards appeasement of the Nazis, and some analysts, such as Carl Jung, began openly working with and apologizing for National Socialist organizations.[4] Reich was eventually placed on both Hitler's and Stalin's death lists in the 1930s, and had to flee to Scandinavia, and later to the USA. His writings were banished and condemned to flames in both Nazi Germany and in regions under Communist control.

Working in Denmark and Norway, Reich made several breakthrough findings in the biophysics of human emotion and degenerative processes. He undertook some of the earliest investigations of human bioelectricity, measuring the phenomenon of emotional and sexual excitation, to better understand the nature of psychic and somatic processes. He made comprehensive, exacting discoveries on the "mind-body" problem in findings which gain appreciation only within recent years. Reich studied other creatures also, and correlated the whole-body expansive-contractive nature of worms and ameba to a similar process in humans, which in turn was correlated with pleasure-anxiety reactions. In the process of this work, he discovered the microscopical vesicular *bions*, and the process of *bionous disintegration* of cells – what is today mechanistically termed *apoptosis* – a discovery which eventually answered the dual long-standing questions of the *origins of the cancer cell*, and of *biogenesis,* the origins of life itself. His findings were truly remarkable, and grounded in the best traditions of natural scientific inquiry. These discoveries constituted major scientific breakthroughs which laid the foundations for his later scientific work on degenerative biopathic diseases, and his discovery of the orgone energy and orgone energy accumulator.

3. See Reich's clear statements as made in 1952, in *Reich Speaks of Freud*, Farrar, Straus and Giroux, NY 1967.
4. See the chapter "Jung Among the Nazis" in Jeffrey Masson's book *Against Therapy*, for documentation on this issue.

Those discoveries also laid the foundations for much of modern scientific thinking on the systemic nature of cancer and other degenerative illness, and on research into the human energy-field, though typically under different terminology, and without any credit going to Reich.

Exemplifying the axiom that "no good work should go unpunished", Reich was attacked for his findings in the Danish and Norwegian newspapers, in a smear campaign from both the left-wing and right-wing press. Reich's Freudian background and interest in sex-political reforms, his endorsement of greater social freedoms, his laboratory investigations of sexuality and emotion, and findings on the origins of life and cancer – no matter what he did, his work infuriated nearly everyone, though typically for different reasons. This was in addition to his being of Jewish background, which at that time earned additional enmity from fascist thinkers of all varieties. With Hitler's and Stalin's armies invading across Europe, and growing fascist power making life and work impossible for him, Reich boarded one of the last ships leaving Europe to the USA.

By the time Reich arrived in New York, in 1939, his reputation as a serious researcher with new and important findings had preceded him, and he quickly attracted a group of young, enthusiastic scientists and doctors to study with him, and assist with his work. The American period of his research, which lasted until his death in 1957, was exceptionally productive, in spite of similar abusive treatment from American journalists and government officials. It was during this period that Reich experimentally clarified, and made practical use of the biological and atmospheric life energy, which he called the *orgone energy*.

The early bioelectrical currents he objectively measured with millivoltmeters were clarified as small expressions of a more powerful and motile life-energy within the body, which expressed itself in emotion, sexuality, work and activity of all sorts. This was clarified also as a new radiant energy discovered from special bion cultures derived from beach sand. They radiated a powerful blue-glowing energy which could be felt and seen, which would fog photographic plates and generated electrostatic and magnetic anomalies. From this, in efforts to amplify and contain the energy for study, the orgone energy accumulator was developed. And from that came the discovery of the *atmospheric orgone energy,* which also could be absorbed and contained directly inside the accumulator. A wealth of new discovery came flooding forth from these findings, "too much" as Reich noted, requiring one to study and follow the *red thread of logic and reason* (as from the Greek myth about Ariadne) which had led him from one discovery to the next. The life energy, the orgone as he called it, was completely new and different from all other known forms of energy. It obeyed functional laws, and could not be understood from either mechanistic or mystical contexts. Long before Albert Einstein would intuitively search, in vain, for a *Grand Unifying Theory,* it was in fact Wilhelm Reich who made exactly this kind of discovery – one which Einstein would later learn about in personal meetings with Reich. A stunned Einstein actually observed and confirmed orgone energy phenomenon demonstrated to him by Reich, in specialized apparatus. In later chapters, I will flesh out these discoveries and facts with more detail.

The orgone energy, Reich observed, was a real, physical energy, which charged and radiated from both living and non-living matter of all varieties: microbes, animals, humans, and it could be amplified by simple arrangements of certain specific materials. To understand it, one must consider comparative examples, for example of how a telescope or airplane-wing functions. Both are simple but very specific arrangements of materials, immersed into a background ocean of light or moving air, respectively. They both accomplish amazing feats. Reich's orgone accumulator may be considered in the same context. It is quite simple, but functions on the basis of an energy which is omnipresent within the atmosphere and space around itself.

Experiments with the accumulator showed numerous anomalies, such as a spontaneous thermal heating effect, electrostatic effects, and clear reactions in living organisms. Humans suffering from biopathic diseases often experienced a remission of symptoms – though Reich was clear not to claim any "cure for cancer". Chronic pains frequently diminished or vanished, and burns healed dramatically from orgone radiation, which boosted what was then known as the *resistance to disease*, what today is called under purely biochemical theory, the *immune system.* Reich developed a special blood test in which living blood was observed for its ability to resist degeneration on the microscope slide, something which today is copied widely, though usually without reference to Reich's original laboratory protocols. The blue-glowing nature of living red blood cells was documented (a visible expression of what is today termed the *zeta-potential*), and Reich increasingly argued that much of the blue glow of bioluminescence and out in nature were direct expressions of the orgone energy continuum, which like living protoplasm could be excited into *glowing lumination.* Reich later demonstrated how the orgone energy moved about the landscape in greater or lesser concentrations, streaming or pulsating, and affecting the weather in the process. A similar lawful motion of the cosmic orgone energy of space, he argued, created the grand spirals of galaxies and planetary motions, as well as the spirals of hurricanes and snail shells. A similar cosmic pattern of life-energy motion and genesis could be understood from Reich's discoveries, found etched into all of cosmic creation, from the microcosm to macrocosm.

In this, Reich's orgone energy is similar to the older ideas of *cosmic ether of space,* which astrophysics claims was never demonstrated (wrong! see the Appendix), but continues to resurrect under new terms such as the *neutrino sea,* the *dark matter wind, intergalactic medium,* or *cosmic plasmas.* In the Appendix and other Chapters, I show how Reich's orgone energy has many similarities to the cosmic ether factually documented in the ether-drift experiments of Dayton Miller and others. Biology also keeps stumbling into the same bioenergetic or bio-cosmic phenomenon. While older less-developed theories of *animal magnetism* or *vital force* are today relegated to ancient history, it was Chinese medicine's *acupuncture* and European *homeopathy* which brought the life energy straight back into the front door of modern biology and medicine – even if the doctors and biologists keep trying to slam that door shut! No matter how often modern mechanistic science and medicine, or dogmatic deistic spiritualism and religion keeps smacking down the life energy, new evidence for its existence keeps popping back up in newer discoveries – rather like the children's mechanical "whack-a-mole" game, where one toy mole is whacked down with a rubber club back into its hole, only to have an identical one immediately pop up in another location. Over the course of this book I will provide the basic details, and give guidance from my own years of study and research.

New Information on Reich's Persecution and Death

Wilhelm Reich unfortunately became one of the crushed-down victims of a deadly mid-20th Century medical-academic assault upon unorthodox scientific discovery. Significant social forces were at work, but not according to the usual "politically correct" narratives. In the decades since his death, many publications spread the misconception that Reich was destroyed by American conservatism, "right-wing McCarthy-ites" and such. Historical research has shown that to be untrue. Reich was persecuted and attacked by both Nazis and Stalinists in Europe. In the USA, however, he was brought down by a combination of *Comintern* (Communist International) Stalinist agents, pestilent journalists and MDs, and finally by the US Food and Drug Administration (FDA). Scholarly books and articles are now available referencing newly-exposed Soviet files from long-closed archives, and internal FDA and FBI files using the *Freedom of Information Act*, and other sources. These are cited in the Reference section. Here is a summary of what they reveal.[5]

Over the period 1927-1931, as a young psychoanalyst and physician working within Freud's inner circle of close confidants, Reich was setting up clinics for working-class people in Vienna and later Berlin. In this effort, he formed mutually cautious working alliances firstly with the Communist Party (CP) of Austria and later the CP of Germany. The CP organizations initially allowed him to hold lectures in their halls, and sell his

5. Unless otherwise indicated, most of what follows here is from James DeMeo's *In Defense of Reich*, James Martin's *Wilhelm Reich and the Cold War*, Jerome Greenfield's *Wilhelm Reich Vs. the USA*, John Wilder's *CSICOP, Time Magazine and Wilhelm Reich,* or Wilhelm Reich's unpublished work *Conspiracy: An Emotional Chain-Reaction.* See the Reference section, p.199, for full citation information. For a full citation list of the smear articles mentioned in this section, see: www.orgonelab.org/bibliogPLAGUE.htm

publications in their bookstores. His lectures on sexual health and the needs of children and families deeply interested working-class people, and typically attracted more listeners than the dry and bland speeches on Marxist economic theory, as given by Party functionaries. Reich's following within the *Sex-Pol* organization and movement which he created, grew dramatically, eventually numbering in many thousands of people, with additional professional volunteers from the psychoanalytic movement.

Reich saw the possibility to prevent neurosis en-masse, through legal reforms based upon psychoanalytic principles. Through Sex-Pol, he argued for legalization of contraception, abortion and divorce, and championed the rights of young unmarried people for a healthy sexual life. He worked to protect children from adult sexual predators, to improve the desperate economic situations of abandoned mothers with children, and fought against the stigma of "illegitimate" children, which carried severe consequences for the child's future education and employment. Women were legally subordinated in many ways, and the cruelty of abusive husbands and fathers incurred little social consequence. Compulsive and frequently loveless marriages, along with high birth rates from unplanned pregnancies, plus a bad economic situation following WW-I, led to a permanent marginally-existing poverty-class with high levels of neurosis, emotional resignation, family violence and suicides. Reich was highly critical of the Royal families and the Church, which held great economic and political power, and thereby could have improved upon these aspects of people's lives. But in fact, existing social institutions were paralyzed and did little in the way of such family reform. The goals of Reich's Sex-Pol, however, were to lift people up from such desperate social, family and emotional conditions, towards happier and more productive lives, thereby *making psychoanalytic therapy obsolete*. He joined with and pushed the CP to include his points into their Party platform.

While initially tolerant of Reich, his public criticisms of anti-freedom CP policies and Party bosses, in both lectures and writings, resulted in a total break-off of their relations. He was misbranded a "Trotskyite" for his outspoken challenges to Marxist-Leninist theory and Stalinist dictates, in favor of his own Sex-Pol ideas. Reich eventually criticized both the

Communist and the Nazi Parties as deeply psychopathic, especially in his *Mass Psychology of Fascism*. Reich also lost support from his mentor Freud around this time, and was expelled by the IPA. Leading psycho-analysts rejected his Sex-Pol ideas, also being offended by his criticisms of IPA lethargy in the face of such immense social problems. They also considered his public speeches critical of the Nazi movement as an unnecessary provocation. Reich was therefore at great risk, and had little support if he stayed in Germany. He fled to Scandinavia shortly before Hitler came to power, and within a few years was on both the Comintern and Nazi death-lists, his books banned, impounded or burned by both the Communists and Gestapo.

Upon arrival in Scandinavia, Reich soon found himself being openly attacked in both Nazi and CP newspapers. Worse, unbeknownst to Reich, he was at that time also being tracked by the Soviet NKVD (forerunner of the KGB). A 1936 Comintern/ NKVD document marked *Top Secret* and identifying *"Trotskyists and other hostile elements in the emigre community of the German CP"* obtained from Soviet archives after the collapse of the USSR,[6] included his name. That was tantamount to a Soviet arrest warrant and death-sentence, a Comintern/NKVD death-list. While Reich was never a follower of Trotsky, the accusation alone was sufficient for his name, and that of one of his Denmark-Norway contacts, Otto Knobel, to appear on the official NKVD list in several places. Knobel's offense was having been a known associate of Reich, indicating Reich was the primary target and offender. The document carried notations on others who had already been apprehended and sent into prisons or off to the Siberian gulag, or executed. Knobel was in fact later arrested by the NKVD and imprisoned, or "disappeared" (executed).

While his time in Scandinavia allowed for new lines of research to be developed, Reich eventually fled to the USA in

6. See Document 20, *"Memorandum on Trotskyists and Other Hostile Elements in the Emigre Community of the German CP, Cadres Department"*, dated 2 Sept. 1936, in the Yale University Archives: www.yale.edu/annals/Chase/Documents/doc20chapt4.htm This document is also partly reproduced as "Document 17" in *Enemies within the Gates? The Comintern and the Stalinist Repression, 1934-1939*, by William J. Chase, Yale Univ. Press 2001, p.164-174.

1939, just ahead of the outbreak of WW-II. In the USA, Nazi sympathizers were few and suppressed, and so he was relatively safe from their agents. By contrast, the American Comintern had a very large network of organizations, front-groups, supporters, Comintern and NKVD spies, and *fellow-travellers* (Comintern agents who did not formally or publicly join the CP, so as to more easily carry out spying and Soviet plots). While initially ignoring Reich, American leftists and the Comintern would later turn on him with a fury.

For nearly two years, Reich was left alone to work, unmolested. He abandoned the public Sex-Pol work from his years in Vienna and Berlin, and instead focused upon the natural scientific and medical research he had begun in Scandinavia, building up a cancer research and biophysics laboratory, and therapy training facility in Forest Hills, NY.

Following the Japanese attack upon Pearl Harbor in December 1941, which brought America more directly into WW-II, the FBI arrested for questioning many German, Italian and Japanese emigres. Reich was one of them, and he remained incarcerated for nearly a month until such time as the FBI was satisfied he was against Hitlerism, and constituted no threat. Reich continued to live safely and productively in the USA, and without significant harassment for the next six years. He continued with clinical, biomedical and physical orgone energy research, starting a new institute, and published journals for publication of his findings — the *International Journal of Sex-Economy and Orgone Research*, which was later followed by the *Orgone Energy Bulletin*, and another entitled *Cosmic Orgone Engineering*. These journal titles reflected his growing interest in orgone biophysics.

A group of American physicians, scientists and educators studied with Reich and supported his efforts, helping in the work. He moved to a larger rural facility in Rangeley, Maine, giving it the name *Orgonon*, and which hosted a large observatory building and student's laboratory. His plans included eventual construction of a medical treatment clinic, centered on the orgone energy accumulator.

Reich's orgone energy experiments occasionally attracted hostile commentary from a few physicians in the medical community, and his writings on sexual freedom also attracted complaints by a few moralists of this period. But these had no serious affect upon his work. His books, such as *Function of the Orgasm*, were given sneering reviews by mainstream medical journals as early as 1942, stimulating a rumor campaign which he addressed by public exposure and rebuttals in his own new *Journal*. No legal attacks or organized persecutions came from any of these early American annoyances. This would change, however. In 1946, shortly after the first English edition of his *Mass Psychology of Fascism* appeared in the USA — one of his works from the 1930s which got him on the Nazi and Comintern death-lists in Europe — he came under serious attacks from American Communists and pro-Soviet operatives.

The *New Republic* magazine figured centrally in the renewed campaign against Reich. Developed from the family fortune of Willard Straight, an American investment banker, *New Republic* was originally liberal-progressive but pro-American in outlook. By Reich's time, however, it was taken over by the young Michael Whitney Straight, who by his own later admissions had been recruited as a Soviet spy in 1935, while attending Cambridge University. Straight was an important American member of the NKVD-controlled *Cambridge Five* spy ring, which worked primarily out of the UK, and included the notorious Anthony Blunt, Guy Burgess, and Kim Philby. Together they provided the Soviet Union with American and British atomic and other top secrets during the period of WW-II until around 1952, when they were exposed. Straight successfully concealed his Soviet connections until 1962.

As owner of the *New Republic* and NKVD-KGB agent, Michael Straight brought many open and cloaked communists onto their staff, such as former US Vice-President (1941-44) Henry Wallace, as editor. Wallace's unconcealed Soviet and CP sympathies, his white-washing of Soviet gulag death-camps, open meetings with Comintern operatives, and other factors forced President Roosevelt to drop him as VP in 1944, in favor of Harry Truman. Newly-released materials from Soviet archives confirm Wallace was in fact working covertly for the Soviets.

Under Straight's oversight and Wallace's editorship, the *New Republic* obtained its direction from the Comintern and KGB, to steer old-fashioned and healthy American liberal democratic sentiments towards pro-Soviet and Comintern agendas. In this regard, assaulting anti-communist freedom-fighters like Wilhelm Reich, who had personally seen and wrote about the poison of Red Fascism, was certainly a central part of their mission. It appears, the newly-published 1946 English edition of Reich's *Mass Psychology* came to the attention of the Comintern and *New Republic* staff, triggering a renewed interest to destroy him.

Under the editorship of Henry Wallace, the *New Republic* firstly published a slanderous "book review" of Reich's *Mass Psychology,* authored by Fredric Wertham, a socialist-oriented psychiatrist who eventually made his fame in books and articles denouncing the ill effects of comic books upon American youth, advocating censorship. The article misrepresented Reich as a dangerous political radical out to do harm to the USA, accusing him of having "utter contempt for the masses", as if Reich's criticisms against the murderous Nazis and Communists were ill-conceived. Comrade Wertham called upon *"the intellectuals in our time ... to combat the kind of psycho-fascism which Reich's book exemplifies."*

But the Wallace-Wertham slanders would pale by comparison to the public sexual slander and smear campaign started the following year, 1947, by the Communist writer Mildred Brady, in both *Harper's* and the same *New Republic* magazine. Her smear articles *"The New Cult of Sex and Anarchy"* and *"The Strange Case of Wilhelm Reich"* made additional unwarranted accusations, which stimulated copy-cat articles within other magazines, newspapers and professional publications of that time.

The Bradys — Mildred and her husband Robert — were intimate with the Straight and Wallace networks of Comintern friends and KGB agents. Robert Brady's academic post at the UC Berkeley campus was identified by the FBI as a meeting ground for contacts and go-betweens stretching back to the Soviet Union. The Bradys also had a long relationship with the largest and most successful Soviet spy-ring working in the USA, as established by *Nathan Gregory Silvermaster*, which also was involved in taking atomic secrets to the Soviet Union. The Bradys had years earlier been central in founding the *Consumers Union* organization, a lobbbying group which had a powerful influence within the FDA and medical organizations. Mildred Brady had actually written some of the specific language for legal codes later used by the FDA to attack natural healing methods, such as the "interstate transportation" and "mislabeling of merchandise" clauses. While nominally overseeing the safety of foods, drugs and cosmetics, a perhaps more central goal of the FDA starting from its earliest years, and apparently due in part to pernicious Comintern subterfuge, was to concentrate Federal Government control over large sectors of the economy, public behavior and health issues.

The Bradys played a key role in setting up that dictatorial "health" infrastructure, even after being fired from their jobs at the *Office of Price Administration* in 1941, during the Roosevelt Administration, due to their open Soviet CP sympathies. The *Dies Committee* of the US Congress had publicly identified the Bradys as Soviet agents, resulting in their firing. One of the employees of their *Consumer's Union* (which later went on to publish *Consumer's Reports* magazine) was also identified in FBI files as a Soviet courier and get-away car driver for the assassin in the 1940 murder of Leon Trotsky in Mexico City. Once Wilhelm Reich was identified as a possible threat to Comintern goals in the USA, this same network of Soviet agents and sympathizers began orchestrating a serious and deadly assault against him.

Brady's smear articles denounced Reich by putting falsehoods into his mouth, implying he ran a sex-racket, and repeated defamation from old Socialist and Communist newspapers which had attacked him ten years earlier in Scandinavia. Brady also denounced Reich for his criticisms of Stalinist sex-repression — factually, the Bolsheviks and later Stalinist dictatorship had progressively betrayed every human right and freedom as existed during the early authentic Russian Revolution, or even as left-over from Tsarist days. As a skilled writer, Brady smoothly lied about nearly everything, implying also that Reich was advertising the orgone accumulator as a cure-all, which was never the case. Her article used standard Soviet methods of public disinformation, with ridicule and half-truth mixed with lies, with the goal to isolate and destroy her target. She ended with an open call for government investigation of his work.

The Brady smears were quickly picked up and reprinted verbatim, without any fact-checking, by other publications, including by hostile medical journals. The influential *Bulletin of the Menninger Clinic* reproduced the entire Brady article, as Karl Menninger had been strongly influenced by various anti-Reich psychoanalysts and psychiatrists, whose animus dated back to Reich's European period. The *Journal of the American Medical Association* also happily joined in, publishing a derogatory item based upon the Brady article, given their on-going war against all forms of natural healing that competed with their beloved and very profitable pharmacy drugs. Short versions of the Brady article, or new ones drawing from it, and salted up with even more salacious commentary, appeared in *Colliers, The New York Post, Everybody's Digest, Mademoiselle, Consumer's Reports* and others, as well as in chapters or sections of new books on medical and psychoanalytical issues. These publications reached tens of millions of people.

Brady's smears were significantly amplified a few years later by the Marxist "humanist" Martin Gardner (later of CSICOP[7] fame). His 1950 article in the *Antioch Review* presented Reich to the academic world as a misguided crackpot. In Gardner's influential 1952 book *Fads and Fallacies In the Name of Science*, which contained a chapter on "Orgonomy", Reich was subjected to what later became a trademark of Gardner and CSICOP — a litany of false and exaggerated cartoon-like caricatures of serious work, with slanderous distortions of public dangerousness, and hyena-like laughing ridicule. Reich was branded as a crackpot and charlatan. Together, Brady and Gardner got the anti-Reich bonfires stoked and roaring hot. The orgone accumulator was by then being publicly called a "sex box" in men's magazines such as *Sir!*, and Reich became the object of public scorn and ridicule, with open calls for "government action" to "protect the public" from "medical quackery". It was, as Reich noted, a *communist conspiracy* playing upon sexual anxieties, with a subsequent *emotional chain reaction.*

At the height of this anti-Reich press smear campaign, the Brady articles were delivered into the hands of top FDA

7. CSICOP: *Committee for the Scientific Investigation of Claims of the Paranormal.* (Today re-branded but without any change in character, as the *Committee for Skeptical Inquiry.*) An unethical "skeptic" group which has warred against natural healing methods, and against Reich and orgonomy. See: www.orgonelab.org/csicop.htm and www.orgonelab.org/gardner.htm

officials by influential medical doctors, which triggered the start of an official but exceedingly biased "investigation". What was the FDA like at this time?

By the 1940s, the FDA was financially energized and socialist oriented, a "do-good", "consumer activist" and "anti-corporation" organization, with a considerable amount of its resources dedicated to snooping out and eradicating independent medical pioneers of all sorts, under the authority of "stamping out medical quackery". Even without active Comintern agents working within its ranks, it was a decidedly socialist outfit and did not need a whole lot of encouragement to go after yet another unorthodox physician — and they had entire ready-made departments dedicated to such efforts. The FDA's mandate also placed it into a close working relationship with the MD-hospital physicians and pharmaceutical companies. Their economic motivations and mechanistic allopathic ideology influenced the FDA to such an extent that it became an agent for destruction of the many less-costly natural healing clinics and methods as applied by non-MD health-care practitioners. In this regard, towards building up a gigantic bureaucratic power that could crush down anyone they cared to, the Comintern moles, MD-hospital physicians and FDA bureaucrats shared common goals.

The FDA had previously destroyed Harry Hoxsey's popular cancer-treatment clinics, whose Native American herbal remedies were used widely with much success. They had smashed down the many *healing water health spas* which existed across the nation, where *orgone-charged blue-glowing waters* (see Chapter 10) flowed up from the Earth, like Lourdes in France, and were used and accepted by most of the natural-healing physicians and ordinary people of that period. Historically, the Indian tribes would smoke the peace-pipe and enjoy sweat-lodges around these waters, to regain health and heal old injuries. Other natural healing clinics and pioneering physicians such as Max Gerson, were shut down through deceit and brute force by the FDA fanatics, working closely with the MD-hospital system, American Medical Association (AMA) and pharmacy companies. Most of this occurred years before Wilhelm Reich came to their attention.

The FDA assault upon Reich was primarily led by W.R.M. Wharton, Chief of the Eastern Division of the FDA, and by

Resident FDA Inspector for the State of Maine, Charles A. Wood. Wharton was described by other FDA personnel and biographers as a ruthless and pornographic, sex-obsessed character, who kept a ceramic phallus in his office, placing it provocatively on his desk when his secretary would take dictations. He wrote internal FDA letters and notes repeating the salacious accusations of the Brady articles. Inspector Wood, who took the key evidence-gathering role in their legal case against Reich, also was prejudicially influenced by the Brady articles. Early in his investigation, he declared to one of Reich's employees that "the accumulator was a fake...and Dr. Reich was fooling the public with it..." and would "soon go to jail." His investigation thereby, from the start, assumed the Brady smears were factual material, and Reich was running some kind of "sex racket" or "fraud".

By ironic coincidence, the name Charles A. Wood also appears some ten years earlier as a trial examiner for the *National Labor Relations Board* (NLRB) as established under Roosevelt's administration. Today, from Soviet archives, we know the NLRB had been heavily infiltrated by Soviet moles, to steer the American labor movement towards Communist agendas. NLRB Examiner Wood ruled against independent American labor groups in favor of the *Congress of Industrial Organizations* (CIO), which the US House *Dies Committee* had identified as being a Soviet-controlled labor outfit. The NLRB Wood also made rulings in favor of fired Communist members of the *Consumer's Research* (CR) organization,[8] who shortly thereafter went on to form a separate Comintern-directed *Consumer's Union* (CU).. NLRB examiner Wood very likely came into contact with Mildred Brady while determining the CR case, some ten years before Brady would later write the most destructive smear articles attacking Reich – articles which would later influence FDA Inspectors Wood and Wharton, to prejudice their investigation against Wilhelm Reich.

Upon his first arrival at Reich's research facility in rural Maine, the FDA Wood began romancing the daughter of the carpenter who actually built the orgone accumulators for

8. *An Inventory to the Records of Consumers' Research, Inc., 1910-1983, bulk 1928-1980*, by Gregory L. Williams. January 1995. Special Collections and University Archives, Rutgers University Libraries www2.scc.rutgers.edu/ead/manuscripts/consumers_introf.html

Reich, and converted her into a spy for the FDA investigation. Within three months, he had married her. For a time, the unsuspecting Reich cooperated with Wood, until the allegations of "sexual rackets" came up. Legitimately infuriated, Reich gave no further interviews or assistance to the FDA "investigation". Wood's report to the FDA home office eventually denounced Reich and the accumulator as "a fraud of the first magnitude".

Other than from Wood's reports, FDA officials in their Boston headquarters overseeing the Reich case put great stock in gossip and rumor from the Brady smear articles, which had gained "respectability" through uncritical republication in medical journals. Finding no evidence of a "sex-racket", however, they shifted focus and went after the orgone accumulator. Their investigation could not find anyone who complained about the accumulator, nobody who found it unhelpful and who therefore might be abused to level complaints against Reich. Quite the contrary, in fact. So the FDA bureaucrats began securing the cooperation of biased "expert" hospital-MDs and dogmatic scientists from their "quack-busting" lists. They had no familiarity with or interest in the scientific facts involved, but could nevertheless be called upon to cobble together a few "experiments" guaranteed to produce negative results, or render an armchair dismissal.[9]

For example, I have in my files a letter from the son of one of the primary scientists who worked with the FDA at the time — physicist Kurt Lion of MIT — wherein he states, he clearly remembered his father being asked by the FDA to "prove that the [orgone] box was just a box and that Dr. Reich was a fraud". Now, that is quite a different thing from being asked to *honestly investigate the orgone accumulator*, which they never did, and never intended to do. Many breaches of legal, moral and scientific ethics occurred as FDA officials, and a number of psychiatrists, psychoanalysts, and physicists, teamed up to put an end to Reich's work. In this, they were steered and guided by the smear articles, and by Chief Inspector Wood. By the end of 1954,

9. See: Richard Blasband and Courtney Baker: "An Analysis of the United States Food and Drug Administration's Scientific Evidence Against Wilhelm Reich" in three parts, *Journal of Orgonomy,* 1972-1973. Full citations in the Reference section, p.199.

the FDA had spent around $10 million on their investigation of Reich, a significant percentage of the entire FDA budget. Other pro-Soviet moles popped up in the Reich case. One of Reich's personal attorneys at the time, Arthur Garfield Hays, a prominent New York lawyer and founding member of the then (and now?) predominantly fellow-travelling *American Civil Liberties Union*, was also pro-Soviet, and a founding member and associate of the Brady's *Consumer's Union* organization. Hays was virtually up to his eyeballs in many different pro-Soviet, communist front-organizations and legal-defense activities. Publicly, however, Hays was known only as a mainstream liberal civil rights advocate. In this capacity, Hays dissuaded Reich from filing defamation lawsuits against Brady and Gardner for their smear articles, and offered no suggestions for legal intervention against the FDA's clearly prejudicial investigation. Hard-hitting lawsuits against both the smear-writers and the FDA might have brought their investigation to a crashing halt. There were many things a good lawyer could have done to confront, slow, and possibly even thwart the FDA investigation and newspaper attacks. Hays wrongly advised that nothing could be done, however, and thereby unethically protected his Comintern confidant Brady, and the FDA-medical conspirators.

Reich knew nothing of Hays' Soviet sympathies or connections with the Bradys, and Hays never informed Reich about it. Reich was thereby manipulated towards disaster at critical points. The smear articles and legal machinery of the FDA ground onwards, with scant opposition other than Reich's letters of protest to FDA officials and newspapers, and articles in his journals, trying to set the record straight, and making public pleas for honesty and an end to rumors.

From this, it is clear the FDA was hot to "get Reich" on whatever charges they could, and had been urged in this direction by various highly-placed individuals within the medical community, by smear articles authored by Comintern agents, and by probable Comintern agents working in key FDA posts. Reich was aware of the Communist backgrounds of some of his major detractors, of their unethical actions, and a number of his co-workers had been professionally hurt by the gossip, slander and FDA actions. Such attacks and betrayals made Reich understandably furious.

When in 1954 the FDA finally sought a *Complaint for Injunction* against his research in the Federal Court at Portland Maine, yet another betrayal became apparent. Reich's former personal attorney Peter Mills then appeared in the role of the State prosecuting attorney. Mills was an opportunistic social-climber, a former minor politician in the State of Maine legislature, and delighted in his new post as high-ranking Prosecuting Attorney. Consequently, he refused to remove himself from the case, which would have been the ethical thing to do. In a 1986 video interview about the Reich case, Mills stated the FDA had arrived at his offices with full and complete paperwork prepared for the prosecution, all ready to go, so he didn't have to do anything except sign off on it. He declared he wasn't about to give up his job for the sake of Wilhelm Reich, and nervously laughed and became evasive when asked about the book-burning, calling Reich "coo-coo".

Following the years of smear articles and betrayals, and finally the FDA Complaint before the courts, Reich refused to appear personally, to act, as he put it, *"as a 'defendant' in matters of basic natural scientific research"*. Instead, Reich wrote a compelling *Response* ("Motion to Dismiss") to the judge, wherein he recounted the history of unethical FDA abuses and lying journalist smears. He also refused to grant authority to the courts regarding the validity of his orgone research, making arguments from the viewpoint of a natural scientist. This prompted a harsh and punitive judicial ruling against Reich which is unique in American history, and which holds far greater significance for our Constitutional protections than the better-known *Scopes Monkey Trial*, where public school teaching of Darwin was temporarily forbidden in one small Tennessee town. The judge simply ignored Reich's written *Response,* which in fact should have been accepted and acted upon as the legal document it was, leading to the next step in the defense proceedings. Instead, the judge ruled Reich had *not responded* at all, and thereby lost the case by technical default.

The FDA was then granted all they wanted, in a Federal Court *Decree of Injunction* which declared the orgone energy "does not exist" and reclassified all books bearing the forbidden word "orgone" as "advertising literature", forbidding their interstate transportation. This included books into which the taboo term appeared only in the preface, or introductory remarks. Additionally, all publications discussing the orgone energy in detail were *ordered destroyed*, and devices using the energy, dismantled or destroyed.

Case #1056, March 19, 1954, US District Court, Portland, Maine, Judge John D. Clifford, Jr.

"BANNED, until expunged of all references
to the orgone energy:
The Discovery of the Orgone
  Vol. I, The Function of the Orgasm
  Vol. II, The Cancer Biopathy
The Sexual Revolution
Ether, God and Devil
Cosmic Superimposition
Listen, Little Man
The Mass Psychology of Fascism
Character Analysis
The Murder of Christ
People in Trouble

BANNED and ORDERED DESTROYED:
The Orgone Energy Accumulator:
  Its Scientific and Medical Use
The Oranur Experiment
The Orgone Energy Bulletin
The Orgone Energy Emergency Bulletin
International Journal of Sex-Economy
  and Orgone Research
Internationale Zeitschrift fur Orgonomie
Annals of the Orgone Institute"

And so, in the late 1950s and early 1960s, Reich's books and research journals, even those which were "only" banned, were periodically seized by FDA agents and Federal Marshals, and sent for burning in Maine and New York incinerators. No scientific or professional organizations, nor journalist's, writer's or "civil liberties" unions publicly objected to the book burning, or acted to help Reich in any manner. His laboratory headquarters were, as a final insult, invaded by FDA agents, who destroyed orgone accumulators with axes. In addition to the above actions, the court ordered Reich to cease "disseminating information" on the orgone energy, effectively censoring his writing and speaking on the subject.

Several years later, Reich was charged with *Contempt of Court* when without his permission, an assistant moved a truckload of books and accumulators across state lines, from Maine to New York, thereby violating the "interstate commerce" clause of the original Injunction. This happened at a time when Reich was more than a thousand miles away, engaged in field work in the deserts of Arizona. Still understandably distrusting of lawyers, Reich acted as his own attorney. But he was forbidden from introducing evidence on his research findings, and was found guilty on the narrowly-defined "Contempt of Court" charge, where no testimony was allowed other than regarding the issue of whether or not the transport of forbidden items across a state line had actually occurred.

Though he appealed all the way to the US Supreme Court, Reich lost the case on the "Contempt" charges, again by technical default, and was hence incarcerated in Lewisburg Federal Penitentiary, where he died less than a year later, in 1957. His death in prison occurred two weeks prior to his parole hearing and probable release, at a time when he was anticipating freedom and being reunited with his loved ones.

Whatever we may think of Reich's response to the court challenge, the principles upon which he stood were very important, and date back at least to Galileo's trial by fire with the Catholic Church. The lesson from Galileo's time was that *no Court, Tribunal, or religious or scientific organization on Earth has the capacity to say, on the basis of textual comparisons or divine revelation, just what is or is not Natural Law.* The results of an experiment cannot be judged by those who have never reproduced it, and the unresearched opinions of doctors and scientists are no better than the unresearched opinions of anyone else, be they members of the American Medical Association, the National Academy of Sciences, or the same Country Club attended by the President. Galileo urged his critics to *look into the telescope*, to verify his observations in a most direct and simple way. But they refused to do so on moral principle, and derisively mocked him. Reich's critics have taken the same approach, in their adamant refusal to reproduce his experiments, and in most cases, to even review the published evidence. Today, many years since Reich's 1957 death in prison, his most vocal critics still take the same anti-scientific approach, and condemn what they have not personally read or investigated.

Let us summarize: The major responsibility for the campaign against Reich included: 1) Comintern propaganda writers publishing salacious smears in major magazines edited by Soviet KGB operatives; 2) socialist-oriented "protect the public" finger-wagging and power-drunk government bureaucrats in the FDA, influenced by the Brady smears, who predictably condemned Reich as "a fraud"; 3) malicious psychoanalysts, psychiatrists and medical doctors, and their Big Medicine allies in the FDA; 4) one compromised lawyer with Soviet sympathies and another too busy climbing the social ladder to care about ethics; 5) plus, additional unethical journalists cooking up sexual scandal to print. Soviet NKVD/KGB operatives stand out in the efforts to apprehend and kill Reich in Europe, and later in the American press smear campaign, with another Soviet enthusiast giving him questionable legal advice. When the case was referred to the courts, we see other elements coming into play, notably the dead hand of bureaucratic lethargy within the US court system, where Reich was slowly crushed down within the gears of legal machinery. The judges displayed an exacting adherence to the *Letter of the Law*, but a pathological neglect of the *Spirit of the Law*, which did not allow for throwing written *Motions to Dismiss* (Reich's *Response*) into the garbage can, much less book-burning. This was equally as bad or worse than anything done by the Soviet agents or FDA, where the rigid court judges, for reasons still unknown, fully ignored the US Constitution's provisions on *Freedom of the Press*, and allowed book-burning and jailing of a scientist for defending his experimental findings to happen on their watch. And all for technical violation of a crummy cosmetic labeling law!

For all of this, nobody can be excused. Nobody except Reich, who was surrounded and outnumbered, betrayed by nearly everyone. He was supported only by a few close friends and professional associates, who wrote letters and articles on his behalf, trying to gain support and help from everyone they could contact. At one time, they actually filed a *Certiorari Petition* to the US Supreme Court on Reich's behalf. Nothing worked. While the press and FDA may have been awash with Soviet sympathizers and zealots for the MD-hospital system, *every prosecutor and judge knew book-burning was impermissible and illegal,* as was throwing physicians into prison for thought-crimes and development of successful new therapies — but somehow they all voluntarily ignored their oaths to *protect and defend the Constitution.*

Today we have a similar situation, where new smears and assaults against Wilhelm Reich's *research legacy* have continued, hardly missing a beat after his death. There is a new specter, of highly organized and well-funded "skeptic groups" on the social landscape, whose sole mission in life is to wipe out new scientific discoveries under the false-flag of "scientific rationalism". These organizations were founded by old Communist Party hacks or hard-line Marxists who cloaked themselves in slogans such as "protecting the public against medical quackery", much as the "do good" FDA. Some of the same people appear in this post-Reich pogrom against orgonomy, such as Martin Gardner of CSICOP, but many new smear-writers have appeared as well. It is therefore not accidental that the left-wing media — *New York Times* and *Time Magazine* chief among them — frequently attacks Reich and orgonomy with lies, often repeating the original Brady smears, in a most unethical manner.

These facts about the Communist and Soviet role in the persecution and death of Reich came to light in new studies only since around 2000, as well as from various Soviet archives. Notable in exposing this new material has been the book by James Martin, *Wilhelm Reich and the Cold War,* which lays out the details and documentation abundantly. I've personally examined some of the same source material, and found additional support for Martin's conclusions, and so can attest to it's authenticity (see my book *In Defense of Wilhelm Reich*).

These new revelations came years after the major biographies of Reich were written. Reich's older biographers, all of whom were liberal or left-wing in personal views, simply failed to investigate the backgrounds of Reich's major detractors. They frequently mischaracterized Reich's rational anticommunism – and his clear insight as to the communist background of his major detractors – as off-the-mark at best, or evidence of "paranoia" at worst. Most people today who know about Reich, for example, will reflexively blame his death and the book-burning upon "right-wing America", "Christian conservatives" or "McCarthyism". But there is scant evidence to support this charge, nor the charges against Reich either, which would try to suggest that anti-Communist sentiments are some proof of emotional illness (and by extension, that Communists, who slaughtered 100 million people in the 20th Century, must be "emotionally healthy"!). There is, however, plenty of evidence to indict the Communist Party and their cadres of left-wing supporters for destructive and malicious social terrorism, both during Reich's lifetime, and in the decades after his death. It is past time that we accept these facts, if only to realize who is friend, and who not, in the current struggle against political irrationalism and repression of our hard-won social freedoms.[10]

Based upon these historical facts, it is clear that **the FDA, and indeed, all courts, academic bodies and governmental agencies of all kinds, have forever relinquished any moral authority or ethical right to say anything about what the average citizen may or may not do with respect to the orgone energy accumulator.** The discovery of the orgone is in much safer hands among the average citizen, than in the hands of the various politicians, academies of science, and medical organizations. This *Handbook* is therefore not primarily directed towards an academic or medical audience. Instead, the case of Dr. Wilhelm Reich and the orgone energy accumulator is taken directly to the general public. Like the sunlight, the air and water, the orgone energy is a part of nature, existing everywhere, and ought to be available to everyone, free of restrictive regulation and control. As an invention, the orgone accumulator is also now in the public domain, unpatentable, and cannot be dominated by any single individual or corporation. It is also still *perfectly legal* for citizens to build, own, and use orgone accumulators.

Of course, with this right comes a great deal of responsibility, as the proper use and maintenance of an accumulator makes

10. Also see the author's article on continuing FDA repressions:
www.orgonelab.org/fda.htm

both social and environmental demands upon its owner. The atmospheric orgone energy ocean can, like our air, food, and water, be disturbed and contaminated such that it loses some of its life-supporting qualities. Knowledge of how to avoid such contamination is imperative. This *Handbook* will give a basic overview of the orgone energy, the accumulator, and the construction and safe use of orgone accumulating devices. For scientific details and data, the reader is encouraged to obtain and review the published materials listed in the Reference and Information sections.

Within a few years after Reich's death, his home and laboratory were opened to the public as the *Wilhelm Reich Museum*. Today, his major works have been republished in multiple languages, and are found in bookstores and libraries worldwide. Starting in the late 1960s, Reich's co-workers also founded new organizations and research journals, such as the *Journal of Orgonomy*. These efforts reflected new investigations and scholarly studies documenting the scientific legitimacy of Reich's discoveries. The author's *Orgone Biophysical Research Laboratory* was likewise founded in 1978, with a new research journal *Pulse of the Planet*. (See the Reference section.) Interest in Reich's works has gradually increased over the years, and many new experimental studies verifying his findings on the orgone energy and the accumulator have taken place, worldwide. College courses focusing upon Reich's life and works now exist, and his orgone energy experiments have been openly reproduced and verified within universities or medical clinics, yielding positive results in favor of Reich. He has also been the subject of many reviews, biographies, and short films. In spite of some mystical distortions (see page 163) and continued smears by the "skeptics" and mainstream media, a new generation of scientists, clinicians and ordinary concerned citizens are rediscovering the authentic Wilhelm Reich.

The effort to kill the discovery of the orgone has failed.

Part I:
Biophysics
of the Orgone
Energy

3. What Is the Orgone Energy?

Orgone energy is cosmic life energy, the fundamental creative force long known to people in touch with nature, and speculated about by natural scientists, but now physically objectified and demonstrated. The orgone was discovered by Dr. Wilhelm Reich, who identified many of its basic properties. For instance, the orgone energy charges and radiates from all living and nonliving substance. It also can readily penetrate all forms of matter, though with varying rates of speed. All materials affect the orgone energy, by attracting and absorbing it, or by repelling or reflecting it. The orgone can be seen, felt, measured and photographed. It is a real, physical energy, and not just some metaphorical, hypothetical force.

The orgone also exists in a free form in the atmosphere, and in the vacuum of space. It is excitable, compressible, and spontaneously pulsatile, capable of expanding and contracting. The orgone charge within a given environment, or within a given substance, will vary over time, usually in a cyclical manner. The orgone is most strongly attracted to living things, to water, and to itself. Orgone energy can lawfully stream or flow from one location to another in the atmosphere, but it generally maintains a west to east flow, moving with, but slightly faster than the rotation of the Earth. It is a ubiquitous medium, a cosmic ocean of dynamic, moving energy, which interconnects the whole physical universe; all living creatures, weather systems, and planets respond to its pulsations and movements.

The orgone is related to, but quite different from other forms of energy. It can, for instance, impart a magnetic charge to ferromagnetic conductors, but it is not magnetic itself. It can likewise impart an electrostatic charge to insulators, but neither is it fully electrostatic in nature. It reacts with disturbance to the presence of radioactive materials, or to harsh electromagnetism, much in the manner of irritated protoplasm. It can be registered on specially adapted Geiger counters. The orgone also is the *medium* through which electromagnetic

31

disturbances are transmitted, much in the manner of the older concept of *cosmic ether* (or *aether*) of space, though it is not itself electromagnetic in nature.[§]

Streamings of orgone energy within the Earth's atmosphere affect changes in air circulation patterns; atmospheric orgone functions underlie the build-up of storm potentials, and influence air temperature, pressure, and humidity. Cosmic orgone energy functions also appear at work in space, in gravitational and solar phenomena. Still, the mass-free orgone energy is not any one of these physico-mechanical factors, or even the sum of them. The properties of the orgone energy derive more from life itself, much in the manner of the older concept of a *vital force*, or *élan vital*; unlike those older concepts, however, the orgone also has been found to exist in a mass-free form, in the atmosphere and in space. It is primary, primordial cosmic *life energy*, while all other forms of energy are secondary in nature. The scientist detects the orgone energy as *ether* or *plasma-energy*, describing it mechanically as something dead, while the ordinary person feels the life-energy as love, in the sexual embrace and orgasm, or when out in nature, or during meditations or prayer, but often mystifies it as other-worldly.

In the living world, orgone energy functions underlie major life processes; pulsation, streaming, and charge of the biological orgone determines the movements, actions, and behavior of protoplasm and tissues, as well as the strength of "bioelectrical" phenomena. Emotion is the ebb and flow, the charge and discharge of the orgone within the membrane of an organism, just as weather is the ebb and flow, the charge and discharge of the orgone in the atmosphere. Both organism and weather respond to the prevailing character and state of the life energy. Orgone energy functions appear across the whole of creation, in microbes, animals, storm-clouds, hurricanes, and galaxies. Orgone energy not only charges and animates the natural world, much like a *cosmic protoplasm*; we are immersed in a sea of it, much as a fish is immersed in water. More, it is the medium which communicates emotion and perception, through which we are connected to the cosmos, and made kin to all that is living.

[§] See the Appendix, and my book, *The Dynamic Ether of Cosmic Space*.

4. Wilhelm Reich's Discovery of the Orgone Energy, and Invention of the Orgone Accumulator

Reich's initial work on the question of a biological energy began in the 1920s, when he was a student of Sigmund Freud, the originator of psychoanalysis. Freud's early theories on human behavior discussed in metaphorical terms the energy of the drives, which he termed the *libido*. While Freud and most other analysts eventually ceased using this term, Reich found it to be a very useful concept, and he continued to seek evidence for this force, which governed human emotion, behavior, and sexuality.

Reich's extensive clinical work led to the observation of *vegetative streamings* or *currents* of emotional energy in the body, which occurred in healthy individuals during states of great relaxation, as following a strong release of emotion, or after a very gratifying genital orgasm. The free, uninhibited expression of emotion, and natural sexual excitation and gratification during orgasm were identified by Reich as expressions of unimpeded energetic movement in the body. When the individual experienced great pain, as from childhood traumas, when the emotions were rigidly suppressed and held back ("big boys don't cry", "nice girls don't get angry"), or when chronic sexual stasis and starvation was experienced, the entire nervous system and musculature participated in the process of emotional suppression, or warding off of feeling. This "holding back" of feeling was also accompanied by a greater or lesser anxious retreat from pleasurable, or even potentially pleasurable situations, which would otherwise stir up suppressed and unpleasant feelings. Reich observed that when this kind of response to feeling and pleasure became chronic, so too did the individual experience a chronic stiffening and desensitization of the body, along with a reduction in respiration and contactfulness.

This chronic neuromuscular *armoring*, as Reich called it, was not a natural condition, though it had a certain rational survival value for situations of pain and trauma. When the armoring became chronic, however, as a *way of life*, it would thwart the individual's natural biological functioning, and affect their behavior even in circumstances where pain or trauma was not likely. The armoring effectively perpetuated the individual's pleasure-avoiding behaviors and emotion-censoring attitudes. Deep seated fears, and pressures to conform to the prevalent armored form of social life, usually prevented the individual from moving towards emotional health, or taking effective steps to change their situation. The bulk of Reich's early writings focused upon these social, sexual, and emotional concerns.

Reich also argued that the heterosexual genital orgasm played a central regulatory role in the energy economy of the individual, as a means to periodically discharge accumulated bioenergetic tension. The more intense the orgastic discharge of accumulated bioenergy, the more gratified, relaxed and pleasurably expansive one felt afterward. When sexual urges and other emotions were chronically frustrated, dammed-up, and repressed, however, great internal tension could build up to a bursting point, where neurotic symptoms or sadistic urges would appear. Reich developed therapeutic techniques for releasing dammed-up emotional energy within his patients, techniques which led to the release of long-buried feelings, and to a greater capacity for pleasure in life, particularly genital pleasure. As his patients became more healthy sexually, and as they reported an increase in genital gratification, he observed that their neurotic symptoms disappeared, as the quantity of dammed-up emotion and sexual tension was reduced. Some of Reich's early contributions to psychoanalytic theory and technique were at first welcomed. But later on, as he increasingly focused upon the consequences of child abuse and sexual repression, the more orthodox analysts rejected and attacked him. Reich eventually left psychoanalysis altogether, and he articulated his work under a new term, *Sex-Economy*. It was at this point in his research that Reich was forced to flee Germany for Scandinavia, following Hitler's rise to power. In Norway, Reich sought to find a way to confirm his model of human functioning.

Reich's early observations regarding human behavior, emotions, the orgasm, and vegetative streaming sensations strongly suggested a real, tangible nature to the emotional energy. He later used sensitive millivoltmeters to confirm this point of view, and to quantify bioelectrical energy currents, and their emotional correlates. However, he was convinced that the very low levels of observed bioelectrical activity could not fully explain the powerful energy forces observed in human behavior. This was particularly so regarding chronic immobilizing psychic disturbances in catatonic and other completely withdrawn mental patients. When their emotions were finally broken loose, these patients would experience a tremendous outpouring of sadness or rage. Afterward, they would also experience a dramatic relaxation of musculature, a spontaneous deepening of respiration, and a return to more contactful lucidity. In these cases, the patient's emotional energy was held down and bound up, until finally set free in the clinical setting. These observations of energy bound, and energy released, were reinforced by parallel observations regarding the discharge function of the orgasm. Based upon these kinds of observations, the question of exactly how and from where the organism acquired its emotional energy, and its exact nature, became increasingly important.

Pleasure, Reich observed, was identified by an increasing bioelectrical charge at the skin surface, while anxiety was accompanied by a loss of this same peripheral bioelectrical charge. Persons with a deep respiration and a relaxed posture would, he observed, regularly give stronger readings at the millivoltmeter than contracted, anxious, highly armored persons, who had a life-history of trauma, abuse, repressed emotion, and ungratified sexuality. As a child grew to adulthood, and became habituated or conditioned towards pleasure-seeking, or pleasure-avoiding (pain seeking) behaviors, so too would their skin charge, and other physiological measures, reflect a corresponding high or low energy charge. This movement of the organism, and their energy charge, in a direction *toward* or *away* from the world, he argued, was the result of one's life history. Life naturally moved towards pleasure, but retreated away from pain. Chronic painful experience would eventually armor the organism, and make it difficult for them to reach out, towards the painful world. From this central set of observations, he postulated that a similar process could be duplicated and observed in lower organisms, such as the snail, earthworm, or even microscopic ameba.

Reich noted that the ameba had no "nervous system", or "brain", as with the higher animal, yet it expanded towards or contracted away from its environment in a manner similar to the higher animals. He believed that many of the functions attributed to the brain were really functions of whole-body processes, involving the participation of the autonomic nervous system, but primarily being the result of the energetic forces he had documented in a clinical and laboratory setting. These currents of biological energy, he argued, functioned the same in all living creatures, and he sought to test the idea by making millivoltmeter measurements of ameba during states of expansion and contraction. As the story goes, Reich went to the University of Oslo Microbiological Institute, and asked to obtain a culture of ameba. He was told that these kinds of simple organisms were never kept on hand in stored cultures, because they could be cultured directly from a moss or grass infusion. Reich was fully aware of the air germ theory, but was surprised to hear this, as the theory had not at that time been used to explain the genesis of more complex microbes, such as ameba and paramecium. These more complex microbes cannot be cultured directly from the air, for example.

Reich made the moss and grass infusions, but also made extended and careful microscopical observation of the process whereby the ameba developed. He did not see spores on the grass blades, swelling up to become new ameba. Instead, he observed that the moss and grass itself would disintegrate and break down into small blue-green vesicles. The tiny vesicles would, over a period of several days, develop and clump together, after which a new membrane would form around the clump; the clump of vesicles would roll and pulsate inside the membrane for a period, and eventually the whole thing would move away on its own, having *turned into a new ameba*. Moreover, Reich observed that a number of materials, both organic and inorganic, would, when allowed to disintegrate and swell in a sterile nutrient solution, form the tiny blue-green vesicles. These observations were greeted by the university microbiologists with skepticism, and Reich developed a series of stringent control tests to answer their objections, and to more clearly demonstrate the observable process. These control procedures involved lengthy autoclaving of nutrient solutions, and heating over flame to incandescence, of the materials placed in the sterile nutrient medium. His control procedures and observations on this question were repeated and confirmed by other scientists of the day, and were presented to the French Academy of Science in 1938. But this did little to satisfy his critics, who shamelessly refused to reproduce the experiments, while simultaneously attacking him in the Norwegian newspapers.

Reich used very high magnifications, around 3500 to 4500 power, but not the usual microbiological stains or procedures which kill the life in the specimen. These facts made Reich's preparations very different from those of the average microbiologist, who to this day still kill and stain their preparations with a religious fervor, and see little value in observing living microbes under the light microscope above 1000 power. Standard electron microscope images, for example, cannot be made of living specimens.

Reich gave a new name to the unusual microscopic vesicle he had discovered: the *bion*. Bions of similar size, shape, and motility would appear in the light microscope when various materials were subject to a process of slow swelling and disintegration, or when substances were heated to incandescence, and then immersed into sterile nutrient solutions. Boiling, autoclaving, or heating samples to glowing incandescence would not eliminate the bions from the cultures, but could actually liberate them in greater numbers. Reich also studied the process of disintegration and decay of foodstuffs in the microscope, and noted that similar bionous processes were at work. The bions exhibited a *bluish* coloration, and radiant energy effects were likewise observed. It was during these microscopic observations of the bions that Reich first discovered the orgone radiation, and later, the principle of the orgone energy accumulator.

Like his findings on human behavior, Reich's bion experiments are far too intricate and important to be fully reviewed here, but it can be noted that they have been widely replicated by various scientists around the world. Classical microbiology of today has made confirming discoveries of very similar small vesicles, though Reich's priority has yet to be acknowledged. His findings on the bions also resolved two parallel riddles, the origins of protozoa from disintegrated dead plant tissue in the natural environment, and the origins of protozoan *cancer cells* from the energetically (emotionally) deadened tissues of the human body. Reich observed similar processes at work in both dead grass and deadened animal tissue: disintegration into bions, followed by a spontaneous reorganization of bions into protozoan forms. In both cases, of soil or tissues, Reich argued that the process was initiated by *a loss of life energy charge* of the tissues, followed by putrefaction and disintegration.

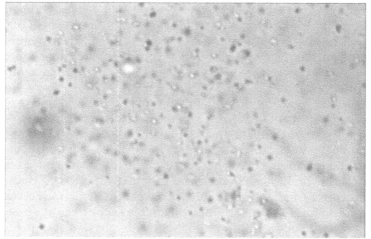

Microscopical bions from autoclaved grass in water, 300x. These are about 1 micron in diameter, and show a clear bluish glimmer, appearing like tiny robin's eggs. This slide was prepared at the author's Orgone Biophysical Research Lab (OBRL) following Reich's protocols, using a Leitz Ortholux microscope with apochromatic optics. (Reich's critics typically sneer: "Only 'Reichians' can see the bions.")

One special bion preparation, made from pulverized beach sand heated to incandescence and immersed into a sterile nutrient broth, yielded a powerful radiant energy phenomena. Lab workers developed conjunctivitis if they observed the preparations too long, while a skin inflammation could be developed by placing the bion solution close to the skin for a period. Working for extended hours in the laboratory, Reich developed a dark tan through his clothing, in the middle of winter. The radiation imparted a magnetic charge to nearby iron or steel implements, and a static charge to nearby insulators, such as rubber gloves. Film stored in nearby metal laboratory cabinets spontaneously fogged. He noted that whatever this bion radiation was, it was rapidly attracted to metals, but just as rapidly reflected away, or dissipated into the surrounding air. Organic materials, however, absorbed this radiation and held onto it. Attempts to identify the new radiation using traditional nuclear or electromagnetic radiation detectors failed.

Reich also noted that the air in rooms containing the special bion cultures would feel "heavy" or charged. When observed at night, in full darkness, the air would visibly scintillate and glow with a pulsing energy. He attempted to capture the energy radiating from his bion cultures inside a special cubical enclosure lined with sheet metal, which he felt would reflect and trap the radiations inside. As expected, the special metal-lined enclosure caught and amplified the effects of the bion radiation. However, to his amazement, he found that the radiation was also present in the experimental enclosure *even when the bion cultures were removed*. In fact, there was nothing which could be done to make the observed radiation "go away". The special metal-lined enclosure appeared to pull the same form of radiation from the air which previously had been observed coming from the bion cultures.

Reich eventually became convinced that the special enclosures were capturing a free atmospheric form of the same energy that he also observed coming from living organisms. He called the newly discovered energy the *orgone*, and he developed ways to amplify the energy accumulating effects of the enclosure, mainly through multiple layering of the metallic and organic materials. No electricity, magnetism, electromagnetism, or nuclear radiations were employed in these accumulating

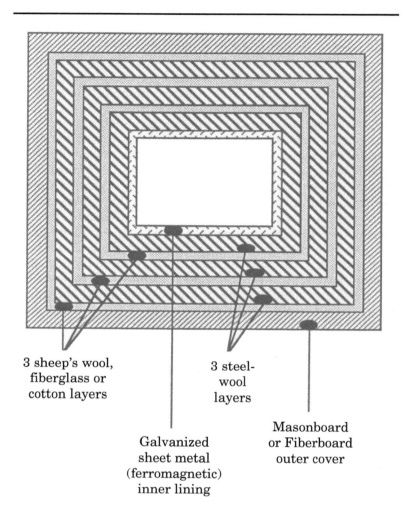

3 sheep's wool,
fiberglass or
cotton layers

3 steel-
wool
layers

Galvanized
sheet metal
(ferromagnetic)
inner lining

Masonboard
or Fiberboard
outer cover

Simplified Diagram of an Orgone Energy Accumulator

A three-ply human-sized orgone accumulator, at center, in the author's laboratory, with a smaller ten-ply charger to the lower-left. A flexible hollow steel-metal cable transmits orgone charge from the charger-box into the large shooter-funnel sitting on the chair inside the accumulator, for local applications. Section III gives construction plans for all these simple devices.

41

structures, which were entirely passive in design. The special enclosures were thereafter called *orgone energy accumulators.* The full sweep of Dr. Reich's clinical findings, his experiments with bioelectricity, the bions, on biogenesis and the origins of the cancer cell, and his discovery of the orgone energy and the orgone energy accumulator, is too extensive to be given, but a few points are summarized here, and in later Chapters. The orgone accumulator was found to have specific life-positive effects upon plants and animals exposed to the concentrated life force inside it. A host of quantifiable effects upon the physical properties of the air, or other materials charged up inside the accumulators, were also discovered and documented. Reich and his co-workers published a host of research articles on the orgone energy accumulator, its unusual physical properties, and its life-positive biomedical effects. These effects have been repeatedly confirmed, and a research tradition in orgone biophysics continues to this day. Briefly, we may identify some of the known properties of the orgone energy, and effects of the orgone energy accumulator.

Properties of the Orgone Energy:
A) Ubiquitous, fills all space.
B) Mass-free; cosmic, primordial in nature.
C) Penetrates all matter, but at different rates of speed.
D) Spontaneously pulsates, expands and contracts, and flows with a spinning wave characteristic.
E) Directly observable and measurable.
F) Negatively entropic.
G) Strong mutual affinity and attraction to/by water.
H) Accumulated naturally by living organisms through foods, water, breath, and through the skin.
I) Mutual excitation and attraction of separate orgone energy streams, or of separate systems charged with orgone (*cosmic superimposition*).
J) Excitability via secondary energies (nuclear, electromagnetism, electrical sparking, friction) to the point of irritation, or glowing *lumination.*

Physical effects of a strong orgone charge:

K) Slightly higher air temperature as compared to surroundings.

L) Higher electrostatic potential, with a slower electroscopical discharge rate as compared to surroundings.

M) Higher humidity and lower water evaporation rates as compared to surroundings.

N) Squelching or magnification of ionization effects inside gas-filled ionization Geiger-Muller tubes.

O) Development of ionization effects inside non-ionizable vacuum tubes (0.5 micron pressure or lower), called *vacor tubes*.

P) Ability to transmit, impede and/or absorb electromagnetic waves.

Biological effects of a strong orgone charge:

Q) General vagotonic, parasympathetic and expansive effect upon the entire organism.

R) Sensations of tingling and warmth at skin surface.

S) Increased core and skin temperature, flushing.

T) Moderation of blood pressure and pulse rate.

U) Increased peristalsis, deeper respiration.

V) Increased germination, budding, flowering and fruiting of plants.

W) Increased rates of tissue growth, repair, and wound healing, as determined through animal studies and human clinical trials.

X) Increased field strength, charge, integrity of tissues and immunity.

Y) Greater energy level, activity, and liveliness.

Above: Orgone Energy Charger Box, fitted with an optical lens and camera bellows, for direct observation of orgone energy phenomenon. Below: Orgone Energy Darkroom. Human-sized accumulators at rear. Both photos from the author's Orgone Biophysical Research Lab (OBRL).

New Instrumentation: A commercially-available, solid-state version of Reich's original Orgone Field Meter, the Experimental Life-Energy Meter. It is the only known meter which gives a sustained non-contact reading of the energy-field strength or charge of living creatures. The stronger your charge, the greater the deflection of the needle. It also has uses for experimental evaluation of the life-energy charge of liquids, fruits, or other objects. A standard millivoltmeter will, by comparison, either require contact electrodes, or it will exhibit an initial reaction, but then quickly return back to the zero-line.

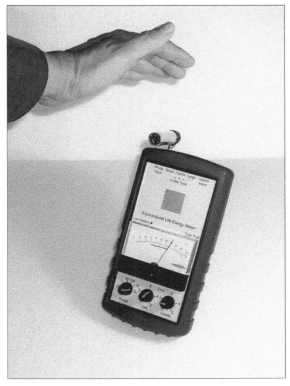

See: www.naturalenergyworks.net

5. Objective Demonstration of the Orgone Energy

A number of techniques were developed by Reich, and by others over the years to document, measure, and objectify the orgone energy. These techniques are briefly listed below, but the interested reader is directed to Chapter 13 on *Experiments*, and to the Reference section for more details.

A) <u>Bioelectric Fields:</u> Reich identified various bioelectrical phenomenon which he felt demonstrated a more powerful energy current at work in the body. The small millivolt currents of "bioelectricity", he argued, were only a small portion of this stronger energy current in the body, which he identified as being both emotional and sexual in nature, and which was later objectively identified as the orgone energy.

B) <u>Radiant Effects from Bion Cultures:</u> Special bion cultures derived from beach sand emitted a powerful radiation which could be felt and seen in darkrooms. This radiation did not register on instruments for detecting nuclear or electromagnetic energies. Additionally, the radiation could fog film, impart a static charge to insulators, and a magnetic charge to steel laboratory implements.

C) <u>Darkroom and Atmospheric Observations, the Orgonoscope:</u> Reich also observed and categorized various observable phenomena which could be seen by the dark-adjusted eye in the open air of darkrooms. Scintillating fog-like forms, and dancing, luminescent pinpoints of light were observed, and numerous techniques were developed which demonstrated their real, objective nature. One of these techniques involved the development of a new instrument, the orgonoscope, which used hollow tubes, lenses, and a fluorescent screen for magnifying the various subjective light phenomena. Large room-sized orgone accumulators were also constructed, and observations made in them were amplified, clarifying many of the effects. A special corpuscular *orgone unit* was identified, whose lawful behavior changed according to cosmic and meteorological factors. These macroscopic particles were also observed in the daytime sky with the unaided eye, as a generally common phenomenon, visible to most people once they were pointed out. The Earth was observed to possess its own orgone energy envelope, or energy field, much as did individual living creatures.

D) X-Ray Photographs: Reich observed that the x-ray "ghost" phenomenon (spontaneous, unexplained fogging of x-ray films) could be explained as an effect of the orgone radiation, or life energy. He published several photos where the ghosts were purposefully created by excitation of orgone energy within the field of the x-ray machine.

E) Visible Light Photographs: Reich observed that his special radiating bion cultures would fog film stored in nearby metal cabinets. Culture dishes of radiating bions set directly upon the film would also render an image of the culture dish and its contents. More recently, Thelma Moss of UCLA has shown that life energy field photos can be made without electrical stimulation (as with Kirlian electro-photographic techniques), by energy field enhancement; living objects placed directly on a film for a few days within a darkened orgone accumulator will, under the proper conditions, render an image.

F) The Orgone Energy Field Meter: Reich developed this device to measure the strength of energy fields. Using a Tesla coil and special accumulator-like metal plates, the device could quantify the differences in energy level between people or objects. A new solid-state version of this device is available today; see page 45.

G) The Orgone Energy Pulsation Demonstrator: Reich demonstrated how the energy field pulsations of a large metal sphere were capable of setting into motion a smaller metallic/organic pendulum suspended nearby.

H) <u>The Accumulator Temperature Differential (To-T):</u> An accumulator will spontaneously develop a slightly higher temperature than either its surroundings or a control enclosure, on those sunny and clear days when the orgone charge at the Earth's surface is strong. The effect vanishes during stormy, rainy weather, when the orgone charge at the Earth's surface is weak (but strong in the atmosphere). The results of this temperature experiment, which has been replicated many times, demonstrates that the orgone energy functions in opposition to the second law of thermodynamics.

I) <u>The Accumulator Electrostatic Effects:</u> An electroscope kept inside an orgone accumulator will dissipate its charge more slowly than an identical one kept in the open air, or inside of a control enclosure. A partly charged, or uncharged static electroscope which is kept inside an accumulator will sometimes spontaneously charge itself up. As with the temperature differential effect, the electrostatic effects vanished during rainy or overcast weather, when the orgone charge at the Earth's surface is weak.

J) <u>The Accumulator Ionization Suppression/Amplification Effect:</u> Geiger-Muller tubes and counters charged up inside a very strong accumulator for several weeks or months tend to go "dead" for a period, but may eventually yield high count rates for background radiation. Special vacuum tubes, which Reich had constructed and called *vacor tubes* (short for "vacuum-orgone", which mimic the design of the Geiger-Muller tube but are evacuated well below the level at which ionization could occur), will initially not yield any counts when hooked to a radiation detector. After charging up inside a very strong accumulator for weeks or months, however, these same vacor tubes will begin to yield very high counts per minute for background, even at very low exciting voltages. The results of this experiment run counter to the classical interpretation of the ionization effect inside the Geiger-Muller tube, and hence, to the classical particulate interpretation of radioactive decay.

K) <u>The Accumulator Humidity/Water Evaporation Effect</u> <u>(EVo-EV)</u>: More recent studies have suggested that an accumulator tends to attract a slightly higher humidity into itself, and suppress the evaporation of water from an open vessel inside. As with other accumulator phenomena, this effect also diminishes or vanishes during rainy weather.

L) <u>Atmospheric Energetic Pulsation, and the Reversed</u> <u>Orgonotic Potential:</u> Based upon observations of the thermal, electroscopical, and ionization characteristics of the orgone accumulator, Reich identified a patterned and lawful energetic cycle at work within the atmosphere and energy field of the Earth. These observations likewise led to the identification of a reversed energetic potential, or negative entropy at work in the orgone energy, running counter to thermodynamic principles. This explained why natural orgonotic systems (organisms, weather systems, planets, suns, galaxies) maintained a higher concentration of energy than their surrounding environments. The stronger of two orgonotic systems will drain energy from the weaker system, and increase its own potential or charge, until the weaker system is drained, or some maximum capacity level is achieved. Discharge may occur thereafter. Under sunny, clear weather, the orgone charge at the Earth's surface is quite strong, and in a state of expansion, preventing any significant growth of clouds. When the Earth's orgone energy field goes into a state of general contraction, a higher charge develops within the atmosphere, leading to a build-up of rain-clouds and lowering of charge at the Earth's surface. This loss of charge at the Earth's surface during rainy weather slows down the activity of living creatures, and the accumulator will not function well at those times.

M) <u>The Millivoltmeter:</u> Virtually all objects and organisms within a given environment, to include the air, water, and the Earth itself, have an orgone (OR) charge that will increase and decrease in a cyclical or pulsatory manner, timed to cosmic and meteorological factors. In living creatures, high OR potentials produce more active physical and emotional periods, while low OR potentials signal less active periods. In Nature, high *atmospheric* OR potentials signal cloudy periods with stronger storms, while high *Earth* OR potentials signal cloud-free conditions. These OR potentials produce small electrical charges, detectable with a sensitive millivoltmeter, and are excellent predictors of deeper-lying and more powerful biological or environmental processes. The millivolts are secondary expressions,however, being too slight and weak to be the causative agent. Reich and other researchers who have examined these small electrical charges (such as H.S. Burr), viewed them as indicative of a more powerful, ubiquitous natural phenomena which energetically links together the Sun, Moon, Earth, weather systems, and all living creatures.

N) Plant Growth Enhancement Studies: Seeds and plants correctly charged up inside an accumulator demonstrate higher growth rates and yields of fruit. This is one of the more telling, and widely replicated experiments with the orgone accumulator. In my own trials, I have seen an approximate doubling in the length of mung bean sprouts charged inside a strong accumulator, as compared to a control group of sprouts. Germination rates, growth rates, budding, flowering and fruiting can be increased by charging seeds or growing plants directly inside the accumulator. The seeds can be sprouted directly inside the accumulator, or charged up for a few hours or days prior to planting. Growth enhancement effects may also occur when the water alone is charged, and then externally given to the plants.

O) Non-Human Animal Studies: Controlled studies on the effects of orgone radiation from an accumulator on cancer mice and wounded mice have been performed. These studies generally confirm Reich's earlier arguments that tissues with a stronger energetic charge will heal more quickly, and develop tumors more slowly, or not at all, as compared to energetically weakened tissues. These findings invalidate many aspects of the DNA theory of cellular differentiation, which appears to be more directly under the structuring influence of the organism's own life energy field.

P) Human Studies: Aside from those clinical trials performed by Reich and his co-workers in the 1940s and 1950s, very little work has been done in the USA regarding the bio-effects of the accumulator on humans. All research into these questions was halted by medical police actions in the 1950s. Recent studies from Germany, Austria and Italy, however, have confirmed such bio-effects. In general, a person sitting inside an accumulator will feel a variety of warm, glowing, or sometimes tingling sensations at the skin surface; their body core temperature will rise and skin flush, while blood pressure and pulse rate will trend towards moderate levels, being neither too high or low. When properly used, it has a distinct vagotonic, enlivening effect. Chapter 11, on *Physiological and Biomedical Effects* will provide details on these questions.

Q) <u>Spectroscopic Studies:</u> New findings have been made at the DeMeo Orgone Biophysical Research Laboratory identifying high ultraviolet (UV) absorption in orgone-charged distilled water samples. When a dish of water is placed inside a strong orgone energy charger for a few days, it deveops a significant absorption of far-UV light in the 220-300 nm range which does not appear in a control sample of the same distilled water kept under an ordinary cardboard box. Orgone charged water also develops a significant near-UV and blue glowing fluorescence when excited by far-UV light, documenting a combined absorbance-fluorescence reaction, the latter being shifted off to longer visible blue wavelengths. This work is a direct verification of Reich's concept of *orgonotic lumination* and the blue color of the orgone energy.

6. Discovery of an Unusual Energy by Other Scientists

Reich was not alone in his discovery of the life-energy. Studies by various natural scientists have, over the years, demonstrated energetic principles at work in the natural world which are similar to the orgone energy. Early Chinese medicine acknowledged the existence of such a force, called *Chi,* and the traditional method of acupuncture is based upon the existence of such an energy principle within the human body. Acupuncture points do not correspond directly with nerve endings, and the most able acupuncturists do not rely upon the Western models of physiology to explain its effects. Given the absence of a vital energy principle, Western medicine cannot explain acupuncture, and for years resisted its adoption in the United States. Acupuncture furthermore works on animals, invalidating invocation of the placebo effect. Ancient texts from India have also referred to the life energy, called *Prana,* and provide maps of *Nila points* (similar to acupuncture points) on elephants. The texts from ancient China and India speak about an energy that is taken in through the breath, and flows through the body along the various meridians. Health is constituted by a free, unimpeded flow of this energy, while sickness occurs when the flow of vital energy is blocked. This is very similar to Reich's ideas on the orgone energy, though the Asian sources say little about the free expression of emotion; they also often advocated a conscious control of emotions and sexual feeling (*orgasm avoidance*). In contrast, Reich demonstrated that such chronic restraint or self-control was the reason why the life energy became blocked or dammed up to create illness in the first place.

In the Western tradition, the vitalists of the eighteenth and nineteenth centuries also discussed the existence of a biological energy or life force, which was called *animal magnetism, the odic force, psychic force, élan vital,* and so on.

Indeed, Mesmer spoke of animal magnetism as an atmospheric fluid which surrounded, charged, and animated living creatures, and could be projected across a distance by a therapist. Mesmer was a teacher of Charcot, who was, in turn, the teacher of Freud, who was one of Reich's early mentors. Reich also studied with other vitalists, such as Kammerer and Bergson, and the vitalist tradition has persisted as a quietly spoken minority viewpoint in biology. Besides Reich, the more recent advocates of a vital or dynamic energy principle in nature included the late Harold S. Burr of Yale University. Burr argued for the existence of a powerful *electrodynamic field* at work in nature, affecting both weather and living creatures. The biologist Rupert Sheldrake has similarly developed a theory on *morphogenic fields* which also takes from this tradition. Like Burr's work, Sheldrake's theory provides a dynamic, energetic explanation for inheritance, challenging mechanistic biochemical DNA theory unnecessary. Most recently, editors for the academic publication *New Scientist* called Sheldrake's book the "best candidate for burning" they had seen in a while.

The surgeon Robert O. Becker developed these prior principles to a most amazing state of advancement, as detailed in his book *The Body Electric*. His early research led to the development of a class of devices for the electrical stimulation of bone healing and pain relief. His later work took these principles, and developed them to the point that he could artificially stimulate the *regenerative growth of amputated limbs of laboratory mice*, in a manner similar to the way in which a salamander or spider will regrow a lost limb. This kind of regrowth is by nature limited only to less complex creatures, and does not generally exist among mammals, such as mice, rabbits, and humans. Regrowth of an amputated limb had never been previously demonstrated in a mouse, or any mammal for that matter. Becker's work was a severe blow for both the biochemical DNA theory of cellular regulation, and the theory that the bioelectrical field of a creature was just a meaningless "by-product" of chemical metabolism, like the electric field surrounding a running automobile engine. His work proved that the energy field of the animal was a primary determinant of growth and repair, as was the case with Reich's work. Becker was preparing to replicate the limb regrowth experiments on humans, when the biomedical community reacted with severe outrage against him, pulling dirty tricks of all sorts to have his research funding cancelled, and his laboratory shut down. Another vitalist of our era is Bjorn Nordenstrom, director of the Karolinska Radiological Institute in Sweden. Nordenstrom, like Reich, made a study of the x-ray "ghost" phenomena, which is an unusual spontaneous fogging of x-ray films. It appears as a wispy, smoke-like or blob-like form on the x-ray images of patients, and sometimes can be seen on the monitors of airport baggage x-ray equipment. It cannot be predicted, and most radiologists consider it to be a nuisance. However, Nordenstrom studied it, and observed distinct patterns correlated to his patient's bioelectrical fields. Like Reich, he also discovered and measured currents of bioelectricity in the body. His meticulous research was summarized in a book titled *Biologically Closed Electric Circuits: Clinical, Experimental, and Theoretical Evidence for an Additional Circulatory System.* After being heavily advertised in medical journals in the USA, it sold less than 200 copies, evidencing a contempt among mainstream medical doctors for any new findings that would support the principle of a life energy, even one of a purely bioelectrical nature. Unable to find support for his work in the West, Nordenstrom was forced to go to China to pursue his clinical research.

Other biological scientists have inferred the existence of such a vital energy principle, on the basis of their experimental work. When they provide good confirming evidence, they are hotly attacked. The French scientist Louis Kervran, for example, spent years developing very elegant and simple experiments demonstrating that the basic elements of chemistry were being *transmuted* by living creatures. Chickens fed a diet free of calcium, for example, would not lay mushy or fragile eggs, unless dietary silica was restricted. With a restricted silica intake, however, they laid mushy and fragile eggs, and it did not matter how much calcium they ate. Likewise, laboratory mice would heal broken bones very quickly when fed a diet high in organic silica, but not so fast when silica was minimized and only calcium was provided. These experiments strongly suggested that dietary silica was being transmuted into calcium in the bodies of animals. Kervran also experimentally demonstrated other likely transmutations, and other scientists in Europe and Japan confirmed his findings. He eventually came to the conclusion that there had to be some unknown form of powerful biological energy at work to drive the transmutations. But when he wrote to a prominent American scientist for assistance in obtaining equipment for an important experiment, he was impolitely told to go "read an introductory textbook on biology". In the United States, Kervran is better known among homeopathic doctors and organic farmers than by university professors. However, if Kervran is right — and the experimental evidence suggests that he is — then the textbooks of biochemistry will need to be rewritten. As Kervran pointed out, biology and biochemistry are two entirely different disciplines and should not be confused. Biology is concerned with observable fact, while biochemistry attempts to explain observed facts by a chemical theory which assumes elemental constancy and no life energy. It is with this basically wrong assumption that great error is found.

Another French scientist, Jacques Benveniste, actually demonstrated such an energy principle at work in homeopathic dilutions. His experimental work was successfully replicated by independent laboratories in other countries, to satisfy his obstinate critics. But that was not good enough. For making this offending discovery, which lent some support to homeopathic physicians (who are often prosecuted and jailed in the United States), the science journal *Nature* dispatched a hit-squad of non-scientist "fraud investigators" and skeptic-club members to his laboratory, under the guise of "evaluating" his laboratory procedures. The *Nature* science cops made a mess of Benveniste's lab, distracting laboratory workers, performing slight-of-hand tricks, and shouting, before finally being told to leave. *Nature* subsequently tried to smear Benveniste in their editorials, but did not factually refute his work through replication of experiments. Such is the warp and weave of traditional academic science.

In the atmospheric sciences, the tradition of dynamic energy forces which affect entire regions was preserved for a period by older weather forecasters, who used streamline analysis, rather than frontal theory to predict weather. Streamline analysis more coherently focused upon streaming movements of air, or jet streams as they are called today. For example, when you look at the dynamic images of clouds, as seen from a satellite in space, you do not see "fronts". But you do see *streaming movements of clouds*. Reich independently discovered the basic configurations of these streams, years before the first weather satellites were launched. Likewise, the older atmospheric scientists often argued for a great interconnectivity in the atmosphere. Charles G. Abbot, head of the Smithsonian Astrophysical Observatory for 40 years, from 1906 to 1944, used related energetic concepts to predict the weather months into the future. But he was ignored and ridiculed for his findings, in spite of their uncanny accuracy. Irving Langmuir, one of the originators of cloudseeding techniques, once objectively demonstrated that cloudseeding in New Mexico would trigger rain storms all the way into Ohio, and he warned the newly-developing cloudseeding industry about this danger. The cloudseeders of today, funded by millions in Federal dollars, act as if Langmuir's work never took place, and refuse to replicated his simple experiment. They deny the existence of long distance effects from cloudseeding, knowing that if such effects became public knowledge, they might be forced to stop.

Among the physical scientists, energy in space was embodied in the concept of an *cosmic ether* (or aether), which dates back hundreds of years. In his old age, the theologian/physicist Isaac Newton forcefully argued that this cosmic ether *had to be static*, in order to prevent it from directly participating in the movement and ordering of the heavens. That role, the elder Newton argued, belonged only to the anthropomorphic God (who at that time was demanding that unbelievers be ruthlessly tortured and burned at the stake). And, over the years, a dead, unmoving ether has never been detected. However, an *ether with more dynamic properties* was objectively demonstrated by the physicist Dayton Miller. Miller also explained why prior attempts to measure the ether had failed. First, he observed that the ether is *entrained* at the Earth's surface, and moves faster at higher altitudes than lower altitudes. Prior attempts to measure its movement had taken place only at lower altitudes, or in heavy stone buildings or basement locations. Second, Miller's ether was *reflected by metals*, and prior attempts to measure it used instruments with the critical parts housed inside metal enclosures. Miller found that by doing the crucial ether-drift experiments on a mountain top, inside a thing-walled building without metals or dense materials, that it was readily detectable and measurable. He made over 200,000 separate measurements, over the course of two decades of investigation. Contrast this to the famous Michelson-Morley experiment, which involved a grand total of six hours of actual measurement time, made over four days in 1887. The Michelson-Morley experiment is widely misquoted as having completely failed in the detection of the ether. It was a hinge-point in the sciences, after which the evidence for the ether was swept aside in favor of the "empty space" theories of Einstein's relativity, Big Bang-ism, and quantum theory.

Miller's extensive work on the cosmic ether question was never rebutted when he was alive, but his research was contemptuously compared with "searching for perpetual motion". After his death, the adherents of empty-space theory misrepresented his work and erased his existence. Today, every physics textbook starts out with the falsehood that "the ether was never measured or demonstrated". It should be pointed out that the theories of relativity and quantum dynamics, plus the expanding universe and "big bang" theories, are utterly shattered by the discovery of an energy in space, and many physicists, who cling to their theories religiously, simply refuse to look at this kind of evidence. Worse, the discipline of physics has become a multi-billion dollar industry supporting very questionable technologies, such as nuclear reactors, "hot" fusion research (which has never produced enough power to run a single light-bulb), and massive particle accelerators. This kind of Big-Science research has not brought forth any real benefits or fruits for humankind, but is composed of sacred-cows which, like the MD-hospital-pharmaceutical industry, are threatened to the core by these discoveries of a primary, cosmic life energy. The physics community has unfortunately reacted to these new findings with the same arrogance and viciousness that characterizes the medical communities' reaction to the life energy. My book *The Dynamic Ether of Cosmic Space: Correcting a Major Error in Modern Science*, gives a detailed history of these early ether experiments, and presents evidence that the detected cosmic ether of the early 1900s is functionally identical to Reich's orgone energy.

Of interest for Reich's work is that Miller's dynamic ether was *more active at higher altitudes*, and *reflected by metals*. The capacity to be reflected by metals, with a more active state at higher altitudes, are basic properties of the orgone energy, as independently discovered by Reich. Both ether and orgone are also dynamically similar. and the orgone satisfies many other basic properties and functions of an ether medium, being ubiquitous and mass-free, and as a medium for the transmission of light and electromagnetic waves. However, the orgone also spontaneously pulses, superimposes, and directly participates in the creation of both matter and life. But even without using the taboo word "ether", or the more offending word "orgone", other physicists have detected or inferred the existence of dynamic energy currents at work in deep space.

For example, the American astrophysicist Halton Arp made so many photographs of energy/matter bridges between deep-space objects, where those energy/matter bridges should not have been there, that he was actually banned from using the big American telescopes. His simple photos demolished the theories of empty space, the expanding universe, and the "big bang" with a single camera click. So great was the hatred against his work that he ultimately had to go to Germany to continue with his research. Hannes Alfven, another famous physicist, also deeply offended his contemporaries by suggesting, like Reich, that space was filled with streaming currents of plasmatic energy. The space scientists to this day refuse to send satellite probes where he says they should, as to do so might confirm that space is energetically rich. In fact, physics theories of today are in a state of turmoil, desperately trying to explain away the newer evidence for an energy in space, to better preserve various other-worldly theories, such as Big-Bang creationism, Einstein's relativity, and "multi-universe" quantum dynamics. "Empty space" has become a religion, with an academic priesthood.

Few of the above ideas, nor the findings on related things such as sunspot-climate correlations, are given much funding or investigation today. Science journals still routinely carry the false statement that "no mechanism" has been found for solar-terrestrial correlations, just as physics textbooks carry the falsehood that "the ether has never been detected". And it is true that these relationships cannot be true, nor do they make any sense, from the standpoint of the "empty space" theories of physics. They require a medium in the atmosphere and in space, through which excitations and influences can pass, independent from thermal or pressure phenomena, a force which propagates in the atmosphere faster than air currents, and which can likewise quickly propagate influences across the depths of space. Again, Reich's orgone energy fits such a description.

Other research has been done to show that living creatures, and the physical chemistry of water, are sensitive to weather or cosmic factors in a manner than cannot be explained according to simple mechanical phenomena, such as light, temperature, humidity, or pressure. Frank Brown, of Northwestern University, spent decades demonstrating that the biological clocks of various living creatures were sensitive to lunar cycles and other cosmic forces. Nobody could refute him when he was alive, but today, after his death, his findings are widely ignored. Likewise the works of the Italian chemist, Giorgio Piccardi, who demonstrated that the physical chemistry of water was changed by magnetism, sunspots, and other cosmic phenomena. His work helped to fuel an interest in the magnetic treatment of water in Europe, leading to new methods for reducing scale deposits in household plumbing, and in industrial boilers. Magnetism, correctly applied, can alter the solubility characteristics of water, allowing dissolved substances to remain in solution at concentrations higher than normal for a given temperature. In the USA, these findings have been greeted with derision, as every physics textbook says magnetism has no effect upon water. Also, almost every chemical laboratory uses magnetic stirring devices to mix their chemical solutions, instead of the "old-fashioned" hand-operated glass stirring rods; these magnetic stirring devices would, if Piccardi is correct (and he is) alter the chemistry, precipitate quantity, and titration curves for every chemical reaction exposed to them. And so, the new findings are ignored in the USA, while abroad, new products based upon the discovery are entering the marketplace. Simple magnetic water treatment systems for the home are now common in Europe, replacing in many cases the ion-exchange water softeners, with their bags and bags of salt. In the USA, meanwhile, the water softener industry, in collusion with dogmatic academics and politicians, has managed to have laws passed in a few states to forbid the sale of magnetic water treatment devices.

Piccardi's work extends beyond the issue of simple magnetic treatment of water, however. At one point he attempted to isolate an unknown cosmic energy which was affecting his chemical experiments, in a manner similar to strong magnetism. In order to block out the unknown radiation, which was correlated to sunspots, he constructed an electromagnetic shield around his experiments, in the form of an Earth-grounded metal box enclosure. Then, in order to stabilize the temperature inside the metal box, he placed a layer of wool around the outside. To his amazement, the metal box did not extinguish the cosmic phenomena, but amplified it. He and his co-workers spent decades performing chemical experiments using similar enclosures, which mirror the construction of Reich's orgone energy accumulator. This independent corroboration of the orgone accumulator principle by Piccardi was also confirmed, though in a less direct manner, by the biologist Brown. Brown observed that hermetically sealed *metal enclosures*, with a constant pressure, temperature, light and humidity inside, would not extinguish cosmic influences upon biological clocks, but would instead allow them to be more clearly observed, or even add an unusual dimension to their behavior. For example, inside the metal box, the metabolism of potatoes followed a cycle that correlated with lunar, solar, and galactic parameters. Potato metabolism additionally demonstrated a correlation to local weather; *not the weather today, but the weather two days into the future!* In the enclosure, the energized potato would respond to external energetic factors in the environment which were also determinants of future weather events.

The above are just a few of the kinds of evidence that exist for an energetic principle similar, or identical to the orgone energy. In many cases, these researchers had not known of Reich's work. In a few cases, I know from personal contacts, they hated Reich's guts, and would hardly tolerate mention of his name by their students! And yet, the facts speak powerfully for their own independent, though indirect, corroboration of

Reich's orgone energy. It must be stated, however, that Reich's findings on the orgone energy are far more inclusive, comprehensive, and tangible than any of the above concepts. In addition to having been quantified, photographed, and measured, the orgone can be seen, felt, and, as noted in this book, accumulated and put to practical use within special experimental enclosures.

An additional word must also be given regarding the response of the scientific and academic communities to these new discoveries. The reader will note that most, if not all, of the above researchers were hotly attacked, or isolated and ignored for their findings, irrespective of their credentials, reputations, or the amount of evidence they provided. This emotional reaction, of attacking new ideas which upset the older ways of viewing the world, was explained by Reich as the results of a specific emotional disorder, which he called the *emotional plague*. It is found at its worst within religious institutions, where the heretic and disobedient are assaulted and burned. Special *emotional plague characters* are attracted into large social institutions, building their reputations *not* upon productive work, research, or uplifting humanity, but rather upon political power, and the number of scalps they have taken. Gossip, slander, political tactics, the sneak attack, and even manipulation of the courts and police are standard tactics of the plague. Their secret goal, like the Grand Inquisitors of the Church, is to kill anything more alive than their own emotionally-dead selves, such as disturbing new life-positive findings, and the men and women who make them. The history of medicine and science is filled with evidence for this kind of behavior. The reader is encouraged to read Reich's discussion on the emotional plague, in his *Selected Writings, Character Analysis (3rd Ed.)*, *People in Trouble*, and *The Murder of Christ*, as it still constitutes the major obstacle in the way of human social progress, and scientific research.

For more information, see my article *"The Suppression of Dissent and Innovative Ideas In Science and Medicine"*, here: www.orgonelab.org/suppression.htm

Part II:
The Safe and Effective Use of Orgone Accumulating Devices

7. General Principles for Construction and Experimental Use of the Orgone Energy Accumulator

A) The interior surface of all accumulators must be composed of bare metal. Paints, varnishes or coatings on the metal will interfere with the accumulating effect, though zinc galvanizing does not.

B) The outer, exterior surface of all accumulators must be composed of an orgone-absorbing, generally organic, non-metallic substance.

C) Metals and non-metallic materials may be alternated in multiple layers within the walls of the accumulator for stronger energy accumulation. The more layers, the more powerful the accumulator, though one does not simply double the strength by doubling the layers. A three ply accumulator will have about 70% of the strength of a ten ply accumulator (one "ply" consists of a layer of metal plus a layer of non-metal). Accumulators of different sizes may also be nested one inside another, to develop an even stronger charge. Points A and B above must be strictly followed, however. In multiple ply accumulators, you can double-up the final outer organic, non-metal layer, and the innermost metal layer, for additional energy accumulating capacity.

D) A major common error made by some who reproduce Reich's orgone accumulator experiments is the use of inappropriate accumulator materials. For accumulators used on living systems, and particularly for human use, copper, aluminum, and other non-ferrous materials must be completely avoided as they yield *toxic effects*. Similarly, certain types of polyurethane foams, rigid or soft, do not have a good effect upon the living system when used in an accumulator. Any type of material impregnated with formaldehyde, or made with other highly toxic glues or resins should not be used.

Good non-metals
- rough wool, raw cotton
- acrylics, styrene plastic
- fiberboard, masonboard
- soundboard
- cork sheeting
- glasswool, fiberglass
- bees wax, candle wax
- natural shellac coating
- soil, water

Poor or toxic non-metals
- solid wood or plywood
- urethane or polyester
- pressboard, chipboard
- organic materials
  containing asbestos
  or other toxic materials
  and chemicals

Good metals
- steel or iron sheet
- galvanized steel
- steel wool
- stainless steel
- steel/tin can alloy

Poor or toxic metals
- aluminum, sheet or screen
- lead
- copper

Also see the *Additional Notes on Orgone Accumulator Construction Materials* at the end of this Chapter.

A general principle is, the metal composition must be *ferromagnetic.* That is, a standard magnet will stick to it firmly. The organic-insulation layers must be composed of materials with a *strong dielectric* property. This means it is a very good electrical insulator, and can also hold a strong electrostatic charge along its surface. There also is another issue, which for lack of a better term, I call the *"fluffiness factor"*, in that the organic-insulation layer works best when it has some "fluff" with tiny pores where air can reside or "breathe" into the material. Air also is a good dielectric material. Hence, porous organic fibrous materials with waxy coatings appear to work the best.

One way to look at the orgone accumulator is that it composes a *hollow capacitor*. We know an ordinary electrical capacitor, as used in electronics, will store up an electrical charge, which is then released later on. The alternating layers of metallic-conductive and strong dielectric insulator materials of the orgone accumulator are analogous to such a capacitor, except being hollow on the interior, where people can sit or objects can be placed for charging-up.

E) Some individuals have experimented with accumulators composed of *buried metal boxes*, surrounded with *rich dark soil,* free of pesticides and herbicides. The larger of these kinds of accumulators give the appearance of a root cellar or "burial mound". Some authors familiar with ancient archaeological sites have even speculated that the life energy principles were known and used by ancient peoples. Certain ancient mounds and structures have a layered characteristic, using clay soils or stone of high iron content, covered over with other layers of organic-rich soils or peat.

F) An exceptionally powerful accumulator can be made by using *bees wax* or other strong dielectrical materials for the outer, non-metallic layers. These materials may be quite expensive for a larger accumulator, and are also fragile. If you use a fragile or crumbly material for the outer non-metal layer, you can coat the outer surface with *clear shellac*. This has been tried by many people, and adds to the orgone accumulation or life enhancing qualities of the energy. However, never use shellac or bees wax on the interior surfaces.

G) Experiments have demonstrated that the *shape of the accumulator* is a factor of lesser importance than its material composition. However, accumulators made in the shapes of cones, pyramids, or tetrahedrons have yielded occasional unexplainable life-negative effects. Unless one is testing for such effects, accumulators should be constructed in rectangular, cubical, or cylindrical shapes. These have given the best results, and are also easier to construct. One anecdote here: in 1980, the author visited Egypt, and went into the Great Pyramid of Cheops. While inside, I was struck down by a most intense choking, and could not get a breath. The feeling was relieved by emptying my canteen of water over my head and chest. Later, I heard reports of whole groups of tourists being similarly stricken, to the point that some people had fainted away, and had to be resuscitated outside. I cannot say if this is an effect of poor ventilation or not, but in my own case, I was the only one out of 8 people in a tour group to be badly affected. Given my observations of stunted and killed seedlings within conical and pyramidal accumulators, it seems possible to me that these effects are the result of a toxic accumulation or overcharge effect. More work needs to be done to clarify these factors related to shape, as well as accumulator use in energetically stagnated environments, such as deserts. See Chapter 8, on *The Oranur Effect and Dor* for more details.

H) Corners of accumulators do not have to be precisely constructed, nor do layers have to be air tight or precisely fitted, though one certainly wishes to have as neat and clean of construction as possible. In some cases, I have seen metal boxes loosely wrapped with layered steel wool and cotton, felt, or wool. Also, some have used *tin cans*, as used for food preservation, wrapped with plastic, and then placed inside another larger can which was, in turn, wrapped with more plastic. These tin-cans were nested inside each other to make reasonably effective four or five ply accumulators, for seed charging or other purposes. They do not look especially neat or "scientific", but they do function quite well.

I) Accumulators should be kept where fresh air can circulate. The door or lid to the accumulator should also be kept partly open when not in use. Its interior may be kept fresh and sparkling by keeping an open basin of water sitting inside when not in use. Periodically wipe the interior and exterior clean with a damp cloth.

J) Larger accumulators used by humans or farm animals are best kept outdoors under a sheltered area, where rain will not fall on it. Good air circulation and sunlight will assist with the accumulation affect. The best location for accumulator research would be inside a large wooden barn in the countryside,

The shape of an orgone accumulator is less important than its material composition and environment. The above photo shows the interior galvanized steel sheet metal of six matched accumulators (upper back row) and cardboard controls (lower front row) used in a seed-sprouting experiment conducted by the author in 1973. Left-to-right: tetrahedron, Cheops pyramid, cone, cube, cylinder and sphere. The most ordinary accumulator shapes, such as the cube or rectangular boxes, and cylinders, always gave the best seed sprouting results. The pointed shapes (tetrahedron, pyramid, cone) frequently killed many of the seeds before they fully sprouted. The accumulator effect was also stronger than the shape effect, in that the best seed-sprouting results from the different control shapes was not as good as the least results from among the accumulator shapes. Similar experiments were run by the author testing out different metals. Standard ferromagnetic materials always gave the best results. If a magnet won't stick to it, don't use it!

away from all kinds of electrical transmission lines, electromagnetic devices, and nuclear facilities. This finding on the best environment for the life energy is in full agreement with more recent findings on *house ecology*, wherein a constructed habitat is critically reviewed for toxic effects upon its inhabitants. See Chapter 8, on *The Oranur Effect and Dor* for more details.

K) The accumulator will not develop a strong charge during wet, rainy weather. On such days, the orgone charge at the Earth's surface is very low, most of it being taken up into the storm clouds overhead or at a distance. The strongest orgone charge is found in the accumulator on clear, sunny days, when the orgone charge at the Earth's surface is also quite strong.

L) Orgone accumulators used at higher altitudes tend to yield stronger charges than at lower altitudes; lower latitudes may yield stronger charges than higher latitudes; lower humidity atmospheres tend to yield stronger charges than higher humidity atmospheres. Periods with many sunspots and solar flares coincide with periods of stronger orgone charge, as compared to periods with few sunspots and flares. Alignments between the Earth, Sun and Moon, during full and new moon periods, appear to yield an increased, more excited charge in the atmosphere, and within the accumulator.

M) If you run a controlled experiment with the accumulator, do not place any relevant instruments immediately adjacent to it. Remember that the accumulator has an energy field, and will partially influence nearby objects in a manner similar to those kept inside it. The electrical or electromagnetic fields of various instruments, including computers or wireless devices, might also disturb or otherwise affect an accumulator, making this caution doubly important for the research scientist.

N) Do not use any household electrical appliances connected to a wall plug inside or near to the accumulator. Neither should cell-phones, portable computers, TV sets, or other radiating devices be used. These will disturb the energy inside. The interior metal walls also conduct electricity, and there may be a danger of electrical shock. For human-sized accumulators, use a battery powered reading lamp if light is desired, or place a strong lamp just outside the door opening. Many people use such a light to read a book while sitting inside. Radio *receivers* do not appear to have a negative effect if used in the same room, but the effects of radios or other portable electronic music players or headsets *inside* the accumulator are unknown.

O) For experimental accumulators, realize that any organic or moisture-bearing materials which are placed inside will absorb the orgone charge. Do not unnecessarily store or bring items inside an accumulator.

P) For human sized accumulators, one wishes the interior walls to be no more than 2 to 4 inches from the skin surface. When sitting inside, it is best to partially or completely disrobe, as heavy clothing will interfere with absorption of the orgone radiation. A wooden chair or bench may be used as dry lumber is a relatively poor absorber of the orgone. Metal chairs are also OK, but may be uncomfortably cold to sit on.

Q) NOTE: A too-frequent or too-long use of the accumulator may lead to symptoms of overcharge, such as pressure in the head, slight nausea, general ill-feelings or dizziness. In such a case, leave the accumulator immediately and rest in the fresh air for a moment. Such symptoms will go away in a few minutes. However, Reich warned persons with a history of overcharged biopathies (see Chapter 11) to use the accumulator only with caution, and then only for shorter periods. These overcharged biopathies include: hypertension, decompensated heart diseases, brain tumors, arteriosclerosis, glaucoma, epilepsy, heavy obesity, apoplexia, skin inflammations, and conjunctivitis.

According to newer research findings, leukemia is yet another overcharge disorder where the orgone accumulator is generally counter-indicated. Patients on anti-inflammatory medications (such as corticosteroids and immunosuppressants like Prednisone) or undergoing radiation therapy should wait several days after the last dosage or treatment before using the accumulator. If in

doubt, consult with a physician trained in orgonomic medicine. (www.orgonelab.org/resources.htm)

R) The question of "how much is enough" is related to one's own energy level, and is primarily a subjective determination, different for each individual. No one ever tells you how much water to drink to quench a thirst. You simply drink until you have the feeling of "having enough". The same is true regarding the use of the accumulator. When you have the feeling of "enough", then get out. With most people, this will be sometime after they have reached the point where their own energy field is gently *luminating*, or glowing with a warm excitement at their skin surface, and after sweating has commenced. If you are unsure about these kinds of feelings, be patient, as with some people, it may require many sessions before they can really feel the energetic effects. A good rule of thumb is to limit the sitting period to no longer than about 30 to 45 minutes. It may be used more than once a day, however. One should not attempt to "nap" inside for prolonged periods. Additional information on these bio-effects is given in Chapter 11 on *Physiological and Biomedical Effects*.

S) The qualitative state of the orgone, as well as its absolute charge, are constantly varying at any given location on the Earth's surface. Weather cycles cause the accumulator to vary its charge, and toxic environmental conditions (oranur and dor, see below) may periodically or chronically contaminate the accumulator, making its use potentially unsafe. Experimental use of the accumulator therefore demands that one learn about weather cycles and other environmental factors.

New Information and Updates on the Orgone Energy and Orgone Energy Accumulator

Orgone research continues worldwide, and with the wonders of internet new information can be made available, allowing periodic updating as needed. The following webpage has been set up for this purpose:

www.orgonelab.org/orgoneaccumulator.htm

Additional Notes on
Orgone Accumulator Construction Materials

Since the 1940s, when Reich first published his findings on the orgone accumulator, he and others (myself included) have advocated *Celotex* for construction of the outer, non-metallic layer of the accumulator. However, "Celotex" is in fact a brand name of the *Celotex company*, and does not today designate any one specific product. Originally, the Celotex company made only organically-based *soundboard* material, which is formed from the crushed and pulverized stalks of sugar cane and other herbaceous farm plant residues. The crushed organic material was mixed with binders and glues, pressed into a flat sheet to dry, and then painted white on one surface. It was reasonably firm and could be cut with a razor box-cutter knife. Such *fiberboard or soundboard* material continues to be available from many different sources, and is typically used for acoustic ceiling tiles. However, the Celotex company today makes a number of rigid insulating panels which are totally unacceptable and toxic in the construction of accumulators, such as an aluminum-foil and foam insulation board. Consequently, the term "Celotex" has lost its original meaning and is no longer used.

Another excellent exterior material for the accumulator is called *masonboard,* which is thinner and stronger than fiberboard. It is a dense, hard material, more sturdy than fiberboard or soundboard. It is also made from cellulose plant or woody materials ground into very tiny particles, mixed with binders and glues and pressed into thin flat sheets. Both fiberboard and masonboard can be used, and gains an even better dielectrical orgone-absorbing property if painted with several exterior coats of natural shellac. The shellac coating is really necessary for durability, to seal out moisture, and for better orgone attraction.

It is also now possible to obtain *carded sheep's wool* at sufficiently low cost as to substitute for the fiberglass normally used inside accumulator panels. When wool is sheared from a sheep, it is gently washed and combed to remove debris, yielding a light and fluffy material called *carded wool*, which is later processed into yarn or thread for the ultimate making of wool fabrics. Carded wool can be pulled and teased into thin layers as needed for use within orgone accumulator panels, and has no dusts or toxic qualities whatsoever. Newer biomedical findings suggest *fiberglass* is much more toxic to breathe and handle than previously believed, and so if possible it is all around a better idea to go with the more natural materials, such as the carded wool. Fiberglass can still be used, however, and it has very good dielectrical and orgone-absorbing properties. It is also economical and readily available nearly everywhere. Just take precautions with a breathing mask, goggles, long-sleeve shirt and gloves if you decide to use it.

I continue to recommend *acrylic felt* for making the outside layers of orgone blankets, but one must be sure it is acrylic, and not the more common *polyester*, which is not a good material to use. When in doubt, it is better to go with 100% sheep's wool felt or wool blanket materials with a soft fluff, using cheaper wool batting for the interior blanket layers.

In general, those materials with a strong *electrostatic* or *dielectric property* (such as sheep's wool with its natural lanolin oils, certain plastics, acrylics, fiberglass, shellac, beeswax, etc.) are also good orgone absorbers. While you can acquire the metal, fiberboard, wood framing and fiberglass components for your orgone accumulators from local hardware and lumber shops, a fabric store is best to obtain wool batting or wool felt. Be sure to get it at 100% wool and not a wool-polyester mix. Outdoor or camping supply stores can provide camp-blankets, and often one can find good used 100% wool blankets from thrift or secondhand stores. Steel wool reels are sometimes available from paint or flooring stores, as they are used on large disk-sanders. If you can't get your materials locally, for slightly higher costs due to shipping, try:

www.naturalenergyworks.net

8. The *Oranur Effect* and *Dor*

Reich's observations on the life-energy show it normally exists in a relatively calm and placid state of activity, to which life on our planet has adapted. One can feel this condition as the pleasant warm glowing or even slight energy-boost typically experienced inside the orgone accumulator, or when out in nature. However, he also discovered that, under conditions of exposure to moderate or high levels of nuclear radiation or electromagnetic fields, and a few other irritants, the orgone changes in its characteristics. The orgone can be driven into an irritated, chaotic state of hyperactivity, which Reich identified as the *oranur effect.*

Oranur – which is short for *Orgone Anti-Nuclear Radiation* – was inadvertently discovered after small amounts of nuclear material were introduced into a strong orgone accumulator. This was done during the Cold War period, as part of a larger experiment evaluating the accumulator as a benefit against nuclear fallout and radiation sickness. Reich kept several large, 20-ply accumulators inside an even larger room-sized orgone accumulator at his laboratory in rural Maine. When the radioactive material was introduced into this highly-charged environment, the orgone energy field of the entire laboratory was quickly driven into a state of wild agitation, which could be readily felt and seen as an intensive blue-fog surrounding the laboratory. Oranur assaulted the body with symptoms of over-charge, giving the feeling of sunburn with fever, and pressure inside the head, with nausea, restlessness and over-excitation. At Reich's laboratory, workers became quite ill, and experimental mice kept in another building died in large numbers. The oranur effects then spread over a larger region surrounding his mountain-top laboratory, causing considerable concern.

Oranur tends to affect each person at their weakest point, to drive latent medical symptoms to the surface. One may feel a constant agitation with fast heartbeat. Others may mildly contract into an anxious sweat when it is present, or faint, while tempers may flare among others. The palms of the hands may exhibit a mottled characteristic, and sleep may be nearly impossible. There is a tendency towards inability to maintain a coherent focus upon work or other activities. In short, oranur effects mirror some of the biophysical reactions typically seen in people exposed to moderate or high levels of nuclear or electromagnetic radiation. However, in the case of Reich's oranur experiment, atomic radiation was not itself present beyond the confines of the small accumulator into which the nuclear materials were deposited. The effects were instead being produced by the concentrated orgone energy, which amplified the effects and spread them out beyond the immediate confines of the laboratory.

Reich found the oranur effect persisted even after the nuclear materials were removed from the strong accumulators in his lab. This clearly indicated, the phenomenon was one of the irritated life-energy itself, and not of the nuclear material. This rendered his research facilities almost unusable for several years. Under such persisting oranur agitation, he observed, the orgone energy eventually developed a stagnated quality, with the subjective feeling of having become immobilized and still, or "dead". Reich identified this energetic state as *dor*, which was short for *deadly orgone*.

The atmospheric expression of oranur is also one of overcharge. Skies may maintain a strong blue color, but significant haziness will appear on the horizon, usually of a milky-white color. Well-formed clouds may appear, but do not coalesce or grow under oranur conditions, partly because the highly charged and agitated atmosphere no longer pulsates, and cannot contract. The charge within clouds cannot build beyond a certain point. Winds may be chaotic under oranur conditions, as if confused or agitated. Approaching rainstorms usually begin to fragment or "smear out" into flat layers or dissipate as they approach an oranur-affected region. The atmosphere may have a "tense" or "strained" quality, reflecting the generally overcharged conditions. Rains will generally decrease, particularly as oranur is eventually replaced by its antithetical quality, of deadened, immobilized dor conditions.

Biophysically, exposure to dor conditions will also produce a deadened quality, of immobility. One gains a feeling of a lethargic "deadness", of a stuffy air quality, and it will be hard to get a good breath out of it. One also feels constantly dehydrated, given the water-hungry nature of dor. Some people react to dor with edema, and a particular extreme form of *dor-sickness* was identified by Reich and his co-workers which is akin to severe flu symptoms. The organism responds with lethargy, immobilization, restricted breathing and emotional contactlessness. These effects are quite tangible, sensible, and in some cases, measurable as a diminution of light, as if the atmosphere can no longer fully luminate or glow with sunshine.

Dor has an atmospheric expression as well, and when sufficiently widespread, is associated with drought or desert conditions. It appears on the landscape as a steel-grey haze that reduces visibility, and gives sunlight a burning or scorching quality. Reich also observed a blackish quality in the skin color of people exposed to prolonged dor, and both trees and rock surfaces acquired a similar blackened "soot like" deposit at the height of the oranur-dor crisis at his laboratory. Combined oranur and dor-material in the atmosphere can observably blacken rocks and trees, creating an opaque greyness in the atmosphere which blocks cloud-growth and rainfall, or turns rains acidic. Clouds under dor conditions appear tattered or "eaten away", similar to slightly dirty, shredded cotton. Or, they are blocked and never grow beyond a certain small size. In some cases, small clouds with a black or very dark grey coloration would appear and maintain their dull or blackish coloration even when directly illuminated by sunlight. These are what Reich called *dor clouds*. They often form and reform continually over certain locations on the landscape, as if energetically attached to that location. One also may find them over entire regions, where the atmospheric scientist typically calls them a "brown cloud" or "pollution cloud", even if they are located in rural or ocean regions very distant from cities or industry. Marine scientists typically also describe unusual "dry fogs" which appear to be desert-dor clouds found in association with coastal desert regions.

A great deal was learned about the atmospheric life energy from the experimental accident at Reich's laboratory, and his 1951 publication *The Oranur Experiment* describes the dramatic events. From his observations on how people and other life-forms reacted to oranur, Reich drew analogies to ordinary experiences most people will already know. For example, he compared oranur-dor irritation of the life-energy to the initial and prolonged reactions of a wild animal placed into a cage. At first, the animal reacts with fury, attempting to break free of the constraining enclosure. A caged lion or bear, for example, reacts with furious rage, throwing itself against the bars, biting them, and smashing about to try and break free. Later, the animal exhausts itself, and becomes inert and lethargic. It resigns to the cage, sits in a corner, and hardly moves. Typical small zoo cages almost uniformly produced this kind of emotionally deadened animal. Reich also compared the healthy and calmly-moving orgone energy to a snake which moves with natural oscillation, and irritated oranur to a similar snake which is caught and held down in one spot, whereupon it writhes and thrashes about. The same is true of how certain kinds of "civilized" life, inside the *social cage* of straightjacket conformity (ie, the compulsive authoritarian school system), can produce a similar result in humans. Biophysically speaking, it is the same kind of natural biophysical reaction at work.

Besides nuclear energy, Reich later identified a number of other sources of mild to severe oranur-production which could disturb the orgone energy, such as fluorescent lights and sparking motors. Today, there are many more orgone-irritating gizmos around, which will be described shortly.

While oranur and dor typically exist together within a given region, one expression will generally predominate over the other. They are initially radiant effects locked to a specific landscape. As such, oranur and dor cannot be "blown away" by winds, though a good rainstorm may sequester and clean them out. Under exceptionally strong oranur or dor conditions, rainstorms are blocked and diverted, giving rise to prolonged drought. Desert locations are generally charged with great quantities of dor, particularly on the lower-lying portions of the topography, and large masses of dor-charged air can spill outwards from a desert region to trigger drought elsewhere. Regions with multiple nuclear power and waste storage facilities, or with uranium mines or refining facilities, also tend to be very highly charged with both dor and oranur. Sequential episodes of drought often occur in those areas, given that the life energy is rarely in a natural state, and is periodically overexcited, or deadened.

Contrast the above descriptions of oranur or dor conditions

Above: Atmosphere choked with greyish dor-haze, obscuring the horizon and blocking cloud development, in the deserts near Phoenix Arizona. Below: The same landscape under different atmospheric conditions, with well-formed clouds and the sky having a rich blue color. The black bar marks the same spot on the horizon. Experimental work from both classical atmospheric science and orgone biophysics has indicated that only a portion of this kind of obscuring atmospheric haze — which also appears frequently over the open oceans at very low humidity and is given the contradictory name of "dry fog" — can be explained by the presence of atmospheric aerosols and dust particles. (See: DeMeo, J., Journal Am. Inst. Biomedical Climatology, Vol.20, pp.1-4. 1996)

with that of the orgone energy in its normally sparkling and pulsing condition. When the orgone continuum maintains a state of healthy and vigorous atmospheric pulsation, regular cycles of rain-dry-rain-dry occur. The atmosphere is clean and transparent, sparkling and crisp, and does not have any notable atmospheric haze. The contrast between clouds and blue sky is apparent all the way down to the horizon. The open sky has a deep blue color, and cloud boundaries are sharp and well-defined. Clouds maintain a rounded shape, like buds of cauliflower, and build vertically without leaning sideways, or collapsing. Distant mountains maintain a bluish or purple coloration. The vegetation is also lush and crisp, full of life. Birds are active and soaring, and other animal life is also active. The sunlight warms, but does not scorch or burn as readily. The general subjective feeling during clear weather conditions is of great expansion, abounding energy, contactfulness, and liveliness. Breathing is so easy that the air literally pushes into your lungs. Most people feel exceptionally alive and alert, and more relaxed than usual. All of life is pushing upwards, against gravity, as an expression of the surging, gently pushing and expansive nature of the life energy. During rainy conditions, one may feel less energetic, even drowsy, but still comfortable, relaxed and at ease. Rains occur with a cyclical regularity.

Most older people are aware that this quality of atmosphere is increasingly rare. It was more commonly observed in the past than today. Hazy, stagnant dorish qualities are fast becoming the "norm", such that many young people, particularly in the big polluted cities, do not know what a really crisp and sparkling day is like. For example, older airline pilots remember when dorish haze was present only over a few industrial areas near to the big cities. Today, however, dorish haze can be observed in unbroken fashion, from coast to coast, and also a considerable distance out to sea as well! Likewise, in areas subjected to rampant deforestation and desertification, dorish desert conditions are spreading into regions that were once much more lush and wet. In wetter regions, as the atmosphere becomes dorish, regular rainstorms are replaced by foggy acidic drizzles. Naturalists report that the blue glow over mountains vanishes about two years prior to the onset of forest death, a phenomena which is likewise associated with hazy and stagnant air pollution. Indeed, the blue orgone glow of the oceans, rivers, forests, and

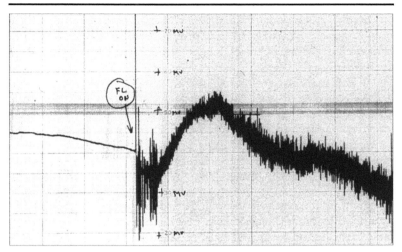

Above: Bioenergetic disturbances created by oranur agitation from a fluorescent light, detected by measuring the bioelectrical field of a nearby philodendron with a sensitive millivoltmeter (HP-412-A VTVM) both before and after the light was turned on. Below: A similar disturbance from a cathode-ray type TV set. In both cases, no light from the apparatus reached the plant, which was shielded behind heavy cardboard.

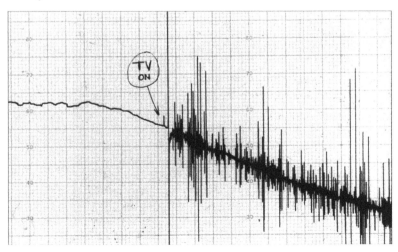

atmosphere is a reasonable predictive measure of the vitality of ecosystems. Just when the life energy has been documented and objectified, we should be concerned that it not be polluted out of existence, and killed.

A common issue with use of the orgone accumulator is that *it will typically accumulate the quality of energy that is locally available.* One must be concerned about the energetic conditions of the place where it is to be used. The orgone energy in the atmosphere or inside buildings is sensitive to certain kinds of disturbance and agitation. Much in the manner of living protoplasm, orgone energy can be *excited or irritated,* and certain environmental influences can drive it towards the toxic conditions of oranur and dor. If the energetic atmosphere in your home or neighborhood has been made toxic in this manner, use of an accumulator will require shielding from, or removal of the irritants, as it will otherwise be very difficult to accumulate anything except an irritating or toxic charge.

Orgone accumulators, particularly those intended for health care or biological experiments, should never be used close to or in rooms with the following orgone-irritating devices:

- strong alternating (AC) electromagnetic fields
- fluorescent lights, long tube variety or
    compact fluorescent bulbs (CFLs); also LED bulbs
- television sets, cathode-tube or flat-screen varieties
- computer desktops, laptops, pads or tablets
- other cathode ray tube devices or electronics
- microwave ovens, or eddy-current induction stoves
- cell phones, "handys" or cordless phones
- wi-fi networking devices, keyboards
- electric blankets (even if only plugged in, and off)
- diathermy, x-ray machines
- sparking electric motors, induction devices or coils
- hand-held video devices, game-boys, playstation
- other electromagnetic or pulsed-DC devices
- ionization-type radioactive smoke detectors
- clocks, wristwatches, or other devices containing
    radioactive, glow-in-the-dark materials
    (phospholuminescent materials, which work on
    the principle of absorbed visible light, are OK)
- other radioactive materials, or strong chemical fumes

- active transmitting TV or internet satellite dishes
- "smart" meters and appliances; 4G or 5G devices

Orgone accumulators should not be used even in the same buildings where the more powerful of the above kinds of devices (such as x-ray machines) are used, or were recently used. Experiments by Reich and other clinical workers in hospitals have demonstrated that x-ray equipment will destroy the life-enhancing effects of the orgone radiation. Additionally, there is a *persistence effect*, wherein toxic energetic conditions remain for a time after the irritating devices are shut down and removed from a room or building. **Orgone accumulators should likewise not be used in the immediate neighborhoods or vicinities where the following facilities are located:**
- airport radar systems
- cellular telephone towers, 4G or 5G, etc.
- intensive wifi networks
- high-tension alternating current (AC) power lines
- AM, FM, or TV broadcast towers
- nuclear power plants, storage facilities
- nuclear waste dumps, uranium mines
- military installations with nuclear bomb storage
- past or present nuclear bomb testing areas

Reich and others associated with him made warnings about these devices in the 1940s and 1950s, but only today do we see epidemiological studies corroborating their life-negative effects.

Part of this problem has hinged upon the difficulty that, by simply demonstrating a correlation between two events, you do not prove causality. One has to show or demonstrate just what the mechanism is, and objectively demonstrate each step between the two correlated events, before cause and effect are proven. This is in most cases a very wise policy, but it is very unevenly applied in the world of the sciences. Orthodox theorems are rarely subjected to valid critical review based upon their failures to meet a strict causality (eg, "bad genes", "hiding viruses", etc.) while unorthodox theories are denied funding or simply thrown out or repressed for whatever weaknesses they may have. Industrial polluters may also raise this issue to avoid taking responsibility for the environmental damage they have done.

Regarding energetic questions, according to the best calculations of the physical scientists, low-level radiation *ought not* to have a deleterious effect upon the living system. The energy present in the low-level radiation, *as detected with conventional radiation detection instruments,* is simply not sufficient to do significant damage. And yet, according to many biological scientists, the damage occurs. I emphasize the concern about "conventional radiation detection instruments", because a major fallacy of physics is that if an instrument does not measure an environmental disturbance, then no disturbance has occurred. The error here lies in the false assumption that their energy detection instruments must be detecting 100% of any disturbance. This unprovable assumption is, of course, challenged by biological or epidemiological evidence which demonstrates that an effect does exist, even though it cannot find any easy explanation within mainstream accepted theories. There is furthermore a great distrust of the body, of the organism, in the modern sciences, in that average people who are made sick by our modern energy radiating devices often are not believed, or are viewed suspiciously. People living around the Three Mile Island nuclear power plant during its major accident in 1979, for example, reported anomalous blue-glowing fogs, intense feelings of sunburn and headache, difficulty to breathe and other things Reich had reported in *The Oranur Experiment* nearly 30 years previously. Those people were dismissed as having "psychological reactions", and not taken seriously, even though large numbers of birds were found inexplicably dead, and the region remained bird-free for some time thereafter. Similar phenomenon were reported around the Chernobyl atomic power plant at the time of its 1986 accident, with similar dismissals by the authorities.

It is precisely here that Reich's findings on the orgone energy provide a clarification, as the life energy (and disturbances within it) are typically documented primarily in living biological reactions. There are methods for making experimental detection of radiation-induced oranur effects, but they require specialized experimental apparatus which is not available commercially. Or, one may observe strange reactions in standard radiation detection devices. So for example, Reich noted his Geiger-counter detection devices would "race" or "jam" and "go dead" when exposed to oranur effects, something which I confirmed years ago when living close to the Turkey Point nuclear reactors in South Florida. Those reactors were not having any accidents, just "routine release" of toxic low-level radiation, and creating a tremendous oranur reaction in their vicinity.

The orgone is also an *energy continuum*, which provides a connection between the offending facility or appliance (nuclear plant, microwave tower, fluorescent light, cathode-TV set, smart meters and appliances) and the living creature that is affected. As the local orgone energy field of the Earth, or the energy field of a home is badly disturbed and agitated by nuclear radiation or electromagnetic devices, so too does the orgone energy field and health of a person in that environment become affected.

Modern physics partly acknowledges these connections, in that all nuclear bombs, nuclear reactors, and related facilities are said to radiate nearly unshieldable, undetectable, and very theoretical *neutrinos* in tremendous quantities. These neutrinos race out from the facilities, penetrating all forms of radiation shielding, and penetrate the bodies of everyone for miles around.

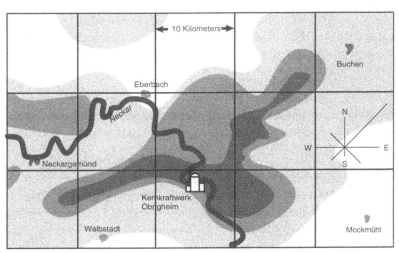

Distribution of forest-decline and death surrounding the German nuclear power facility at Obrigheim, from a study by Prof. Günter Reichelt. Other atomic facilities - to include reactors, uranium mines and refineries, showed similar damages. (G. Reichelt, Waldschäden durch Radioaktivitäet? 1985; Also see R. Graeub, The Petkau Effect, 1992.

Theoretically, they do not do any harm or damage, as neutrinos are considered to be of such an exceedingly low mass, they pass right through everything and hence require only the most sophisticated detection devices to show their presence. So how could they harm living creatures? But this is purely a speculative assumption. The major observed fact is that according to the best theories of classical physics, for every nuclear decay event emitting Beta particle (which is to say, most kinds of radioactivity), a separate paired neutrino is also produced and ejected. Beta radiation can be shielded, but not neutrinos. Significant energy is therefore constantly being lost from the heart of the nuclear reactor, through the heavy reactor shielding into the surrounding countryside, which cannot be detected with ordinary radiation detectors.

Neutrino detectors are large and cumbersome warehouse-sized devices requiring entire teams of scientists to operate them, based upon the principle of looking for tiny flashes of blue light in enormous darkened water-tanks, or in the darkened ocean depths, or as observed deep inside the polar ice-cap glaciers, where entire arrays of light-detectors are spread out in deeply-drilled holes. By mainstream calculations, there are an incredible quantity of neutrinos occupying our living and breathing space. The Sun theoretically produces 18×10^{37} neutrinos per second, a very large number indeed (18 followed by 37 zeros!). Of these, the Earth intercepts 8×10^{28} neutrinos every second. The Earth also gives off a cousin particle, the anti-neutrino, at a rate of around 1.75×10^{26} per second. Of these gigantic numbers, *the average human receives about 3 Trillion natural cosmic neutrinos every second, theoretically only from Earth and Sun, racing through our bodies.* A large nuclear reactor also puts out anti-neutrinos, at a rate of about 10^{18} neutrinos per second. The question is, how reactive are all these neutrinos?

By classical theory, neutrinos are claimed to be so "other worldly" that, like ghosts, they basically pass right through us without affect. They are of such a very low mass, without appreciable tangible properties, they can pass through over a hundred-billion miles thickness of solid lead before reacting with one of the lead atoms. And this does not even begin to address the mind-boggling question, of what happened to all the neutrinos and anti-neutrinos created since the beginning of time, from all the nuclear radiation events within the universe, assuming time even has a beginning! Now, that is a number which swells to infinity no matter how you calculate it. It makes no sense, actually, and leaves one breathlessly groping for answers which sound more like metaphysical speculation.

Consequently, some physicist have postulated the existence of a *neutrino sea,* which sounds increasingly like the older *cosmic ether of space,* by a different name. But even this has led to a theoretical conundrum, as obviously an infinite or even "big bang" universe could not allow for infinity-squared numbers of neutrinos all crammed into every cubic cm of space. In fact, the whole theory of neutrinos – which is essential for classical nuclear decay theory – is today so overburdened with contradictions and complexities, and about which so little is factually known, we can easily speculate this "neutrino sea" is in fact *a contiguous ocean of energy*, and not merely a squeezed-together complication of discrete particles. It forces us to emphasize the wave-theory component of the particle-wave dualism, and ask, once again, just *what are the waves waving in? What is their medium of transmission?* Considered fresh from this viewpoint, we can view the neutrino sea concept as being one and the same thing as the *orgone energy ocean*, being similar also to the old *cosmic ether of space.*

From the perspective of Reich's science, all atomic radiation particles emerge from the background orgone energy ocean, and eventually return back into it. Radioactive decay with neutrino emission therefore suggests one pathway for the partial transfer of matter back into the ocean of cosmic energy from which the same matter originally was created. All the stars, galaxies, planets and other matter in the cosmos have slowly built up by a process Reich described as *Cosmic Superimposition* (the title of his primary book offering a new cosmology), which involves the spiral-form movements of the life-energy towards mass-creation. Cosmic Superimposition theory was in largest measure a theoretical set of postulates, but also was founded upon the new observations and findings of orgone biophysics, and hence has an empirical foundation.

I would speculate, using Reich's theory as a starting point, that matter is driven by this same cosmic-energy superimposition, which has gravitational and electrostatic functions, to aggregate and build up from low- to higher-weight atoms, eventually to form unstable or radioactive elements. Very probably, the transmutation phenomenon identified and measured by Louis Kervran (see Chapter 6) is at work in this process. Matter then breaks down through radioactive decay with the direct release of raw cosmic life-energy back into the orgone ocean, partly as lower-weight atomic matter or "daughter products" as they are called, but also through discharges of the typical zoo of atomic particles, including neutrinos and neutrons, the latter of which also remains a mystery particle suggestive of negatively-entropic orgone energy functions. At my laboratory in rural Oregon, for example, it has been possible to produce "neutron counts" of up to 4000 cpm inside very strong orgone energy accumulators, from background radiation sources alone. Typically such high counts should only come from a very strong radiation source, as within the core of a nuclear reactor. This argues in favor of Reich's theory, which suggests most of nuclear-decay events are subordinate to orgonotic life-energy processes, and in many cases may not even be "*discrete* particles".

The lost and nearly indetectible neutrino (or neutron) energy from radioactive matter break-down simply may reflect the interface between matter and the life-energy continuum, where no "particles" per se are discharged at all. By this view, the nuclear decay event merely throws off some of its energy back into the orgone ocean. Reich further speculated along these lines, describing the "life-energy convulsion" which accompanies an atomic bomb explosion, as due to severe oranur reactions within the atmospheric life energy surrounding and penetrating the atomic material, but not being solely due to the fission-process itself. Atomic testing at the Nevada Test Site in the 1950s, for example, disrupted Reich's specialized orgone energy experiments as far away as his laboratory in rural Maine. Below I will give other examples of similar long-distance effects. From this, he became an early critic of nuclear energy. With Reich's theory on oranur, we also have a wealth of both objective and subjective biological reactions for understanding the phenomenon. The neutrino theory of modern physics is very incomplete, but through a simple reinterpretation along the lines of orgone energy functions, suggests a powerful connective and reacative mechanism by which atomic bombs and reactors could influence life and weather over long distances.

Atomic reactors, we may consequently argue, do not radiate discrete "neutrino particles" around the countryside, but instead are constantly discharging cosmic energy back into the localized orgone energy continuum, which then becomes greatly agitated and overcharged. This could be the source of the intensive blue-glowing nature of so much of atomic processes, such as the "Cherenkov radiation" seen in every nuclear reactor, as well as during the severe reactor accidents at Three Mile Island and Chernobyl, as previously mentioned. Similar orgone functions would be at work in "neutrino detectors" or "cosmic-ray detectors" which all function by the recording of blue-light flashes. It would be analogous to how the atmosphere around a steaming pot of boiling water is disturbed, even though the air already has some thermal energy and water-vapor in it. Or, how a powerful wave-making machine located in the center of a large and otherwise calm lake, would create disturbances out to the distant shore-line. The artificially-created disturbances are propagated outwards, passing right through the reactor shielding and every kind of wall or barrier, to affect matter, living creatures and weather in the surrounding area. The effects diminish only with increasing distance.

Likewise, the dilemma of illness provoked from low-level electromagnetism. Such radiation ought not be making people sick, but it does. The theoretical difficulty here is that physics says these electromagnetic waves are transmitted across the countryside and around the globe *without any medium of transmission*. This position is similar to someone studying and working with sound waves, or water waves, but denying the existence of the air or water. But the nuclear and electromagnetic "particle-waves" need a medium through which they can propagate. The big myth of modern physics is that this medium was never discovered, but this fallacy was discussed in Chapter 6, in reference to the work of Dayton Miller. They also claim, there is insufficient energy within the low-level electromagnetic waves to break chemical bonds in living creatures. The assumption is, biochemistry is supreme, and just like the cosmic ether of space, the life-energy does not exist.

Nuclear and electromagnetic devices and facilities do have deleterious effects upon the health of their workers, and of people who live nearby, whether or not one accepts the bioenergetic point of view outlined here. In general, the health hazards are not evenly distributed among a given population. Certain very high energy, or very low energy people, and in general the very young and very old, are more sensitive to these toxic energies, and will react to them more quickly and strongly. In the next Chapters, I will recount several specific cases, with practical suggestions people can do to protect themselves, and their accumulators, from these environmental hazards. But we can firstly outline the problem.

In the average home, the most common orgone irritants are the cathode-ray TV set, the microwave oven, computer systems with associated "wireless" wi-fi technology, fluorescent lights of any kind (the full-spectrum fluorescent varieties reduce, but do not eliminate this problem), and spyware-laden so-called "smart" meters and appliances. Fluorescent lights often produce hyperactive plants, with enlarged, oversized leaves, and so fool people into thinking that the lights are "good". Some studies have even shown that depressed people can be agitated to a greater activity or metabolism by exposure to fluorescent lights. Examples are wintertime emotional depression, depressed newborn infants, and even "depressed" office workers, all of whom are agitated to a temporary increase in activity under fluorescent oranur. In many cases, the increased activity was linked to light color or frequency, and this also has its influence. But the problem of fluorescent oranur excitation is usually not addressed as a factor in those studies. Oranur is, however, produced by all types of fluorescent lights, TV sets, computers, wi-fi gadgets, cell phones, microwave ovens and smart meters. It can be objectively measured through the disturbed electrical potential of a house plant exposed to such devices, and sometimes through use of a standard or orgone charged Geiger counter. Or, a scientific evaluation can be made through extended measurements of accumulator functions, and observing the perturbation which occurs during oranur and dor conditions.

In any given city neighborhood, radio broadcast towers, airport radars, wifi and cell-telephone communications fixtures also constitute hazards, and producers of oranur. Like microwave ovens, and cathode-tube TV sets, they are allowed to leak relatively high levels of radiation into their local environments. The newer flat-screen LCD TV sets and computer monitors are much safer in this respect, if viewed from arms length.

Some early versions of infrared automatic door opening sensors or automatic light switches also emitted an *active* signal which was detected by sensors, turning things on and off. Mostly those are today replaced by *passive* technology, which merely detects your body heat. Passive electromagnetic devices pose no problem, only the devices actively radiating energy do so. In this sense, however, active electromagnetic WiFi-based library or commercial inventory scanners, which are designed to stop petty larceny or now for detection of ID-chips placed into products, may pose a problem for people who work in those environments, day after day; the actual risk here is simply unknown. Like microwave ovens and cathode-TV sets, they are allowed to expose the "average" person with an "average" dose, which is irrationally assumed to be harmless. Until more is known about them, one should err on the side of caution. Do not site an orgone accumulator near any of these devices.

Nuclear power plants likewise are permitted to vent (or rather, dump) significant quantities of diluted radiation into the cooling water and ventilation air that passes through the facilities. Aside from the fact that the local population breathes and often drinks this waste, which can accumulate in the food chain, there is the problem of oranur and dor. Both are created by nuclear power plants, and the atmospheric energy in these areas will be affected, with one qualitative state predominating over the other. Sensitive people can literally feel the difference in a region after a nuclear reactor has been operating for a period, and careful observations will sometimes reveal changes in weather patterns, of haziness and cloud cohesion.

Underground atomic bomb tests are, or were, perhaps the worst offenders, as they badly shock and agitate the orgone energy field of the entire planet. There is some evidence suggesting that severe weather extremes and earthquakes were triggered both locally and at considerable distances following such underground atomic testing (see the Reference section). The most severe example of this came from a series of ten atomic tests carried out sequentially over a short time-span by the Pakistan and Indian governments in May of 1998.

Within days, a major heat wave exploded across the India-Pakistan region, with a 6.9 magnitude earthquake in nearby Afghanistan. Several thousand people died in those events, and other severe weather reactions developed globally in a very short period of time.[§] By classical thinking, all of this was "impossible", but it makes perfect sense when considered as a widespread disturbance of the Earth's life-energy field. Other evidence, from the Japanese researchers Kato and Matsume has suggested the entire Earth is disturbed in its rotational dynamics, and the upper atmosphere overheated and perturbed, by underground atomic bomb tests. Geographer Gary Whiteford also documented changes in global earthquake patterns following underground atomic tests (again, see the Reference section for citations). These kinds of effects make no sense whatsoever from the viewpoint of classical biology, geology and physics, which denies the existence of any vital energy principle, and assumes that space is "empty". From the standpoint of orgone biophysics, however, these effects find a reasonable explanation. It is very much like our prior discussion of the life-energy in the lion or bear, being agitated by captivity or prodding. One is reminded also of the tortured bulls inside the Spanish arenas, where they are firstly stuck with sharp-sticks in the back, creating an emotional reaction of fury! It appears the life-energy charging the earth and atmosphere is similarly reactive, and irritable, like protoplasm.

In fact, the agitated and later lethargic and sick reactions of life-energy within living creatures, firstly documented by Reich in the oranur experiment, has been marvelously corroborated by John Ott in his book *Health and Light*. Ott demonstrated that laboratory mice exposed to agitating radiation from a cathode-type of TV set would at first become overexcited and hyperactive; later, the same mice would become inert and lethargic, eventually developing degenerative diseases. Ott gave many examples where aggressive behavior among breeding animals, such as mink and aquarium fish, were eliminated by removing oranur-producing fluorescent lights, coupled with increasing their exposure to full-spectrum natural daylight. Similar effects are at work upon schoolchildren, from fluorescent lights in the classroom. Ott demonstrated this using time-lapse

§ www.orgonelab.org/oranur.htm

filming, the alarming sequences of which are preserved in the video *Exploring the Spectrum*. Some school teachers have found that disruptive behavior in the classroom is often easily eliminated by simply turning off the fluorescent lights.

I have observed a similar reaction among children who are allowed to spend enormous amounts of time "watching" TV or surfing the internet. These effects are most notable with the older-style cathode-tube TV or computer monitor, so may not be so dramatically apparent with the newer flat-screen LCD displays. In any case, during the early phases of a child's TV or computer exposure, there is often little focus upon program content. The kids simply want the TV on, and they will often busy themselves with other things while sitting in front of it. Computer addiction also shows a similar syndrome. One often sees this strange behavior among entire families, where the evening or weekend family activity revolves around the big color cathode-TV. Nobody seems to care what program is playing, just so long as the TV is *on*. Or, children especially sit immobilized in front of the TV or computer screen, having less outdoor activity or human contact in the process. Like cocaine-eating laboratory mice, both children and adults may become *addicted* to the oranur effects of the computer or TV set. Later, like Ott's mice, they may enter an inert, lethargic, or immobilized stage, what is popularly called the *couch-potato syndrome*, which may be a correlate and precursor to obesity and degenerative disease. Of course, there is an emotional component at work here, where emotionally contracted adults and children may use the TV and internet as a means of escaping an unhappy social or family situation. But recall Reich's discovery that the orgone is the energy of the emotions. The strongly-radiating TV and computer, and for the child, the game-boy, playstation or cell phone for "texting" and other such things, are more than just a "cognitive" escape. They have *distinct bioenergetic effects which may, in the final analysis, be what makes them so addictively attractive to their users.*

This bioenergetic form of electromagnetic/oranur addiction is most clearly seen when someone tries to turn off the computer, cell-phone or TV set. Lethargic children, who were bathing themselves in the radiation of the viewing screen, but being immobilized or brain-dead-frozen, may suddenly become agitated and object quite vocally when attempts are made to shut it off.

Even adults suffering from this syndrome will be discomforted by the thought of shutting off the electronics, forcing them, as it would, out of a mildly catatonic state, into more direct emotional (bioenergetic) contact with other human beings. One sees a reinforcing overlap of this "bioenergetic buzz" for the adults being coupled with alcohol consumption, as in the appearance of electromagnetic TV displays at sports-bars, where the big TV stays on the whole time, and the bioenergetic feeling may be similar to a big electronic's store TV department. Of course, the colorful images give it all a jazzy upbeat feeling, and oftentimes the social atmosphere at the sports-bar may be more congenial than the alone-ness or veiled hostility the person faces at home in a dysfunctional family. In some cases, this can be a real and quite rational *temporary escape*, and not merely "escape-ism".

Of course, program content also plays a role, in that the more exciting and fantastic, or violent, cruel, and sexually titillating it is, the more it will touch upon the repressed feeling, sexual longing and bottled-up anger of the individual, to further feed the syndrome. I do not wish to condemn the use of TV in any sweeping manner, as there are a few islands of exceptionally good program content amid the ocean of *mental junk-food* which floods the airwaves.

Another response that belongs in this category is the widespread use of hand-held video games or increasingly fancy cell phones, typically by anxiety-prone teenagers who spend enormous amounts of time with them. We might call them *hand-held oranur devices*, where the individual gets a personal bioenergetic "fix", much like the addiction of a cigarette smoker. Loss of such an addictive toy can result in great anguish or even violent outbursts. Ott has shown that these devices, TVs (or cathode-ray computer screens) and fluorescent lights in particular, are often a cause of childhood hyperactivity. Other researchers today have observed similar behavioral disorders, reinforcing social isolation and emotional contraction among young children who are addicted to their electronic gizmos. The fluorescent-light and wifi oranur in school classrooms or as compounded by multiple computers, or as seen in TV departments of large stores, which also have many fluorescent lights, assault the body with tangible irritating sensations.

A clear case of TV radiation addiction came to my attention, with three hyperactive children who spent hours each day in front of the set, but paid little attention to program content. The minute they came home from school, the big color TV *had* to be on. When the TV was finally shut down, there was a wail of agonizing protest, and a period of even more agitated behavior. The frustrated mother had to cut the power cord to defeat the clever kids. After about a week of no TV, the kids calmed down and began to develop new friendships and activities, and *the hyperactivity disappeared completely*. The mother got rid of the big cathode-ray color TV, and later purchased a smaller flat-screen LCD set, which produces much less electromagnetic disturbance. Even though the kids were later allowed to watch the flat-screen TV almost as much as they wanted, they never fell back into the same trap, and the hyperactive syndrome did not occur again. In these cases, the energy system of the human had become addicted to the electromagnetic oranur agitation, which took a clear and conscious effort to overcome.

When using the orgone accumulator in an oranur or dor environment, all of the above considerations are most important, as the accumulator will amplify whatever kinds of energy conditions are present in the local environment. If oranur or dor is present, an accumulator will amplify those tendencies, imparting a disturbance to its charge. In some cases, the effects of oranur and dor are both persistent and widespread, and cannot be affected by simply changing things in your own home. This may be the case in some larger polluted cities, and certainly in the regions near to nuclear power facilities. Regarding nuclear power facilities, a distance of around 30 miles is recommended for safety regarding both the biological effects of emitted low-level radiation, as well as for use of an accumulator. (See my conditional note about the distance factor in the Author's Preface.) Similarly, if you are within a few miles of very high voltage electrical transmission wires, or large radio broadcasting towers, use of an accumulator is cautioned. Likewise, do not use an accumulator if your area has been recently subjected to a nuclear accident, and fallout is present. However, the same precaution applies to your own bioenergetic system. Just like the orgone accumulator, your own bio-system life-energy is going to be affected from these same factors. For this reason, some people choose to move to safer locations, typically following feelings they had anyhow, to move out into the countryside where life moves more slowly, with the natural rhythms. Learning about the orgone energy will be beneficial and deeply fulfilling, but it also makes us aware of potentially toxic aspects of our local energetic environment which previously went unnoticed.

One last set of considerations. Accumulators should never be used inside mobile homes or houses with aluminum skin or side paneling. Aluminum imparts a life-negative characteristic to the orgone energy, and it is advisable not to live inside such a structure even if an accumulator is not built or stored there. Mobile homes with wooden siding are safer, and no problem inherently exists with them.

However, note that some mobile homes and buildings are insulated with fiberglass batting that has an aluminum foil backing. If this kind of insulation is widely used, it will act very much like aluminum siding, and turn the house into a large, aluminum accumulator, imparting a slightly toxic or overcharge feeling. Also, houses with metal roofs, or new homes that use steel wall braces, instead of wooden components, may act somewhat like a large accumulator, and thereby amplify whatever effects come from electromagnetic exposures.

I once lived inside an aluminum-skin mobile home for a short period, and even without an accumulator, it developed a high charge of mildly nauseating energy inside. This can disturb a person's sleeping cycle, and lead to further amplification of the oranur effect if fluorescent lights, CFLs, microwave ovens, computers, cell phones, wi-fi communications, smart meters or cathode TV sets are used. Newer homes designed for energy efficiency often are similarly problematic as they typically include the aluminum foil for insulation and lots of spyware-loaded "smart appliances" radiating all kinds of toxicity, and may not have adequate ventilation, which makes their energetic situations even worse. One does not wish to live inside an orgone accumulator, due to the problem of overcharge, and sensitive people may often be driven to insomnia or anxiety by the overcharge which spontaneously develops within such a toxic-home structure.

Biologically we are not so different from the caveman, but we like to consider ourselves as "space-age" creatures, with all our electronic appliances and toys. Factually, however, you can live quite well with a standard land-line telephone, incandescent lights, ordinary gas or electric cooking, and flat-screen displays for both computer and TV, and no "wireless" radiating gizmos. We don't have to go back to kerosene lamps and horse-drawn buggies. It merely requires us to evaluate our technology with some wisdom, to make the technology adapt to our biology, and not the other way around. And who knows, in time, when the anti-gravitational functions of the orgone energy are understood, the human species will become quite space-age and even travel to the stars. Hopefully we won't become electronic cyborgs, or atomic-age mutants in the process.

Learn to recognize dor and oranur, such that if the feeling inside a building or accumulator is disturbed or uneasy, you can take necessary steps and precautions to eliminate those effects. The subjective feeling in an accumulator should be one of warmth, comfort and relaxation. This is where it becomes most important to learn about your energetic environment, and to get in touch with your own body and organ sensations. There are also some reasonably-priced meters for detection of electromagnetic fields (EMF) and microwave radiofrequencies (RF) to aid in this process. Practical steps and guidelines are given in the next Chapter for "Cleaning Up Your Energetic Environment".

9. Cleaning Up Your Bioenergetic Environment

The last chapter identified some potential problems regarding use of the orgone accumulator, or living within an energetically disturbed environment. The following points will help you to create a living environment in which the orgone accumulator will yield its strongest charge, with the most energetically soft and expansive characteristics. If you undertake as many of these steps as possible, it will not only protect your accumulator, but also yourself and family, whether you construct an accumulator or not. See point "N" below, for a discussion on simple measuring devices for detection and evaluation of the various low-level radiation sources discussed in this Chapter.

A) The "Old Barn in the Woods": The best of all possible environments for locating an accumulator would be on the dry floor of a large, airy barn in the countryside. Most people will not have such a barn, but may have a covered outdoor porch, which meets these conceptual criteria. One should try to duplicate these conditions as closely as possible. The "barn in the woods" environment should *ideally* be located next to open fields and forest, at least 30 miles from any nuclear facility, and 5 miles from any large cross-country power transmission wires. (See the Author's Preface for some caveats about the distance factors.) It should also not be on the "path" between microwave transmission beams, nor close to large radio, TV or cell phone broadcasting towers. It is best to have an open, airy structure, with good circulation and sunlight, but shielded from rains and high winds. Under a porch or a sunny room with some ventillation. No TVs, fluorescent lights, computers, cell phones, microwave ovens, wi-fi devices, radioactive smoke detectors, and so forth, should be present near to the accumulator. Only a few electrical outlets, with incandescent lights, should be present. However, place it away from the outlets.

B) <u>Plants, Fountains and Waterfalls:</u> You can enhance the life-positive energy characteristics in a room by filling it with as many living plants as possible, and providing it with continuous, adequate ventilation. Green plants soften the effects of dor and oranur, and additionally oxygenate the air. The same is true regarding the cascading water of a fountain. Most people can feel these expansive and pleasing effects, and indoor plants with waterfalls or fountains are being increasingly used to improve the subjective aesthetics within both large and small structures.

C) <u>Direct Water Cleaning:</u> If your environment is polluted, or is of a dry, desert character, be prepared to routinely water-clean the accumulator by regularly wiping the insides and outside with a damp cloth. You can also keep an open bowl of water inside it during times of non-use, to draw off any stagnant energy.

D) <u>House Building Materials:</u> Books devoted to helping people find safe building materials free of toxic chemicals are now available from bookstores, libraries and internet. These will inform you on the many new nontoxic products on the market. From a bioenergetic standpoint, a concern exists about living within, or building accumulators in, mobile homes or houses with aluminum or steel skins or siding. Aluminum siding makes a dwelling into an aluminum accumulator, which is known to have a toxic influence in and of itself. Any structure composed of metal walls, or even the newer homes using metal studs for interior wall partitions, can create an energy-accumulating effect. While you may want to "charge up" inside an accumulator on a periodic basis, you do not want to constantly live inside one! Remember, the *old barn in the woods* principle.

E) <u>Lighting:</u> Regarding lighting, all kinds of fluorescent lighting, including both the long-tube variety and the small curly compact fluorescent light (CFL) bulbs or their LED cousins which are screwed into ordinary lamp sockets, should never be used near or in the same room as an orgone accumulator. Both CFL and LED bulbs especially give off significant radio frequencies (RF), in addition to 60-cycle powerline electronic disturbances. Most people spontaneously don't like the feeling or the light from these bulbs, without even being told. This warning also is valid for the "full spectrum" varieties of fluorescent tubes and CFL and LED bulbs, which in fact do not mirror the Sun's natural frequencies. At the Orgone Biophysical Research Lab, I have made spectroscopic readings of both the Sun's natural spectra and many different types of light-bulbs. All kinds of fluorescent lights, including the full-spectrum kinds of CFLs and LEDs, yield a very "spiky" and incomplete spectra by comparison (see pages 102-103). Fluorescent lights additionally have an agitating electromagnetic ballast with high-voltage cathodes that excite and disturb the orgone energy continuum.

The best possible type of lighting from both a bioenergetic and full-spectrum consideration, is the simple and economical clear-glass incandescent or halogen bulb. The unfrosted variety where you can see the filament through the clear glass is best. These bulbs closely duplicate the natural solar spectrum, and do not create oranur. Any waste-heat produced will merely warm your home, which is not a problem in cooler climates.

Energy-efficiency claims regarding CFL and LED bulbs also are considerably hyped, as it takes a lot of energy to produce them by comparison to a simple incandescent or halogen bulb, and most CFL and LED bulbs will burn out much quicker than advertised when subjected to normal on-off usage. You will also need several of them to equal the light intensity of an incandescent. *Be skeptical of what Big Government and Big Environmentalism claims on these issues.*

Furthermore, the CFL bulbs contain toxic mercury, thus complicating disposal and presenting an environmental hazard. Some of the stronger CFL or LED bulbs also carry an radiofrequency- emission warning on the packaging, which is a good indicator not to buy them. The non-continuous spiked color spectra of fluorescent tubes, CFL and LED bulbs often looks ghostly, or irritates the eyes, even if they fool you into thinking they might be similar to natural sunlight. "Old fashioned" incandescent or halogen bulbs remain the best lighting choice overall. In any case, *Big Brother Government should not be dictating what kind of light bulbs you can or cannot use.*

F) Cooking: Regarding your cooking, stay away from microwave ovens and stoves that work on electromagnetic eddy-current

Spectral Comparison of Different Light-Bulbs to Natural Sunlight.

The top spectrum graph on the opposing page is natural sunlight, which shows a frequency distribution from around 300 to beyond 900 nm, peaking at around 520nm. This is what living creatures, plants and animals, have been exposed to and evolved with over millennia. Just below that is the spectra of a standard clear-glass incandescent bulb, which gives the best-possible duplication of the solar spectra of all bulbs currently on the market. It functions by electrical heating of a filament inside a partial vacuum, which produces the light by an uncomplicated thermal process. The bulb is much cooler than the Sun, however, and so peaks out at about 625 nm, also producing some beneficial trace ultraviolet radiation down to around 350 nm. This mild trace ultraviolet radiation is life-positive, necessary for both skin and eye health, and is not harmful. The clear incandescent bulb also shows a smooth spectral curve which gives it a bright and full Sun-like appearance. Below that, at the bottom, is a so-called "full spectrum" compact fluorescent light bulb (CFL). Its spectra is composed mainly of sharp spikes from high-voltage electrical excitation of selected fluorescing phosphors. When mixed together, those spikes try to fool your eyes into believing they are similar to natural Sunlight. In fact, they produce an unpleasant effect which most people spontaneously do not like. Not only do they produce "junk light", but the bulbs emit radiofrequencies which at close proximity rival the output of a cell phone. They are not life-friendly, and yield up a toxic light and biological irritation. Many different bulbs have been tested at OBRL, and the clear incandescent ones always outshine virtually every kind of fluorescent tube or bulb on the market. Currently, LED bulbs yield a light similar to the "spiky" fluorescents, and also emit significant radiofrequencies. Time will tell if the light bulb manufacturers can produce an authentic full-spectrum variety of low energy-consumption. Meanwhile, *trust your eyes!*

Cleaning Your Bioenergetic Environment

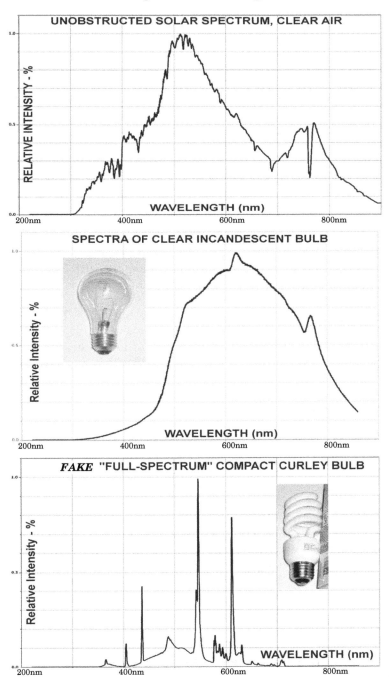

UNOBSTRUCTED SOLAR SPECTRUM, CLEAR AIR

RELATIVE INTENSITY - %

WAVELENGTH (nm)

SPECTRA OF CLEAR INCANDESCENT BULB

Relative Intensity - %

WAVELENGTH (nm)

FAKE "FULL-SPECTRUM" COMPACT CURLEY BULB

Relative Intensity - %

WAVELENGTH (nm)

principles. While microwave ovens are certified as "safe" by the federal government, the standards used to set this criteria are quite out of date, and a collusion between oven manufacturers and the government exists. Ovens, stoves and toasters that work through standard electrical resistance heating are safer, but they do emit some electromagnetic disturbances in the extremely low frequency (ELF) range. Another drawback with electrical resistance cooking appliances is that they are not very efficient in their use of energy, given the inherent inefficiencies of burning fuel, transforming it into steam, using the steam to turn a turbine to generate electricity, then pumping that electricity down a long wire, then converting that electricity back into heat in the home. From a biological and energy efficiency standpoint, it is best to use pilotless, electric-spark gas stoves and ovens for cooking. Microwaved food also reportedly often loses flavor, and is nutritionally suspect, with creation of radiolytic by-products which cannot be healthy.

G) Television: Regarding television, big color TVs using cathode-ray tube (CRT) technology are the worst offenders. They have three electron guns in the cathode tube, all aimed directly at your face, and operate at relatively high exciting voltages. The standard cathode-TV emits a wide spectrum of noxious energies, to include extremely low frequencies (ELF), soft x-rays, radio frequencies and pulsed magnetic fields. They rapidly build up the levels of oranur and dor in a room or house.

As an alternative, the newer technology of liquid crystal display (LCD) TVs are advised, and appear destined to replace the CRTs entirely. LCD technology is used in the flat-screen high-definition TVs, which are increasingly available at a reasonable price. Also acceptable from a bioenergetic standpoint are the projection TV sets, which do not have a cathode ray tube, and project the image onto a screen or wall. The electronics of both the LCD and projection TVs still have some disturbance upon the orgone energy, however, and should not be used near an accumulator. However, *plasma*-screen TVs consume more energy and have a stronger disturbing field than the LCD varieties, and so are disadvised.

H) Computers and Pads: Here, the same precautions are advised as with TV sets. Computer monitors using CRT technology are *worse* than the TV, in that a worker sits quite close, and spends a lot more time in front of them. The big CRT TVs and displays should be junked or recycled, as they produce ELF, radiofrequencies, soft x-rays, and pulsed magnetic fields, and have been linked to fetal deformities and miscarriages. If you use a computer a lot, then definitely switch to a flat-screen display using standard LCD technology, as described in the above section on televisions.

Aside from the computer screen, the internal circuitry of the desk-top computer will also produce electromagnetic disturbances and oranur, and should be placed as far away from the user as practical. For this reason, it is best to use the portable lap-top computers that run off rechargeable batteries and DC current, with a temporary connection to the wall-socket for battery recharging. Coupled with their internal liquid crystal display, they are probably the safest computers on the market, and additionally require a minimum amount of electrical energy to operate.

However, *lap-top computers should never be used in your lap*, as they do produce considerable radiation in close proximity to their case. Same with "pads", which often demand constant connection to internet by internal wifi radiation. If you cannot work them with a hard-wired ethernet connection, then my advice is, *don't buy or use*. Use them on a desk. Some people also use an external hard-wired USB keyboard and mouse, to avoid exposing their hands to the same proximity radiation, which is associated also with carpal tunnel syndrome. Typically that syndrome is described as the product of "repetitive motion" but in fact it could be the result of electromagnetic overdose in the hands. Also, use hard-wired connections in all cases. No "wi-fi" connections for the keyboard or mouse, and hard-wire also for the connection to your router and internet system. Better to have some cables strung on the floor or ceiling, than to get "strung out" and sick from chronic low-level microwave exposure! Regardless, *you should never use any kind of computer, pad or television inside or near to an orgone accumulator*.

I) <u>Electric Blankets and Space Heaters:</u> Regarding electric blankets, these have also been linked with increased miscarriages and spontaneous abortions among pregnant women. Even when off and only plugged into the wall socket, they can emit a powerful AC electrical field with toxic influences. It is advised that you get rid of them, and go back to the wool blanket, down comforter, or heavy quilt. *Electric blankets should never be used with an orgone blanket,* or in an accumulator. By inference, this caution regarding electric blankets should be extended to cover portable electrical resistance space heaters. Used at a distance from your body there is no problem. And better to move the orgone accumulator indoors over winter if it would otherwise be too cold and left unused. Or, use an orgone blanket indoors.

J) Radio or TV Broadcasting Towers, and Power Line Emissions: Regarding radio or TV broadcast towers, and large overhead electrical transmission power lines, the environmental hazards are only recently being documented. Do not be surprised if the local power company, or even environmental groups, have little information on these subjects. Educate yourself about the dangers, purchase appropriate EMF/RF meters, and make an assessment based upon your proximity, and the measurements. According to my own study of the problem, 2-5 miles is a safe distance for both the larger, cross-country, very high voltage power lines, and for radio broadcast or telecommunication towers.

Electromagnetic (EM) fields from local power distribution lines also pose a much lower hazard, along with the power transformers on the power pole which feed a line coming into your home. The power surge is sent down that powerline with a pulse of 60 cycles per second in North America, or 50 cycles in Europe. Each pulse of electrical power creates a magnetic and electrical field surrounding the powerline. The pulses of energy race down the powerline and through the transformer which lowers its voltage from several thousand volts down to around 120 to 240 volts. It is then routed into the circuit-breaker fuse-panel of your home or office, which then distributes the power to the various wall sockets where you plug in your appliances.

Unfortunately, if the electrical wiring of your home is not properly and adequately grounded, this may create a large EM field inside your home. This can happen, for example, if the building contractor used your water-plumbing system for the earth-ground, as often is the case, or if the copper rods pounded into the earth have only an insufficient electrical grounding themselves. Additionally, one can almost always find strong

EM fields in nearly every home where the electrical power-supply wires enter the home, and also near to the fuse-panel of the home, where power supply is split up into multiple circuit breakers. You would not wish to locate an orgone accumulator, nor your bed or work-desk, close to those "hot spots" inside the home. And if for reasons of poor grounding, your entire home is "hot" with EM fields, then it is best to know about it, and take possible protective measures. The same is true with respect to cell phone and tower radiations in your neighborhood.

K) <u>Microwave Emissions from Radar, Cell Telephone Towers and 4-5G:</u> A major controversy is brewing about the biological effects of microwave radiation, which is finding increasing applications. In addition to use in household ovens, microwave frequencies are used for industrial drying and materials processing, and for weather, airport, and police radar systems. They are also used for long distance and cellular telephone communications, and now also for a plethora of "wireless wi-fi" devices such as computer networks, internet connections, wireless keyboards and so on. Also new "smart" appliances and electrical/gas meters use microaves to spy on you while reading your usage. *Your orgone accumulator must never be plced closed to these "stupid" appliances or meters*, and people also should avoid them when possible, keeping or switching back to "old-fashioned caveman" hard-wired telephone lines, computer connections, appliances and meters. If you must use a cell-pone or wi-fi connect for internet, then use ethernet cables to separate yourself from the radiating antenna components, which is where the "hot" and damaging radiation is emitted. Orgone accumulators should never be sited close to these gadgets.

L) <u>Smoke Detectors:</u> The cheaper *ionizing* smoke detectors use a bit of toxic radioactive waste as a source of ionization, as part of the operating mechanism. While they do function well for smoke detection, they should not be used in rooms with orgone accumulators, nor where people are living or sleeping. The radioactive irritation constantly produces oranur, and can rapidly agitate the energy within a room or small apartment. As an alternative, there are commercial smoke detectors that use the *photoelectric* principle as an alternative to ionization and radioactive waste. Photoelectric smoke detectors meet or exceed all zoning requirements and fire safety codes.

M) <u>Nuclear Facilities:</u> If you live in an area close to a nuclear power plant or waste storage facility, you should make a serious assessment of the danger to yourself and family. Get information on these facilities from local environmental groups. Usually, there are one or more of such groups trying to clean up or shut down nuclear facilities at any given location. These citizen's groups are the best informed regarding the health hazards of any given nuclear facility. Regardless, it is reasonable advice not to not live or work closer than 30 miles of such a facility.

Documentation on this was originally presented by Ernest Sternglass many years ago, in a small but important book *Low Level Radiation*, with more detail in Jay Gould's *The Enemy Within*. They demonstrated high rates of spontaneous abortion, low birth-weight and low IQ births, and increased cancers among populations living close to nuclear power plants, with the deleterious effects falling off with distance. Additional documentation is found in Gould's *Deadly Deceit*. These books introduce a substantial body of evidence on large problems with low-level atomic radiation exposure from nuclear power plants and similar facilities. Orgone Accumulators should therefore never be used close to any kind of nuclear facility. (See the Author's Preface and Chapter 8, on oranur effects).

N) <u>Radiation Detection Instruments:</u> Professional instruments for detecting electromagnetic fields or ionizing nuclear radiation are available today at fairly reasonable prices, and made for use by the ordinary consumer. Several excellent meters can be purchased to make a detailed assessment of your home, workplace, your child's school, and neighborhood. These would include a meter for detecting both low-level electromagnetic powerline frequencies (EMF), and microwave radiofrequencies (RF) for wifi, microwave oven, cell tower and radio tower emissions. Also I recommend a sensitive atomic radiation detector such as a Geiger-counter. Below I will give some details on these. If the price seems too high, it must be compared to the price of a serious disease, or low-level illness that reduces your work productivity. I know cases where several neighbors collectively pooled their resources to purchase a set of meters, and other cases where an entrepreneur purchased them to set up a new independent business, making environmental surveys for other people. I will also explain how to develop several simple and inexpensive devices. Once you have measured or approximated your toxic exposures from radiation sources in the neighborhood, home or office, and can precisely locate them, you can then take steps to mitigate against them.

Microwaves: The frequencies used for microwave ovens typically peak around 2 gigahertz (GHz), which is slightly different from that used for cell phones, cell towers and AM/FM broadcasting (up to 3 Ghz), while "smart" meters and newer 5G networks range out to 6 Ghz. Microwave ovens typically use much more intense radiations and are hence more toxic if you are constantly around them. The best and most reasonably priced broadband, combined EMF-RF meters we have tested are the *Trifield TF2,* and the *Cornet ED88T Plus.* They will detect both powerline EMF and RF microwaves, as from microwave ovens, cell phones and towers, AM/FM broadcast towers, and "smart" meters and appliances. Some years ago I began using and recommending these meters to others, and today they are widely available (as from Natural Energy Works: www.naturalenergyworks.net)

While you can decide to use or not use a microwave oven, or to use or not use a cell phone, you rarely have a choice when it comes to your exposure from cell phone towers, which provide the signals to each individual cell phone. The Telecommunications Act passed during the Clinton-Gore years specifically forbids local towns, counties or states from setting their own more stringent safety standards, which had the effect of allowing the cell phone companies to run rough-shod over the American landscape and populous. To protect yourself from "smart" meters, you must use existing laws to challenge them, but this is not always possible, it depends upon local laws and the presence of activist citizen's groups interested in this issue applying legal pressures. When you try to fight a cell phone or power company in the courts, you wind up fighting both governments and large corporations, so look for allies in your local region.

The major environmental groups have meanwhile grown in size and political power, and fell into the trap of typical Washington schmoozing, glad-handing and selling out their principles for flawed Big Government and Big Science agendas — or more crassly for money. Electromagnetic field safety standards were never high on their priorities, and they took their donation bribes, and "got with the program". So we now have cell towers, "smart" meters and appliances, and 5G relay stations sprouting up all over the place, including on the roofs of buildings, atop church steeples and in school playgrounds, often disguised as chimneys, stovepipes or placed within plastic palm trees. The public health isn't seriously considered here, because the same companies who make the devices sit on government panels where decisions are made about how much low-level radiation the public will be exposed to. And that calculus is dependent upon the lowest costs for making the technology function, which means, higher levels of radiation so that your teenager can get good cell phone reception even when down in the basement, hiding under a box.

I firstly came to understand the widespread nature of microwave exposure in the early 1990s, after installing a sensitive police radar-detector in my automobile. At one apartment where I used to live, my police radar detector would start chirping whenever I parked my car facing a certain direction. The detector gave an indication similar to being only a hundred yards or so from an operating police radar. The activity was stronger on the second floor of my apartment than at street level, and I later discovered that my apartment building was constructed along the path of a microwave telecommunications beam, that was being transmitted overhead from one tower to another. The people on the upper floors were receiving a significant dose of microwaves in their apartments, and the oranur agitation in those upper floors was quite apparent. Today I can drive through entire towns or counties where my TF2 or Cornet meters will give a strong signal from a variety of sources. Local people were being constantly bathed in the microwave energy coming from every direction!

How strong are these signals compared to what comes from nature? Basically, there is little or no exposure from nature in those frequency bands, which is why they were chosen for communications -- they are "naturally quiet zones". In the countryside, you may typically measure 0.002 micro-watts per square centimeter (μw/cm^2) exposure for radiofrequencies and microwaves, which is extremely low. Drive into the nearby city, and the levels can quickly shoot up to 1.0 or 10 $\mu w/cm^2$, or to levels in the hundreds of $\mu w/cm^2$. And it is very irregular in exposures. One home or apartment can be bathed in such radiations, while another is very quiet. Or, one part of the home is quiet, and another "hot". This makes it imperative to purchase a good RF meter to make these determinations. Not only is it very bad to locate an orgone accumulator in such a "hot spot", but you really don't want to sleep or work in such a hot-spot either.

Electrical and Magnetic Powerline Fields: Electromagnetic fields (EMF) from powerlines have two different alternating current (AC) components which must be measured separately, the electrical field and the magnetic field. The best meters we have found for doing this are the same ones used for the RF measurments, the *Trifield TF2* or the *CornetED88T Plus* (www.naturalenergyworks.net), which measure both electric and magnetic components, for both 60-cycle American or 50-cycle European AC calibrations. You do not wish to locate any orgone accumulator in a place with a constant exposure in those frequencies of greater than around 1 milligauss or 20 volts/meter. Nor is it wise to work or sleep in such an environment with those or higher levels of exposure.

In case you cannot find or afford such a measuring instrument, you can also detect these toxic EM fields by using a cheap AM/FM transistor radio, where the tuning dial is set to the extremes of its AM (520-1700 khz) or FM (87-108 mhz) range, where you cannot hear any stations. With this setting, it will give out only background static. You can in fact turn it up to full volume, and only hear a hissing sound. However, if you then hold the radio close to an electrical power outlet, power cord, electrical dim switch, telephone line or jack, computer, television set, or fluorescent light, you will find that the electrical disturbance will dramatically increase the level of interference and noise from the radio. In this manner, your small portable radio has become sensitive to strong electricaland magnetic field disturbances, and will give a clear audio signal when so exposed. By walking around your house and holding the radio close to devices, or even portions of your walls that you may suspect are giving off these toxic fields, you can locate safe and unsafe areas of your home. Use the cheapest possible radio, with a plastic case and with or without an external antenna, as available from consumer electronic stores.

Do not locate an orgone accumulator, or your bed, or your child's bed, near to any of these strong disturbing energy fields.

Nuclear or Atomic Radiation: There are no cheap or simple methods known for detection of low level atomic (ionizing) radiation. Beware also of the cheap bright-yellow Geiger counters being sold on the used market, which are typically old Civil Defense instruments. They would hardly react unless an atomic bomb had exploded nearby! So they are useless for detecting low-level radiation as from a nearby atomic power plant, or as emitted in the soft x-ray band as might from computer CRTs or cathode-TV sets. Likewise, radiation from nuclear facilities is generally rendered dilute, but still dangerous, by mixing it with large volumes of air and water. Sophisticated methods for monitoring over hours or days, or concentration of air and water samples, are required for proper measurement. Holding a simple Geiger counter in front of a TV set or computer screen, or holding one in the air near a nuclear plant, will rarely detect anything, and is generally a meaningless procedure. Likewise, the cheaper pocket dosimeters are generally made to detect fairly high levels of radiation, and will not register low level effects. Even so, I have seen physics professors hold a Geiger counter tube, made for detection of intense gamma radiation, in front of an intense buzzing cathode-TV set, declaring it to be "completely safe". This, of course, is nonsense. What I recommend for neighborhood evaluations or home-use is the *RadAlert* or similar sensitive, broad-spectrum instrument that will pick up the entire range of soft x-ray, alpha, beta and hard gamma radiations. (www.naturalenergyworks.net) With familiarity, you can use such an instrument to judge general background radiation, against which contaminated atmospheric conditions or objects will yield a higher count readily apparent from the background averages.

O) <u>Safe EMF/RF Levels and Protective Devices:</u> While above I provide details for simple and cheap methods for rough determinations of EMF radiations, this should not suggest the issue is insignificant or trivial. If you use the cheaper methods, and discover a significant part of your home or neighborhood is "noisy" and reactive, then you should go to the next step and make more precise determinations, as with the more exacting meters. Anything registering more than around 1 milligauss (AC magnetic fields) or 20 volts/meter (AC electric fields) or 0.1 µw/cm2 (radiofrequency) is probably too much for a chronic long-term exposure, especially for children and pregnant women. My advise for maximum exposures is maybe 1/10th to 1/100th of the Federal standards, so of course "official science" of Big Government would emphatically disagree with my recommendations. But so far, *we do have the right to publicly disagree with and challenge Big Government and Big Corporations.* The decision on "what to do" is also your own to make, so don't rely only upon what is given in this book, but do your own homework and research the issues from a variety of viewpoints. And get the measuring meters so you know for certain just what are your exposures. Don't rely upon guessing or speculation!

Also *beware*, there are many different gadgets being sold as "protective devices", for supposedly "neutralizing" EMF and RF radiations. These range from little buttons you put on your cell phone, to larger pyramid or crystal thingys you put near to your computer or screen, and from there more expensive gadgets you plug into the wall, to "protect your home" with one device. I must express a great skepticism about these claims, because I have never seen any defendable scientific evidence showing they reduce the measured EMF strength. People sometimes swear by them, but as a natural scientist, I must remind people of the power of persuasion. This is why use of a good measuring device is so important. So long as you can measure the EMF or RF, then its effect is still there, still present, no matter what the gadget manufacturer claims. And most electrosensitive people will acknowledge this.

I know of several cases where the measured EMFs were ignored, in deference to some gadget which claimed to "neutralize toxic EMF!" resulting in deaths. In one case, a woman who worked as a secretary developed acute neurological disorders which flared up dramatically whenever using a computer, but lessened when away from them for a few days. Calling me for advice, I recommended changing her job, to something outdoors. Fearing poverty, she kept the secretary job and started wearing a metallized apron and hat, as well as several protective devices on the computer, which had a big CRT display, blasting her in the face and upper chest all day long. Her boss refused to purchase a new low-emission flat-screen monitor, and she refused to purchase a lap-top, to eliminate the source of the problem. But she was willing to go to the hospital doctors for pills to suppress the symptoms of the CRT radiations! She died within a year. Medical practitioners who are confronted by such symptoms usually do not make a diagnosis based upon the energetic ecology of a patient's home and work environment, and may not even inquire about it.

In another case, a woman called up whose daughter had developed acute lymphoma, apparently from living on the upper floor of an apartment where, on the roof, was located a cell phone tower. The apartment management had not informed anyone, and typically this is something which happens when the cell phone company offers a monthly fee to the apartment owner, to rent the space on the roof. In any case, the woman asked me what I thought about the situation. Without hesitation I said "move out of there, immediately". Instead, she purchased a $300 device which claimed to "neutralize toxic EMF". I never heard back until a year later, when she wrote a grieved letter indicating her daughter had died, and how devastated she was for not moving out of the apartment.

In another case, a man with three daughters called me, one daughter having just developed leukemia, and another showing preliminary signs of the same. The family doctor told him it was "something genetic", but the man considered it might have something to do with the large AM-FM broadcasting tower located about 1 mile from his home. He purchased several meters, which gave readings well above my recommended 0.1 μw/cm^2 threshold, and within a week had moved his family to another location in the countryside, with no EMF exposure, good fresh air and clean water. Within a year, his daughters had recovered fully, without any sign of the disorder. He later started reading up on Wilhelm Reich, and while the standard advice is to *not* treat leukemia with the orgone accumulator – it is an overcharge biopathy, not necessarily requiring additional life-energy – he is today quite enthusiastic on the whole subject, and constantly is giving advice to his friends in the old neighborhood. They halfway think he is crazy, but cannot dismiss the recovery of his daughters.

Typical Consumer-Level EMF/RF Meters.
The Cornet ED88T Plus (top)
The Trifield TF2 (bottom)
www.naturalenergyworks.net

From the above, it is clear that you can do a lot to eliminate toxic energetic disturbances inside your home and work place. Dealing with such problems in the local neighborhood is more difficult. Sometimes the only solution is to move to a new location or change jobs.

Another decision some people make, when finding their local environment is being radiated by cell phone towers or nearby atomic facilities, is to organize for social change. This is far more difficult than private-personal change. And typically, when dealing with such issues, you will be fighting government policy that is nearly carved into stone. Most of the major environmental groups, for example, have sold their soul on issues such as EMF and RF safety, just as they have done by endorsing the deeply-flawed CO_2 theory of global warming, for which the biggest beneficiaries always were the nuclear power plant vendors and Wall Street "cap and trade" stock brokers. Most of the Big Environment organizations seem mostly aimed towards socialist goals, of helping Big Brother Government to get more power to tell you what to do, and when to do it, and also to grab more money out of your pockets, to stuff into their own.

However noble "social change" may sound, your first and foremost priority should be to secure your health, and that of your loved ones. Then consider social action, and devotion of some of your time to working collectively with like-minded people. A lot of self education, and education of others, may be required to get even small problems resolved. Still, some people will have the resources and be quite happy to fight City Hall, or effectively take on a local industry or utility. So if you have the time and life-energy to do so, well and good. But firstly save yourself and family. One thing is sure, the problem with radioactive and electromagnetic pollution, and the consequent bioenergtic dor and oranur associated with them, will only get worse in the foreseeable future.

To get started, acquire the proper meters and survey your home and neighborhood. Do internet searches on "stop smart meters" or "microwave hazards" and similar phrases. That will put you in touch with concerned people and groups in your own area. Asking around at local health food stores, or at the public library, is a reasonable place to start, and see what you can learn.

10. Natural Healing
Living Waters

Whenever we take a long soak in a tub of hot water, or relax ourselves with a foot bath, we in part gain that feeling of relaxation because of the energy absorbing capacity of the water itself. Reich observed that water had a strong mutual affinity and attraction for the orgone energy. Water therefore has a special capacity to draw off bioenergetic tension and stasis, including what Reich called *dor*, the deadened, immobilized form of the life-energy. Water can also carry its own intrinsic charge and pulsation, such that when we soak in especially alive or *living water*, we can be revitalized.

A warm-water soak reduces our internal orgonotic charge, and bioenergetic tension, and we relax. The effect may partly be explained by thermal warming of our bodies, and stimulus of our parasympathetic relaxing-expanding nervous system, but other considerations are clearly at work. By soaking in a tub of water, the energetic potential of the body will be reduced, while the energetic potential of the water will increase. We literally lose energy into the water, and relax, somewhat like an inflated balloon that has lost a bit of air.

The energetic absorbing or *drawing* effect of water can be changed in character, into a combined *absorbing and energizing* effect, through use of dissolved crystals, such as Epsom salts, which increase the energy potential of the water, thereby making it a more powerful attractor and mobilizer of our own biological energy. A similar energizing and drawing effect can be brought about by soaking in a tub of water which contains 1 pound each of sea salt and baking soda. Salt and soda baths, lasting around 20-45 minutes, can be used to reduce tension and overcharge, or to drain off a toxic charge of energy, as well as to revitalize and provide fresh life-energy released by the crystalline materials.

The mineral baths at various natural hot-springs where the water has observed healing properties appears to be based upon

117

similar life-energy principles. Many resorts and health spas are built at locations where hot springs, or other waters or earth materials (muds, clays, ash) of an unusual nature exist. Such hot-spring mineral waters were used by Native Americans, who often put sweat-lodges near to them, and pour the high-energy mineral-rich waters onto the red-hot stones inside the lodges. The released steam and energy had healing effects, in a manner parallel to modern natural healing methods utilizing saunas and steam-baths, with aromas and vapors.

European colonials frequently copied the Native American ways, and throughout American history all the way into the 1940s there were many health spas located on natural hot-springs which drew visitors from around the countryside. It is common for people to soak in these mineral waters, or in special mud, sand, clay or ash baths, after which they feel greatly relaxed, uncommonly energized, or even healed of chronic ailments. Medical symptoms may be relieved, temporarily or permanently, by partaking of these soaking baths. These healing waters were often called "radium waters", because of the early 1900s discovery of radium by the Curies in Europe, and the subsequent widespread fad (and frequent abuse) of atomic-radiation therapies in the hospitals. The quantities of radium or radon-gas in natural hot-spring waters has typically been appreciably low, but in the absence of any other known explanation for the healing nature of the waters, this incomplete explanation took hold. In other cases, such as the big grotto spring in Lourdes, France, the healing waters are given a metaphysical explanation.

Today, we may postulate, these are orgone-charged waters, percolating up from deep within the Earth. Evidence for this is found in two forms. Firstly is the oftentimes deep blue-glowing or luminating characteristic of these hot spring waters, and secondly the abundant semi-alive vesicles typically found in such waters, which frequently bubble-up from extreme depths of great pressure and high temperature, where microbes ought not to exist. And these are very strange "microbes" indeed. Called *thermophiles* or *extremophiles* by modern microbiologists, these are frequently claimed to produce the blue-glow, but strangely do not create typical bioluminiscense effects in the microscope, nor "cloud up" the waters in which they are found, as one might see where a clear broth is made cloudy when it spoils from microbial contamination. Instead, the hot-springs maintain a deep blue clarity even when less than a meter deep, something which also negates typical "light-scattering" claims as is usually invoked to explain a similar wonderfully alive intense blue colors observed in deep lakes and oceans.

Reich's work provides a basic explanation for these effects of natural healing waters and earth baths. Reich discovered the orgone energy, or life energy, during experiments which demonstrated that microscopic, energy-radiating vesicles could be derived from the disintegration of various organic and inorganic materials. Clay, soil, ground rock, beach sand, and iron filings were among the inorganic materials that, when allowed to disintegrate and swell in water or sterile nutrient broth solutions, would form the small radiating vesicles, which he later called *bions*. The process of bion-formation could be speeded along by heating the mineral materials to red-hot incandescence, before plunging them into the nutrient solutions.

Certain sands from Scandinavian beaches were found to form bions of an exceptionally strong, bluish, radiating character. The blue bions from these preparations developed energy fields that could irradiate people and objects, and for a period, Reich experimentally used the energetic bion solutions for the treatment of various disease symptoms. Bion solutions were injected into experimental animals, where they had an immobilizing influence upon pathogenic bacteria and cancer cells. Later, poultices made from bions, by which the energy directly liberated from the disintegrating substance could be used to irradiate the body.

Parallel to Reich's discovery of the bions, the Austrian naturalist Viktor Schauberger made a series of findings on the alive nature of natural spring water, as opposed to processed city water. He called such natural and alive spring water, *living water,* as observed during his youth in the Alpine region. Everyone will appreciate the refreshing qualities of such natural spring water as compared to chlorinated city or plastic-bottle water, even though modern chemists and government bureaucrats will typically scoff at the idea. But both Reich and Schauberger appear to have identified, by different directions of research, a fundamental truth about water, the universal solvent, which even today one cannot say is well understood. As noted in Chapter 6, notably in the work of Piccardi, we know that water is a substance which reacts to sunspots, magnetism and other cosmic phenomenon. That it should carry a charge of the cosmic life-energy, the orgone, along with blue-glowing bionous material, would not be surprising, and this would explain quite a lot.

After the discovery of the orgone energy accumulator, which developed its charge directly from the atmosphere, Reich ceased experimental development of bion packs for such purposes. In later years, however, with the energetic and chemical poisoning of the atmosphere, and the consequent problem of contamination of the accumulator, interest in bion packs has been rekindled.

The following simple recipe for the bion pack was developed from a variety of sources. A bion pack can be made from clean beach sand or other earthen or clay materials known to have healing properties. A large handful of the earthen material is wrapped in a thick sock, or other heavy fabric container, like a sausage, about one foot in length and 1/2 foot in width. It should be tied or sewn shut so that the material cannot spill out. The bion pack is subsequently saturated and boiled in water, or in a pressure cooker, for about 15 minutes. Do not use a microwave oven, as this will disturb the bioenergetic properties. After being heated, the bion pack is wrapped in wax paper or plastic and allowed to freeze solid, in the freezer. For the first use of the bion pack, the boiling and freezing process should be alternated several times. It should not be cooked in a microwave oven. The bion pack is used after one of the boilings, being allow to cool, with excess water drained off. The pack is then applied to the body, with additional cloth insulation in case it is too hot. As the beach sand disintegrates from the cooking and freezing, radiating microscopic blue bions will form. The radiation from such a bion pack should continue even after the pack has cooled off, and it can be rejuvenated after drying out by repeating the boiling. Orgone radiation can be obtained from this natural source, even in very dorish, polluted atmospheres, when use of an orgone blanket or accumulator would be problematic. The effect was discovered by Reich early in his research, and both the existence and behavior of the radiating bions has been confirmed by other scientists.

Before the modern era of drugs, health professionals used special kinds of warming, radiant clay or sand packs, or plasters, which were used to relieve aches and pains, or for healing wounds or infections. Many of these poultices or plasters were learned from native healers, who knew which muds or plants gave the best effects. Some of these poultices are still commercially available, but rarely with any health claims being made. One must consult textbooks on herbal medicine, or look for them in the health-food stores. There are many plastic or rubber "plasters" and "warmth packs" available from drug stores, but these are based solely upon thermal phenomena. However, the various health spas and mineral spring resorts, where people soak in special muds or other earth or plant-based materials, are using the principles of life energy radiation, liberated from those natural earthen substances through the principles of bionous disintegration. A similar bionous process may also be at work regarding the use of rock dust fertilizers, for reinvigoration of dying forests and contaminated lakes, and in the "mud facials" or "clay masks" applied to refresh the face, and tighten the sagging skin.

This tradition of the healing waters and poultices eventually attracted the hostility of the American hospital-MDs, in the 20th Century FDA-AMA-Pharmacy war against natural healing methods. Health benefits were clearly observed and documented when soaking in such waters or in mineral or clay baths — as with the disappearance of chronic arthritis and rheumatism. Such waters were typically heavily mineralized, sometimes being quite stinky with sulfides, but would — partly because of such minerals — alleviate various health problems when drank or soaked in. Up into the 1940s, it was typical for these hot springs and mineral-water companies which bottled them for drinking, to advertise their health-benefits. President Franklin D. Roosevelt, for example, frequented the healing waters of Warm Springs, Georgia, which continues to be used as a therapeutic center for polio hydrotherapy. It survives, however, only because Roosevelt bought the place and created an institute to guarantee its survival. Few other of these healing-water health clinics and spas survive into the modern era, however.

Due to demands by the FDA, AMA and local MD-hospitals, and working through crooked or malicious prosecutors threatening health-spa owners with imprisonment, the surviving high-energy healing water hot-springs are today dramatically reduced and constrained as to what they can say or publish about their health benefits. Rarely are clinics located on their premises, and many have been converted merely into museums or national parks, places of historic interest where you can walk around and see photos of people taking the mineral baths, but not do so yourself. This suppression of the healing-water traditions took place about 10 years before Reich's work was assaulted by the same FDA and hospital doctors.

With some searching, however, one can still locate these old hot-springs. In a few cases, they survive and while prohibited from making disease-cure claims, they are integrated with resurgent natural healing methods such as massage therapy, which poses little threat to the doctor's pills.

*Above: Postcard image of Radium Hot Springs, Albany Georgia, characterized by **deep blue waters** where people flocked for healing and recuperation. It is today vanished, the site occupied by a golf course with "no swimming allowed". Such natural healing hot-springs, spas and clinics existed by the hundreds across the USA before the rise of the FDA, AMA and MD-Hospital monopoly, which worked tirelessly to shut them down.*

In Europe, by contrast, the spa traditions are still being preserved. Like the Native Americans, Europe has a long history of using such *mineral health baths*, or *healing baths*. There are hundreds in Germany alone, for instance, appropriately called *Heilbäder*, with physicians in attendance to help people who have come to find a nature-cure, all under the auspices of their official health-care system. German physicians may actually prescribe a visit to such a hot spring/mineral water health resport, and have it paid by the German health-care system. And the science is developed such that all Heilbäder are officially identified for benefiting specific organ systems, and for stimulating healing effects for their respective ailments. The physicians will write their prescriptions accordingly.

There are six recognized major categories of healing baths: the *Mineralheilbad* (mineral healing bath), the *Moorheilbad* (peat-healing bath), the *Seeheilbad* (Ocean healing bath), the *Soleheilbad* (salt healing bath), the *Kneippheilbad* (following the methods of Dr. Kneipp), and spas devoted to *Radonbalneologie,* the application of natural radon gas.

This latter application of radon gas constitutes a kind of "homeopathic dose" of radiation, through an effect termed *hormesis* by classical radiation biophysics, to stimulate the whole system. It is suggestive of a mild *oranur effect*, which Reich discovered could have therapeutic values in low doses. However, these life-enhancing effects appear limited only to brief exposures to low-level natural radiation sources, notably radon gas exposures, and not to any kind of prolonged exposure to hard-radiations from processed uranium ore or its by-products. In small careful doses, hormesis (or *oranur medicine*, as Reich termed it) could bring about a healing effect.

This parallels the observations of ancient peoples, as a part of the folk lore and natural healing methods which stimulated the ideas of Hahnemann, who discovered the principles of homeopathic medicine. The "medicine bags" carried around the neck by some Native Americans frequently would have small bits of mineral and plant materials whose mild radiations made them feel stronger or more alive. My personal conversations with a few old-time mineral prospectors indicates that some classes of radioactive mineral made them *feel good*, as if to create a strong bioenergetic expansion, while others yielded not-so-good feelings. And it also is true that, years ago, people would go sit inside caves or abandoned mines and breathe the radon air, with the claim it would cure their respiratory diseases. This is an old body of natural healing methods basically lost to the world, but certainly ought to be studied with some rational inquiry. It should be clarified, here I am speaking about mines where no more drilling or mineral extraction is taking place. Consequently, the air is no longer laden with dusts or particulates.

Another way to clean up the energetic atmosphere within a home or apartment is the use of draw tubes or draw buckets. Like the accumulator, these devices are very simple, passive instruments that function by virtue of basic energetic principles. Draw tubes are hollow metal tubes, made from 1/2" or 3/4" diameter galvanized steel electrical conduit pipe, cut to around 2' lengths. The draw bucket requires a plastic or metal pail, placed on a drain board or in a large sink or bathtub, into which water flows from a faucet, and then is allowed to slowly circulate and overflow. The draw tubes are halfway immersed into the draw bucket, while the other half is allowed to point off into various parts of the room or apartment which needs energetic cleansing.

As the water slowly circulates in the bucket, toxic forms of orgone energy are drained out of the room, and possibly from adjacent rooms as well. Dor tends to be exceptionally water-hungry, and will be removed from the room, assuming that additional quantities are not being created. Oranur will also be lessened, as the draw tubes and bucket gradually lower the energy level in the room, reducing agitation and overcharge. After the draw system has been in place and operating for awhile, you can hold your hand in front of the tubes and sometimes feel a slight tingling or "cool breeze" phenomenon. It is recommended that the tubes be positioned away from where people are resting or sleeping; they should likewise not be pointed to any part of the body longer than a few seconds. They can be set up for occasional or semi-constant use in an office or working environment, to reduce oranur overcharge and agitation. On several occasions, I have seen such a system in use to lessen oranur in rooms with operating computer systems. In these cases, where a sink or drain is not near the areas to be treated, several lengths of hollow, flexible steel condiut can be used to extend the drawing effect from a sink or bathtub full of water into adjacent rooms. Point the open ends of the cable to the areas you want to clean. This kind of cable is used for electrical wiring, and can be purchased at most large hardware or electrical supply stores. Do not use aluminum flex-conduit, and do not run any wires inside it.

It is essential that the grounding water be as clean as practical, and circulating or moving. It must be constantly refreshed, even if only by a trickle of fresh water. A good method is to place a bucket into an existing deep sink or bathtub, fill it, and allow the water to then overflow into the drain. The volume of water-flow can then be cut down to a trickle, and the tubes inserted. In all cases the tubes should be made of galvanized steel. The tubes must be hollow, without dust or dirt on the interior. One end of each tube must be immersed into the water, and a number of tubes should be used.

When draw tubes and buckets are allowed to work in a room for several hours or days, the room gains a softer feeling and sweeter smelling condition; stuffy or oppressive conditions generally vanish. The metal tubes amplify the natural drawing effects of the water, grounding out stale and toxic forms of the orgone energy, changing it from a life-negative to life-positive character. They should work their influences within a couple of days at most. Unless the space is exceptionally badly contaminated, use them periodically, not permanently.

The principles of the draw tube and bucket are based upon Reich's findings that water has the capacity to strongly attract and absorb orgone energy, and that hollow metal tubes has the capacity to focus or extend the drawing influence of the water some distance outward. At one point in his research, Reich developed a device called the *medical dor-buster*, which was used experimentally on patients, to remove overcharge and dor from the body.

11. Physiological and Biomedical Effects of the Accumulator

It will be useful to review the biological effects of the orgone accumulator, as given by various people who have actually worked with it, and know just what it can and cannot do. However, this chapter should not be considered as a definitive or comprehensive overview of Reich's findings on cancer, the biopathies, or even the biological effects of the accumulator. It is not, and only constitutes a bare-bones summary, to let the reader know what kinds of things to look for if the accumulator is ever used in a health-related context. Selected citations for the materials summarized below appear in the Reference section.

The actual discovery of the orgone energy and accumulator was first announced by Reich in the 1942 issue (Volume 1) of the *International Journal of Sex-Economy and Orgone Research*, in a section on "The Construction of a Radiating Enclosure". That journal focused also upon the *emotional* aspects of the cancer biopathy, the relationship of cancer to emotional resignation, sexual starvation, and chronic energy depletion. Reich also published his findings on the spontaneous organization of cancer cells from the patient's own bionously disintegrating tissues. Additional information was later published in *The Cancer Biopathy*, the *Orgone Energy Bulletin*, and the *Orgonomic Diagnosis of Cancer Biopathy*. Reich's findings on cancer were confirmed by others, who likewise published in his journals. But he never saw the accumulator as a simple "cure" for cancer, and explicitly said so on a number of occasions. However, he did lay claim to the following discoveries:

1) Cancer is a systemic biopathic disorder, and not just a localized tumor.

2) The cancer biopathy starts in early life, with a major component related to early childhood trauma, and the consequent respiratory block and suppression of emotions; later in adolescence, and in adulthood, the individual has great difficulty

establishing a love life, and eventually resigns from sexual pleasure, and from joy or meaning in life.

3) The cancer patient possesses significant bioenergetic neuromuscular contraction and tension (armoring) that restricts circulation and oxygenation in primary organ systems, including the sexual organs.

4) The cancer patient suffers from a chronic loss, and gradual depletion of bioenergetic charge of body tissues.

5) Shortly before onset of tumor development, the individual experiences a powerful emotional blow, such as loss of a special loved one, which reinforces their emotional resignation.

6) The cancer cell originates from bionous processes, arising from the disintegration of the patients own energetically weakened tissues.

7) A specific *t-bacilli* is found in copious quantities in the tissues and blood of cancer patients; t-bacilli are culturable, and when inoculated into mice will cause tumors to form.

8) Use of the accumulator could not by itself reverse the deeper biopathic nature of the cancer disease; in a limited way, however, it could stimulate the bioenergy system to expand, recharge the tissues, and even disintegrate tumors.

While this last point may sound like a cure for cancer, Reich was cautious about this, though clearly optimistic. Of the case histories given in his writings, he emphasized the failures over the successes. He was constantly making careful evaluations of the patient's blood, and also developed a new bioenergetic blood test, that allowed even precancerous tendencies to be identified. He also observed that the gentle vagotonic, parasympathetic excitation the accumulator provided would often deepen the respiration of the patient, and help to bring long-buried feeling to the surface. Reich also worked with his patients characterologically, to overcome the emotional and respiratory blocking and sexual stasis associated with the cancer. The highly-charged blood would distribute new life energy from the accumulator throughout the body, into every organ and tissue, as patterns of emotional holding were likewise being relaxed, and the respiration deepened.

It was clear that the accumulator could recharge the organism, and even in a limited way help to overcome many secondary complications of the disorder. People would often regain lost organ functions and an increase in energy, for a few years, or sometimes in association with a complete remission of symptoms. But often, at least in the published accounts, a relapse would occur. In some cases, it was apparent that as the patient's tumors began to disintegrate, they would become debilitated by the toxic breakdown products of the tumor, and die of secondary complications, such as kidney or liver failure. This was a particular problem when tumors deep inside the body were being broken down, and easy discharge of toxic tumor debris was not possible.

In some cases when the patient's bioenergy level was being recharged by the accumulator, they began to feel a welling-up of buried feelings, which they often did not want to deal with. In some cases, as they began to recover, they developed pains in the genital area or thighs, related to their sexual stasis. Reich found that almost all of his cancer patients had not had sexual intercourse for years, and were trapped in a loveless, compulsive marriage. In such cases, overcoming the obstacle of sexual stasis and blocked emotion, and restoring their desire to live, was the key to a remission. In a few cases, as these emotional problems surfaced, his patients would discontinue further treatment with the accumulator, even though significant tumor reduction and restoration of body function had occurred.

For these reasons, and also to emphasize his interest in cancer *prevention*, Reich focused upon the central role of emotional and sexual resignation in the life histories of cancer patients. Where this resignation from life and feeling could be overcome, Reich observed that the prognosis was better than where the resignation was left untouched. This factor appears to explain the common observation that cancer patients who become *emotionally mobilized*, who learn to express their sadness, rage, and terror, and who regain a desire to live, will have a better prognosis.

Given Reich's findings on the emotional component of cancer, the following question has to be asked: What effect upon emotional and sexual resignation occurs when radical cancer surgery deforms or incapacitates the sexual organs, or other body areas? Or similarly, what happens emotionally when the body is so badly assaulted by caustic chemicals and radiation, such that visible, frightening deformity occurs, and normal body functions, such as eating, defecation, or sexual arousal, are no longer possible? Such horrific treatments of degenerative illness surely can only *increase* emotional resignation and sexual stasis. Having done so, they cannot help but to also *increase* the rate of degeneration, and likewise *increase* the rate of relapse and metastases. In this context, it is no wonder that the mutilating surgeries and toxic chemical treatments advocated by cancer specialists today do not have any greater benefit to patients than the treatments of 30 or even 50 years ago!

Of course, the better known unorthodox treatments, which are frequently banned in many countries, can do much better than this. They commonly offer the patient natural foods and herbal remedies that energize and detoxify, in a manner similar to the bionous baths and bion packs discussed above. Reich, unfortunately, had his hands full with the discovery of the life energy, and other matters, and spent little time focused upon methods for detoxification. In *The Cancer Biopathy*, he did demonstrate, with use of a special fluorophotometer, that honey had about *eight times* the orgone charge of refined sugar, and also that unpasteurized milk carried *twice* the charge of pasteurized milk. The implication here is that natural foods are highly charged with life energy, as compared with synthetic, devitalized, and refined food products. The treatments developed by Gerson, Hoxsey and others, appear to have independently discovered these kinds of nutritional differences through empirical means, and are clearly more advanced than Reich on the effects of diet and detoxification. These practitioners likewise employ special herbal or nutritional treatments that appear to have a significant bioenergetic component.

Without detracting anything from these alternative treatment methods, however, *Reich's findings more clearly provide a scientific basis for the origins of the cancer biopathy and cancer cell.* His discussions on the emotional roots of cancer have been independently confirmed, and should assist in providing effective emotional invigoration of cancer patients. Reich's findings are also compatible with the various theorems on the causation of cancer from inadequate nutrition or environmental toxins, through the question of *energy level.* The measurable energy level of an individual appears functionally identical to the classical concept of *immunity*, or *disease resistance*, and is a key to understanding why one person gets sick, while another does not, under similar toxic environmental or dietary influences. Social and emotional factors, as well inherited factors, work a powerful influence upon the energy level, or charge of the tissues. Likewise, the discovery of viral/ bacterial pleomorphism (capability of microbes to change form: viruses into bacteria, and vice versa), the independent observations of the t-bacilli, and the rediscovery of the bions by various biogenesis researchers, all confirm Reich's positions on the bionous, self-generated nature of the cancer cell. The following fact cannot be emphasized enough: **the causation, process of development, and reasonably effective, non-toxic therapies for cancer have existed for decades, since the 1940s.** The obstacle has not been a failure of science, but of *too many arrogant MD cancer specialists, the corrupting influence of politics and Big Money Medicine, the slavish attitudes of the average person in the face of questionable medical authority (ie, the emotional resignation and helplessness, coupled with a "Doctors always know best" attitude), along with the abuse of the courts and police by the orthodox medical establishment.* If the reader finds my words unsettling, then I suggest they educate themselves on the authentic history of medicine, as revealed in the biographies of repressed and assaulted health pioneers such as Ignaz Semmelweiss, Harry Hoxsey, Max Gerson, Royal Rife, or Wilhelm Reich.

In spite of many difficulties, a lot of very clear and positive evidence has been gathered on the effectiveness of the orgone accumulator for treatment of a variety of symptoms and disorders. Very effective pain relief for, and subsequent rapid healing of severe burns has been reported. Likewise, a great reduction in pain was reported when the accumulator was used by cancer patients with tumors, and by persons suffering from arthritis. Besides Reich, other doctors associated with his research effort published case studies on the treatment of cancer with the accumulator. These published accounts demonstrated a significant and promising therapy for the disease. Complete remissions were rare, but people always experienced a reduction in pain and other symptoms, with a lengthening of life by at least several months to years beyond the conventional prognosis. Other medical problems were experimentally approached, such as diabetes, arthritis, tuberculosis, rheumatic fever, anemia, abscesses, ulcers, and ichthyosis. In these cases, benefits from orgone radiation and therapy were suggested. Reich also wrote about the promising application of the therapy to leukemia. Additional benefits in the form of an immunity to flu and colds, the elimination of skin problems, and general increased vigor and energy level were also discussed in the pages of his research journals.

To my knowledge, no clinical studies on treatment of human disease with the accumulator have taken place in the USA since Reich's death in prison. Only animals studies have been undertaken, mainly the effects of the accumulator on cancer mice, and on wound healing in mice. These laboratory trials with mice do confirm the wound-healing and anticancer effects of the accumulator. There are, however, human clinical trials from hospitals in Germany, where prescription of *orgone accumulator therapy* can be a standard medical recommendation. Several of the German physicians I met told me that *the somatic effects of the orgone energy accumulator were more powerful in the treatment of cancer than any other form of conventional or natural therapy they had tried.* They reported to me the following effects of the accumulator on cancer patients:

1. Pain was relieved, the appetite was stimulated, and the patients became more alert and active, often leaving the hospital bed, or the hospital itself, to resume activities that interested them.

2. The blood picture cleaned up, with red cells showing a stronger energetic charge, and fewer t-bacilli.

3. Tumors ceased growing, and in some cases, declined dramatically in size.

4. While some patients went on to show a dramatic recovery, others frequently gave only the outward *appearance* of a "cure". Orgone accumulator treatment alone could not touch the life-long emotional aspect of the biopathy, which would continue to deplete the patient in a manner that could not be compensated for beyond a certain unknown point. In those cases, while the accumulator would usually extend the life of the patient by months or even years, reducing their pain and making life dramatically better, they would eventually experience a relapse, with a sudden recurrence of symptoms, and a fairly rapid, albeit

less painful death. Unfortunately, we do not have any statistical measures by which to know the percentage of recoveries versus relapses, given the hostility of "official medicine" to the subject. 5. The German doctors also stated that many cancer patients were presented to them that did not possess the character traits of the fully-blown cancer biopathy, as described by Reich in the 1940s. In particular, many younger people and children came to them with tumors and a very poor blood picture, and with evidence of a greatly depleted energy level; but they did not have the complete sexual stasis or emotional resignation typical of the disorder among older persons. They attributed this to the prior exposure of the patient to environmental toxins and pollutants, and the increasingly devitalized nature of common foods. These observations suggested that, under conditions of environmental and dietary stress, energetically weak individuals are prone to tissue disintegration and tumor formation, while energetically strong individuals are not. In such cases, accumulator treatment gave excellent results, with a much better prognosis for long-term recovery.

Below I give a list from published sources, of various conditions or diseases which have responded favorably to the orgone accumulator — full citations are given in the Reference section or at the provided weblink. The orgone accumulator is best used in coordination with Reich's revitalizing methods of *character analytical emotion-release therapy*, to simultaneously help people to breathe more deeply, and get in touch with buried feelings and to deal with repressive social situations which may constitute the core of their emotional-energetic stasis and blocking. I must also caution, the materials summarized in this *Handbook* are only a preliminary. The accumulator must be used with care and knowledge, and not become merely a substitute for "doctor's pills", where the patient periodically sits inside it and does nothing more. It is necessary to read Reich's original works and the various papers I cite for more details, and where possible, combine it with other natural healing methods. Unfortunately, for most people approaching this subject, in the USA at least, the patient is frequently alone in their efforts, and must engage in somewhat isolated self-treatment, given how the FDA and friends have so utterly smashed down the subject. Nevertheless, as I describe elsewhere, there is reason for hopeful expectation of good, if not also frequently dramatic life-positive results from the orgone accumulator.

Clinical Case Studies of Disease-Treatment

Here is a listing of published papers listing the diseases treated along with the name of the physician who authored the paper, and the year of the publication. For citations, consult the author-year listings here: www.orgonelab.org/bibliog.htm

Disease	Physician/Author	Year
Cancer Biopathy	Wilhelm Reich	1943-48
Cancer, Burns	Walter Hoppe	1945
Mediastinal Malignancy	Simeon Tropp	1949
Multiple conditions	Walter Hoppe	1950
Multiple conditions	Victor Sobey	1950
Rheumatic Fever	William Anderson	1950
Breast Cancer	Simeon Tropp	1950
Ichthyosis	Alan Cott	1951
Manic Depression	Philip Gold	1951
Hypertensive Biopathy	Emanuel Levine	1951
Leukemia	Wilhelm Reich	1951
Cancer	Simeon Tropp	1951
Diabetes	N. Weverick	1951
Coronary Occlusion	Emanuel Levine	1952
Multiple conditions	Kenneth Bremer	1953
Skin Cancer	Walter Hoppe	1955
Pulmonary Tuberculosis	Victor Sobey	1955
Uterine Cancer	Eva Reich, W. Reich	1955
Uterine Cancer	Chester Raphael	1956
Rheumatoid Arthritis	Victor Sobey	1956
Malignant Melanoma	Walter Hoppe	1968
Cancer Biopathy	Richard Blasband	1975
Cancer Biopathy	Robert Dew	1981
Multiple conditions	Dorothea Fuckert	1989
Skin Infections	Myron Brener	1991
Cancer Biopathy	Heiko Lassek	1991
Multiple conditions	Jorgos Kavouras	2005

Controlled Studies on Physiology with Human Subjects

Aside from the many clinical case-studies published by Reich and his associates, as listed above, there are several excellent double-blind and controlled studies of human physiological responses to the orgone energy accumulator. These studies are not directed towards treatment of any specific disease or problem, but rather were organized to evaluate Reich's original claims as to the basic vagotonic, parasympathetic stimulus created by the orgone accumulator in human subjects.

The earliest of these double-blind/controlled studies, undertaken as a dissertation through the University of Marburg, Germany, was later published as *The Psycho-Physiological Effects of the Reich Orgone Energy Accumulator,* by Stefan Müschenich and Rainer Gebauer. A replication study of this same experiment – also controlled and double-blind – was undertaken a few years later by Gunter Hebenstreit at the University of Vienna, Austria. This also confirmed Reich, and both studies are cited in the Reference section, as are other studies. Some indicate Reich's orgone is the long-sought energy of acupuncture and Chinese Medicine. It may also ultimately prove to be the energy of homeopathic effects. Much remains to be clarified experimentally, though a lot is already confirmed.

Controlled Studies with Laboratory Mice

There also are many controlled experimental studies undertaken with laboratory mice, evaluating the effects of the orgone accumulator or orgone medical dor-buster (a related apparatus) upon their health and longevity. This includes mice either genetically predisposed to develop spontaneous tumors or leukemia, or who were given tumor transplants. As noted, these studies showed considerable improvement in the health of these immunologically-stressed or weakened mice when given a daily treatment with the orgone accumulator, as compared to control groups of mice. This was reflected in the overall descriptions and vitality factors of the mice, as detailed in the various papers, but mostly is objectified in their dramatically increased lifespans. Orgone accumulator treatment increased the mouse lifespans from 1.6 to 3 times longer than the controls!

For example:

1. Wilhelm Reich: "Orgone Therapy Experiments", in *The Cancer Biopathy,* Orgone Institute Press, Rangeley, ME 1948 (Farrar, Straus & Giroux, 1973, p.290-309).

This study was undertaken by Wilhelm Reich, evaluating three groups of cancer mice. One group was injected with a special form of orgone-radiating sand-packet (SAPA) bions, while another was treated in the orgone accumulator. These were contrasted to a group of untreated controls. The total number was 164 mice. Average life-spans were as follows:

Lifespans of Mice:	Average	Maximum
Untreated Controls	3.9 weeks.	11 weeks
SAPA - bion treated	9.1 weeks.	28 weeks
Orgone Accumulator	11.1 weeks.	38 weeks

The orgone accumulator approximately tripled the life-spans of the treated mice.

2. Blasband, Richard A.: "The Orgone Energy Accumulator in the Treatment of Cancer Mice", *Journal of Orgonomy,* 7(1):81-85, 1973.

In this study, nine immune-weakened inbred (C3H) cancer mice with transplanted tumors were randomly divided into control (5) and treated (4) groups. The treated mice were put into the accumulator for 80 to 120 mins daily. Control mice, who were otherwise treated identically, lived average of 54.4 days after transplantation, while treated mice lived an average of 87.3 days.

Lifespans of Mice:	Average
Untreated Controls	54.4 days
Orgone Accumulator	87.3 days

The orgone accumulator treated group lived 1.6 times as long.

3. Blasband, Richard A.: "Effects of the Orac on Cancer in Mice: Three Experiments", *Journal of Orgonomy*, 18(2):202-211, 1984. Only the first of the three experiments merits comparison to human trials, as I detail below. Only in Experiment 1 was there a quick treatment of mice, and the use of mice developing spontaneous tumors. In both Experiment 2 and 3, treatments were delayed by a critical 9-10 days, and in Experiment 2, transplanted tumors were used.

The Experiment 1 group used eight C3H cancer mice with spontaneous tumors, four treated with the ORAC starting right after tumor development, with four untreated controls.

Lifespans of Mice:	Average
Untreated Controls	38 days
Orgone Accumulator	69 days

The orgone accumulator treated mice, developing spontaneous tumors and treated early, lived nearly twice as long.

4. Trotta, E.E. & Marer, E.: "The Orgonotic Treatment of Transplanted Tumors and Associated Immune Functions", *Journal of Orgonomy,* 24(1):39-44, 1990.

Here, 50 mice with transplanted tumors were divided into two groups, one Control, the other Treated with the orgone accumulator. The results were:

Lifespans of Mice:	Average
Untreated Controls	4 weeks
Orgone Accumulator	8.7 weeks

The orgone accumulator more than doubled the lifespans of the treated mice.

These controlled studies on cancer mice, coupled with the clear health benefits reported by numerous patients and health-care practitioners in the clinical case-studies, supported further by the several double-blind and controlled studies on basic human physiology, is what has fueled a continued and growing interest in Reich's findings, many years after his 1957 death in prison, and in spite of FDA threats, academic-medical professional hostility and repressions, and book-burning.

The next studies discuss the effects of the medical dor-buster on cancer mice, or are focused upon the orgone accumulator's effect upon leukemia mice, which is a more difficult disorder to treat as, by Reich's discussion, it is the consequence of biopathic overcharge of the red blood cell, and so is not something so directly benefited by the orgone accumulator.

Special chambered mouse-sized orgone accumulators used in the Blasband laboratory, Pennsylvania, c.1976. Each long box has six ventillated mouse-chambers. The chamber box was placed inside a long cylindrical multi-layered orgone accumulator for approximately 1 hour daily.

5. Blasband, Richard A.: "The Medical DOR-Buster in the Treatment of Cancer Mice", *Journal of Orgonomy*, 8(2):173-180, 1974.

This paper detailed use of the Medical Dor-Buster, and not the orgone accumulator. It presented a graphic which indicated initial tumor suppression in the treated group was followed by a rebound of tumor growth close to the time of death. But the most significant result was not summarized in any Table or Graph, but was written on p.178 reporting median lifespans. He did not provide a mean-average, so I calculated that myself, as follows:

Lifespans of Mice:	Average	Median
Untreated Controls	70.7 days	66.5 days
Orgone Accumulator	107 days	102 days

Medical dor-buster treatment alone led to a significant 50%+ increase in longevity.

6. Grad, Bernard: "The Accumulator Effect on Leukemia Mice", *Journal of Orgonomy*, 26(2):199-218, 1992.

Grad was a Professor of Biology at McGill University and an associate of Reich's. He undertook experiments with the orgone accumulator on leukemia mice, with results supporting Reich on the bio-effects of the accumulator, but also showing the importance of how the mice were treated to elicit tumor formation, and other factors. His experiment used around 260 mice, whose leukemia is the product of multigenerational inbreeding. Grad's experiment lasted over several years with testing of the progeny. The leukemia mice, different from the cancer mice Reich and others used, did not show life-prolongation. However, **the orgone accumulator treatment reduced their leukemia incidence by around 20%** (from 90% in controls to 70% in treated group). This was indicative of an influence by the orgone accumulator towards betterment of health, though without life-span influences in this particular experiment. Leukemia in humans, Reich considered to be an overcharge biopathy affecting primarily the red blood cell, which by its irritated condition in the blood plasma provokes the white immune cells to overabundant reactivity. So he advised using the orgone accumulator for leukemia only for short periods, or not at all in some cases. Leukemia mice present a situation quite different from the human clinical condition, in any case, as humans are not inbreeding over generations.

This final study has nothing to do with cancer directly, but was an evaluation of wound-healing in mice, worthwhile to mention.

7. Baker, Courtney F., et al: "Wound Healing in Mice, Part I", *Annals, Inst. Orgonomic Science*, 1(1):12-23, 1984. "... Part II", *Annals, Inst. Orgonomic Science*, 2(1):7-24, 1985.

This study covered approximately seven years of various treatment approaches and methods in 42 separate experimental runs using ~1600 wounded mice. Part I was devoted to discussion of the wounding processes, and observations on how normal untreated control wounds healed naturally. No orgone treatment data was presented in Part I. In Part II, the abstract states (p.7) *"Our findings demonstrate that the healing rate is regularly increased by both the orgone accumulator and medical dor-buster; the results are significant at the level of $p<0.002$ or better."*

The authors admit to variations in result which they attribute to possible seasonal factors which could affect the energy-charge capacities of the orgone accumulator. They also made changes in experimental procedures and mice-treatments in the different runs, which were identified as "A, B and C" to separate them. They note, the "C" runs reflected their final and best experimental protocol, and hence pointed to the C runs as carrying the greatest significance and confidence for benefits from the orgone device treatments, which included the medical dor-buster and orgone accumulator. The "C" series results of 18 runs (42 mice per run, or 756 mice) showed **increased healing by orgone accumulator treatment from a nominal 1% to 12% increase in Therapeutic Index, and were statistically significant.** Unfortunately the authors did not show a separate graph for the "C" group runs alone. When aggregated with the A and B runs, the graphic suggests a dramatic variation in results, where the observed "C" healing effects were obscured.

Conclusions: Overall, these studies indicate *the orgone accumulator is most effectively beneficial when applied quickly after identification of the illness or injury. The most reproducible anti-cancer effects were observed primarily where spontaneous tumor development occured. A lesser, but noticeable and important anti-cancer effect was observed in the case of transplanted tumors.* This is in keeping with observations from published clinical case-studies of orgone accumulator therapy on human cancer patients.

The reader might correctly complain there are only a few studies to show after so many years following Reich's death. However, one must appreciate how all of these physicians and scientists took great personal and professional risks in doing this kind of research. The chronic open warfare against orgonomy by the FDA and medical groups, which has existed since the 1940s, has taken its toll. Nevertheless, ***everything here confirms Wilhelm Reich's original positions, and powerfully suggests the orgone accumulator ought to be available for use in every home, clinic and hospital, worldwide.***

Based upon these kinds of published findings, we may once again summarize the biological effects of a strong orgone charge:

A) General vagotonic, expansive effect on the entire system.
B) Sensations of tingling and warmth at skin surface.
C) Increased core and skin temperature, flushing.
D) Moderation of blood pressure and pulse rate.
E) Increased peristalsis, deeper respiration.
F) Increased germination, budding, flowering and fruiting of plants.
G) Increased rates of tissue growth and repair, as determined through animal studies and human clinical trials.
H) Increased field strength, charge, integrity of tissues and immunity.
I) Greater energy level, activity, and liveliness.

Given these facts, it is not surprising that the orgone accumulator might stimulate the remission of any symptom which is related to low energy charge in the blood or tissues, or to chronic overstimulation of the sympathetic nervous system. However, some medical problems are the result of chronic overcharge, and in those cases, use of an accumulator is disadvised, or advised only with caution, as previously mentioned.

Again, Reich warned persons with a history of hypertension, decompensated heart diseases, brain tumors, arteriosclerosis, glaucoma, epilepsy, heavy obesity, apoplexia, skin inflammations or conjunctivitis not to use the accumulator, or to do so only with great caution and for shorter periods, due to the dangers of overcharge in those cases. Not all people suffer from a lack of energy, or even from "low energy". Quite often, people suffer more from a clamping down, or holding back of the emotional energy which they already have. In some cases, additional energy from an accumulator may simply give a person more energy to clamp down with. One should recognize this fact, and understand that regular accumulator use is not mandated for everyone, nor is it a mystical panacea.

12. Personal Observations with the Orgone Accumulator

In the early 1970s, I met a young woman who had treated her ovarian cyst with an accumulator. Her doctor had urged surgery, but she did not have insurance or much money, and decided instead to try the accumulator. The woman had used the accumulator, a three-ply unit big enough to sit in, for about 45 minutes a day for two or three weeks. Around the middle of the third week, she had a vaginal discharge of blackish blood, which was the disintegrating tumor discharging into the uterine cavity. The woman felt completely healthy throughout the entire process, except for some discomfort during the time of the discharge. Some time after this, she went back to the doctor, who could not find a trace of the tumor. When told of the form of treatment, the doctor was derisive and uninterested.

Around this same time, I constructed a small but powerful accumulator, at a time when I was living only 8 miles away from the two Turkey Point nuclear power stations, in South Florida. I had been advised not to build accumulators that close to a nuclear plant, and had read Reich's account about oranur. Still, I remember thinking to myself, "It's just a small accumulator, and can't do much harm". The accumulator was left in a garage, along with a number of large metal appliances and objects, such as a clothes washer and dryer, refrigerator and filing cabinets. Within a week after doing so, the entire garage became so highly charged that it was impossible to stay in it for long. The sensible agitation and overcharge, which was provoked and amplified by the nuclear power plants, began to spread into the house, and the entire area often felt as if it were subtly resonating or vibrating. I still recall quite distinctly this phenomenon, which was most apparent at night, when winds ceased, and city noise was quiet. Meanwhile, plants inside the house began to die, and my blood began to show signs of deterioration, by the Reich blood test. A small Geiger counter began to yield erratic and racing counts for "background" radiation. In a bit of a panic, I dismantled the small accumulator, and removed other metal from the garage. A small draw-bucket was placed there, and the disturbance gradually quieted down. Still, the nuclear power plants were a constant worry, and we moved out of the area.

A few years later, I built another very powerful ten-ply accumulator, with shooter funnel, as described in the following chapters. One day when I was working outside, barefoot, I accidentally stepped on a hot soldering iron that had been carelessly left on the ground. My flesh was badly seared, and I was in a great deal of pain. However, the new accumulator and shooter were fortunately nearby, so I placed the burned foot into the shooter funnel. Within seconds the pain receded, and in a few minutes there was no pain at all! Without further discomfort, I could clean the severe burn, which had taken away all the layers of skin. The wound healed very rapidly after this, and I subsequently learned that pain relief from burns, and rapid healing of new skin, was one of the most powerful effects of the accumulator.

After constructing an accumulator that was large enough to sit in, I was able to confirm a number of subjective and objective measures that were first observed by Reich. It did indeed make one feel more invigorated and warmer, with a flushed skin. I no longer contracted colds or the flu like before. I have never been sick in any major way, and so have no major "healing" of myself to report. Eventually I ceased sitting in the accumulator on a regular basis, as I just did not feel the need for it. More often, I use the orgone energy blanket. It is easier to store (usually laying over the back of a chair, or on top of a bed near an open window) and can be retrieved for use very quickly. The most amazing effect of the blanket, I found, was its ability to stop a head cold, or at least to prevent it from developing into a chest cold. Prior to discovering the accumulator and blanket, all my colds would spread from head to throat to chest. Since using the blanket, I rarely contract a head cold, and when I do, it can be prevented from spreading by simply resting with the blanket over my chest and throat. Over the years, I have also had a variety of small cuts and bruises, or toes cracked from smashing them into table legs (I still go barefoot a lot), all of which were treated with the shooter or blanket, with great pain relief and healing benefits.

Only on one occasion did the accumulator fail to help me with a health problem. I was bitten on the leg by a poisonous *brown recluse* "fiddleback" spider, the toxin from which killed a piece of skin on my calf about 3 inches in diameter. I did not know about the dangers of that kind of spider, and only began treating the bite after the skin had turned purple and became numb. The wound was treated several times per day with the shooter, while sitting inside the large accumulator. These treatments did not restore feeling or normal color, and the entire depth of killed skin eventually turned black and hard, falling out of my leg, leaving me with a gaping open wound for several weeks. A secondary blood infection was treated with antibiotics, and I was on crutches for weeks. The wound healed over, however, and the leg functions today without a problem. The skin regrew, and only a small scar exists to mark the bite today. A survey of medical literature on this kind of spider bite indicates that, short of questionable cortisone shots into the bite shortly after it occurs, there is no known remedy.

On several occasions, friends of mine who knew about my accumulators would ask if they or their friends could use them. In one such case, a 19 year old female had a disc-shaped encapsulated benign tumor of the breast, measuring about 1" in diameter. The tumor first developed after she became pregnant out of wedlock several years before. Her parents had horribly mistreated her for this, and called her all sorts of bad names. The pregnancy was terminated, but the emotional abuse she had gone through led to a powerful bioenergetic contraction, and to the development of the tumor. She understandably did not tell her parents about the tumor, and had avoided doctors, being afraid of losing her breast. She had been treating the tumor with a vegetarian diet for several years, and it had not grown, nor gotten any smaller. After we discussed the matter, she began the orgone accumulator treatment by sitting inside for around 45 minutes a day, with a large shooter funnel over the breast. After three treatments, the tumor began to break apart, and disintegrate into smaller pieces. She became anxious at this point, however, and was openly agitated and upset about the accumulator, refusing to sit in it any more. Upset feelings related to the treatment she had received during her past pregnancy began to surface. She was also a student of the biological sciences, and, while she had a feeling of desperation about her situation, she had maintained a jocular surface attitude, saying she would try the accumulator only to "humor" her concerned friends. The fact that the accumulator actually appeared to work, when nothing else had, became an intellectual confusion and was simply too much for her. She never sought additional treatment with the accumulator, but friends informed me shortly thereafter that the tumor had almost completely vanished. Here, it is important to point out Reich's observations that, in spite of the emotional components of the underlying cancer biopathy (which clearly emerged in the above case), certain kinds of superficial tumors, such as breast or skin cancer, could be effectively treated with orgone energy.

In another case, a 23 year old woman had been under conventional medical treatment for severe genital herpes for several years, but without any relief from the persisting genital lesions. She sat in the accumulator once, using a vaginal shooter tube. Within days of this, her lesions began to dry up and heal, leaving her symptom-free for the first time in years. She remained free of symptoms for at least several years thereafter.

I know of several cases where the orgone blanket was used for treatment, instead of a large accumulator. An elderly woman was given an orgone blanket to see if it would help her arthritis. She used it and found that it did provide relief from the discomfort and pain, and she regained a bit of movement in the affected areas. After this, she unfortunately used it with her electric blanket, after which all the arthritis symptoms intensified, back to their original condition. (See the caution statement on page 105.) With great disappointment, she refused to have anything more to do with the orgone blanket.

In another case, a young woman treated her baby, which had a persisting slight fever and cold. She simply placed the child on top of the blanket in the crib, and left it there for around 15 or 20 minutes. When she returned, the child had a temperature of around 102°. She quickly removed the orgone blanket from the crib, and walked the child about for awhile. Its temperature soon dropped back to normal, but the cold symptoms also had vanished. Reich noted that orgone irradiation will increase a fever somewhat, even in adults, speeding the process of healing. Small children being treated for any kind of illness with a blanket or accumulator should obviously be watched closely. Also, no small child will feel comfortable being put inside a large accumulator all by themselves; but if the parent will go with them, and make a game of it, the child can sit on the adult's lap, and this will be just as effective.

In another case, an elderly man with fibrosis of the lung, related to a lifetime of smoking and emotional holding in the chest, was predicted to die within a few weeks. He was on oxygen, and could not speak more than a few words at a time or walk very far, given his inability to get a good breath. He began to use a vest-type orgone blanket and large box-type accumulator. Within a few weeks, he was up and about, rowing his small fishing boat. He reported the only time he could get a good breath was when he was inside the accumulator, or when wearing the orgone blanket vest. Many of his symptoms were relieved from the orgone therapy, and he remained active for many months thereafter. However, his condition worsened after he was put on an experimental medication by his doctors (prednisone), who viewed the orgone accumulator with contempt. He died shortly thereafter. Again, no miracles were observed given his original terminal condition, but a good deal of comfort and relief, and an additional 6 months of life.

I once corresponded with a farmer who had a cow with a large gash in its side that had gotten badly infected and festered, refusing to heal. The veterinarians had tried all sorts of different treatments, but nothing seemed to help, and the poor beast was on the decline. Having tried everything else, the farmer made a four-ply orgone blanket, and secured it to the festering side of the cow with heavy duct tape. He left the blanket taped to the cow, not expecting to see any cure, and anticipated a sorry death for the animal. However, within a few days, the blanket had fallen off, revealing a large scab over the sore. He treated the cow a few more times with a new blanket, and says that today you can hardly find a scar on the lively beast.

Another farmer I met was diagnosed as having a fast-spreading form of liver cancer. The doctor told him to get his affairs in order, as he would be dead in 6 months. The farmer made an accumulator out of two steel oil drums, by removing both the tops and bottoms of the oil drums, sandblasting the insides down to bare metal, and welding the two cylinders together, top to bottom. He then wrapped layers of steel wool and fiberglass around and around the steel tube he had constructed. With this tube accumulator laying on its side, he would go inside it, and take a nap from time to time. *"Dr. DeMeo"*, he told me, *"I object to your caution about not staying inside the accumulator for more than 30 or 45 minutes. I've stayed inside my accumulator for 7 hours at a stretch without problems, when I fell asleep inside it!"* Well, I did not know what to make of this fellow, as when I met him, he was very weak and slow-moving, needing help to get around. He seemed so low in energy that, in his case, the danger of overcharge did not exist. At that time, using the accumulator, he had lived for around a year beyond the terminal death-sentence of his doctor. I wished him well, however, and asked him to keep me informed on his progress.

After several years had passed, I got a delightful letter from that farmer, saying he wanted to attend one of my workshops. When I finally met him again, I was absolutely amazed at his condition. He was about 40 pounds heavier, his face was ruddy and tanned, standing firm and strong on his own legs, and he was literally bursting with energy. Sometimes, however, he would appear quite red in the face, as if he would explode, and once he started talking, you could hardly get him to shut up. Characterologically, he had gone from a situation of undercharge to overcharge. I pointed out this danger to him, and he did reduce his accumulator treatments. Anyhow, the story does not end here. It seems that he went back to his family doctor, who saw his changed condition and could not find a trace of the liver cancer. The doctor got real mad at him, and accused him of "going to some big city hospital for a wonder drug". He told his doctor about the accumulator, but the doctor didn't believe him. Since this was in a small town in the Midwest, the fact that the farmer had survived the death sentence of the town's most reputable doctor, and had even thrived in spite of that death sentence, was the cause of considerable interest and discussion. Presently, I've been told, there's a shortage of steel oil drums, fiberglass, and steel wool in that town, as the man's friends and neighbors are very busy building their own accumulators!

13. Some Simple and Not-So-Simple Experiments with the Orgone Accumulator

After you construct one or more of the accumulator designs given in this *Handbook*, you can run a few simple experiments to confirm the effects for yourself. Make sure you monitor environmental conditions during the experiments, as per the factors listed in prior chapters. Consult the various references given in this book for more information.

A) <u>Confirmation of Subjective Sensations:</u> If you are the type of person who works with your hands, who is generally relaxed, with a deep, full respiration, then you will most likely be able to confirm the following effects. Place your open relaxed hand inside the orgone accumulator, about an inch from the metal walls. You should feel a warm, penetrating radiant sensation, or a slight tingling sensation. The effect can also be confirmed by use of the funnel-type metal *orgone shooter,* which can move the orgone charge out of an attached accumulator in a directional manner. The *shooter tube,* which is a heavy glass test tube filled with steel wool, and charged up inside an accumulator, will yield similar discernible sensations when held close to your hand, upper lip, solar plexus, or other sensitive body area. Make sure you try this on clear, sunny days when the orgone charge at the Earth's surface is strong. On wet, rainy days, the effect will be minimal or absent. People with a shallow respiration, who work more with their brains than their hands, or those who carry a greater amount of emotional tension, will require more time and effort to confirm these sensations. One general rule of thumb: If you can feel the life-negative disturbances coming from TV sets, CRT displays on a computer, or fluorescent lights, it is likely you will also be able to feel these subtle and more pleasant orgonotic effects.

B) <u>Observations in Darkened Rooms:</u> Many people remember from childhood the ability to see various foggy shapes or "dancing dot" luminescent phenomena in darkened rooms. Reich proved that these subjective phenomena were real, and not imaginary, nor located only "in the eye". To reproduce these observations, you must be able to discern energetic phenomena from the debris or "floaters" in or on the surface of your eye. Reich identified a *fog-like* form of the energy, and a *pointed* or *dot-like* form, which was a more highly-excited expression. Reports from the 1700s to the modern day have been made by sensitive people who could see radiant energy fields around living creatures and other objects in darkness or semi-darkness. Energy fields around magnets, or weakly-charged electrical wires, have also been observed in darkrooms by sensitive people. These effects are intensified by the presence of a strong orgone charge, as is the case when accumulators are present. Energetic phenomena inside accumulators are also directly observable. For proper viewing, allow your eyes to adjust to the full darkness for 20 minutes or so. To provide a scientific basis to these observations, the reader is guided to Reich's original accounts in *The Cancer Biopathy.*

C) <u>Observations in the Daytime Sky:</u> A dancing dot or *orgone unit* phenomenon is also observable in the daytime sky. This is best seen with a homogeneous background of solid cloud cover or solid blue sky. Trees often appear to be flaming this energy into the sky, or attracting it towards themselves, much in the manner of a Van Gogh painting. One must be relaxed when making these observations; one can also "soften" the eye focus, purposefully looking into the open space in between yourself and the distant infinity. Observing the sky through an open, hollow metal, plastic, or cardboard tube helps to facilitate these observations. The phenomenon is most apparent against plastic window panels and skylights, and especially when looking out of the plexiglass windows of a high flying jet aircraft. Remember that some of these phenomenon will be occurring within the eyeball, though most are not. Again, Reich's accounts of these subjective phenomena are most telling.

By my experience, about half of the human population can see this phenomenon once it is pointed out to them. Some will dismiss it immediately, proclaiming "that's just something floating in my eye", while others will become fascinated. I had one lady attending my summer seminars on orgone research who told a sad but amazing story, about how she had seen these phenomenon as a little girl, and told her mother about it. Her mother got worried and took her to the eye-doctor, who could not find anything wrong. So she was then taken to a psychiatrist, who diagnosed her as having psychotic hallucinations, prescribing antipsychotic medications. So this poor lady had been on the doctors mind-altering pills for years before reading about Wilhelm Reich's orgone energy discovery, and the subjective light phenomenon. She weaned herself off the pills without consequence, except she discovered a capacity to heal people with her hands, the ability to transfer life-energy from her own energy field into that of another person. This also finds a reasonable explanation in Reich's discovery. It is interesting to point out that Van Gogh was also diagnosed as "psychotic" by the modern pill-pushing psychiatrists, in one of their medical journals, in part because of his turbulent life, and the proclamations that he was "seeing things". We can hope that Reich's discovery of the life energy will eventually be taken up into scientific, medical and popular thinking sufficiently to appreciate, rather than condemn, those among us who can directly feel, see, or even project this life-energy with their hands.

Observable luminating orgone units pulse and randomly move through the sky, with lifetimes of about one second.

D) <u>Plant Growth Enhancement Experiments:</u> The life-positive effects of the accumulator may be observed in its charging up of seeds, with subsequent increases in growth when they are planted. Take your garden seeds and divide each type into two separate groups, labeled A and B. Place the seeds in group A inside an orgone accumulator for a day or two, just before planting. Store the seeds in group B in a location away from the accumulator, but with similar temperature, moisture, and light conditions. You can keep the seeds in their plastic or paper packages while this is done, but make sure that neither group is near a TV, computer, wifi, fluorescent light, microwave oven, computer, "smart" meters or appliances, or other EMF/RF oranur-producing device. After charging, plant the various seeds in a way that you can identify the two groups. Monitor and measure the growth in both groups, taking notes and photographs. Count or otherwise measure the yields from each group. The accumulator group should have a greater growth and higher yield. Controlled studies by organic farmers, particularly those by Jutta Espanca of Portugal (see the references), have demonstrated very significant orgone charging effects. Espanca has found that garden seed charging works best if done for only a day, or even a few hours; but this must be done only on a very crisp, clear, and sparkling day, when the orgone charge at the Earth's surface, and in the accumulator, is quite strong and lively. Otherwise, charging may have to take place for slightly longer periods. Also note that seeds can be overcharged; attempts at charging seeds for 30 days or more often result in little difference between controls and charged seedlings, or even stunted growth in the charged group.

Orgone Charging of Potted Plants: This can be done by charging up seeds prior to planting, as discussed above, or by charging up soil or water before using. One can also make a "wrap around" accumulator, using a clean metal food can, with plastic and steel wool layers wrapped around the outside. Be sure that the final outside layer of plastic is fairly thick, and do not use aluminum materials. Leave the steel wool in a fluffy condition; don't compress it.

Home Seed Sprouting Experiments: The life-positive effects of the accumulator may also be observed in the way it enhances seed sprouting. Build an accumulator to house your seed

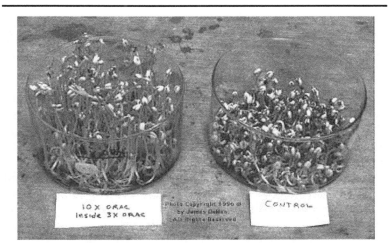

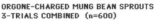

A Controlled Mung-Bean Seed-Charging Experiment

Above: The beans in the left-hand dish were sprouted while kept inside a one cubic-foot orgone energy charger, similar to what is described in Chapters 16 and 17, while the other was sprouted inside a control, non-accumulating enclosure. Below: Histogram analysis of three-years of seed-sprouting experimental data. Orgone-charged seeds sprouted to an average of 200 mm, while Controls sprouted an average of 149 mm, an overall increase of 34% from the orgone-charging, with a statistical significance of p<0.0001. (J. DeMeo: "Orgone Accumulator Stimulation of Sprouting Mung Beans", Pulse of the Planet 5:168-175, 2002.)

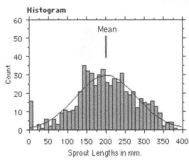

OR-Charged
Average of ~200mm length

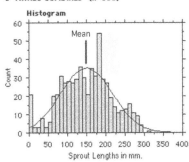

Controls
Average of ~150mm length

sprouting apparatus. Store one sprout container in a darkened area away from the orgone accumulator, and another inside the darkened orgone accumulator. Make sure the temperature, ventilation, and light exposure of the two groups is identical and, once again, keep both groups away from oranur-producing devices. Measure the quantity of seeds going into each container, and make sure the quantity of water in each is about the same. Observe and record any subsequent differences in growth and taste. The accumulator group should have a greater growth and yield.

Laboratory Seed Sprouting Experiments: Obtain two small shallow glass dishes with a flat bottom, or two shallow glass laboratory culture dishes, about 4" diameter with a 1" lip. Into each dish place around 20 or 30 dry mung beans, to form a single layer of beans on the bottom of the dish. Add a measured quantity of water to each dish, which only halfway covers up the beans. The tops of the beans should remain exposed to the air, while the bottoms are wet. Place one dish of beans into a small but strong orgone accumulator, and the other dish into a control wood or cardboard enclosure of similar dimensions, but with no metals. Cover both the accumulator and control enclosure with a layer of black plastic, to seal them against any intruding light. Place the enclosures in a well-ventilated area, of equal temperature, and out of the direct sunlight. The enclosures should be in nearly identical environments with respect to light and temperature, but not placed closer to each other than about a meter. Again, no EMF/RF oranur-producing devices should be nearby. Each day, open the enclosures up and add as much water as is needed to keep the bean dishes wet to approximately the same height in the dish as originally was necessary to cover the beans halfway. If one dish begins to grow more quickly it will require more water, and this should be provided on demand. After one of the dishes of sprouts has reached about 4" high, record your observations of germination rate, length or weight of sprouts, general appearance, and other characteristics. Contrast the two groups. The accumulator group should have a greater growth and germination rate. To do this experiment with some serious interest, firstly review the protocols in my cited research paper, as given on the preceding page.

E) <u>The Accumulator Temperature Differential Effect:</u> Reich demonstrated that the warm glow felt inside the accumulator possessed an objective aspect which could be measured with a sensitive thermometer. An airtight orgone accumulator will spontaneously warm up the air inside itself by a few tenths of a degree, up to several degrees. This temperature increase will make the accumulator interior slightly warmer than the surrounding air temperature, or the air temperature inside a thermally-balanced control enclosure which does not use metals in its construction. This experiment, called the *To-T* (temperature in the orgone accumulator minus temperature of the control) was considered by Reich to be a proof of the orgone energy, and a violation of the second law of thermodynamics. Albert Einstein once replicated the experiment and called it a "bomb in physics"; a fascinating booklet titled *The Einstein Affair* documents the correspondence between Reich and Einstein on the matter. A definitive evaluation of the To-T experiment requires the

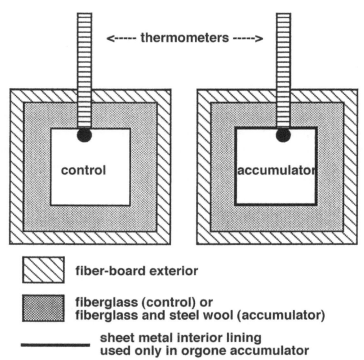

<----- thermometers ----->

control

accumulator

fiber-board exterior

fiberglass (control) or
fiberglass and steel wool (accumulator)

sheet metal interior lining
used only in orgone accumulator

Thermal Anomaly inside the Orgone Accumulator, peaking at Solar Noon by 0.5 °C greater than within an identical Control enclosure, over 11 days in August 2006. Note the predominant positive nature of the anomaly, and the reduction which occurs during cloudy / rainy weather.

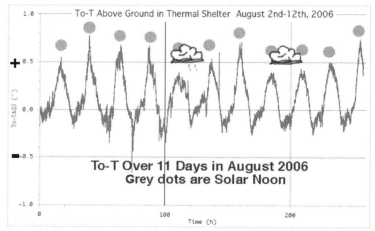

construction of thermally balanced accumulator and control enclosures, careful monitoring of weather and environmental temperatures, sensitive thermometers capable of recording down to tenths of a degree, and prolonged systematic measurements. Those who wish to reproduce this experiment should consult the published reports given in the reference section for details. It is an area ripe for innovative investigation, and I strongly encourage the experimentalist to carefully seek out this effect.

F) The Orgone Accumulator Electrostatic Effects: Obtain or build a simple aluminum or gold leaf static electroscope. If you do not know what this is, instructions can be found in a good library or online. Make sure that the electroscope is calibrated with degree markings, from 0 to 90, such that its degree of deflection can be accurately measured. By running a plastic rod or comb through your dry hair, you can gather a significant static electrical charge and transfer it to the electroscope. Using a stopwatch, or a timer, determine how long it takes for the electroscope to slowly lose its charge into the air, through a predetermined deflection angle. For example, you want to know how long it will take for the electroscope to discharge from a 40 to a 30 degree angle. You therefore should charge the electroscope up to a deflection angle greater than 40 degrees, waiting until it discharges to the 40 degree mark. Once this happens, you can count the number of elapsed seconds that pass until it reaches 30 degrees. The time elapsed is the electroscopical discharge rate. On sunny days, the discharge rate will be quite slow, while on rainy days, the discharge rate will be very quick, so quick that you might not even be able to measure it. If you time the electroscopical discharge rate inside an orgone accumulator, you will find that it takes a longer time to discharge in the accumulator than in the open air. The difference between the discharge rate inside the accumulator, and the discharge rate in the open air, is called the *electroscopical discharge rate differential*. This differential will be large on dry, clear, sunny days, and minimal or zero on humid, rainy overcast days. On rare occasions, an electroscope that is only weakly charged, or even completely discharged, may—if allowed to soak inside an orgone accumulator—spontaneously charge itself up to a higher level. All of these effects will vanish on rainy, overcast days. For more details, see the citations in the "Reference" section.

G) <u>The Accumulator Evaporation Suppression Effect:</u> This experiment requires a sensitive weighing scale that can measure to fractions of a gram. It also requires an accumulator and a thermally-balanced control enclosure of similar dimensions. For this control, do not use water-absorbent materials in the interior; instead, line the interior of the control with a non-metallic waterproofing material, such as plastic, enamel or varnish. Obtain and weigh two small, identically shaped and sized glass dishes of about 4" diameter and 1" deep. Weight the dishes when empty, clean and dry, down to tenth's of a gram. Next, add identical quantities of water to each vessel, filling them about halfway, and weigh again, calculating via subtraction the weight of water in each dish. Place one vessel of water inside the orgone accumulator, elevated on a small wood block, such that the bottom of the dish does not come into direct contact with the metal interior of the accumulator. The lid of the accumulator should be shut, but fixed open with a crack such that air may circulate. It should not be placed in a windy or sunlit area, however. Place the second vessel of water inside the control enclosure in a similar manner, on an identical wood block, and also prop its lid open. Place it in a location at least a meter away from the orgone accumulator, but with similar light, temperature, and wind characteristics. You may wish to drape a piece of black plastic over both the accumulator and control, in order to control for slight differences in light. Wait exactly 24 hours and remove the dishes of water, being careful not to spill any. Carefully weigh the dishes and compute the evaporative loss for the 24 hour period. Make this measurement once per day, preferably in the late evening, such that you can determine the amount of water evaporated each day from each container. You should find that the control enclosure evaporates significantly more moisture on clear, sunny days, when the accumulator suppresses water evaporation. On rainy days, when the accumulator no longer

Water Evaporation Anomaly in the Orgone Accumulator. Amount of water evaporated from an open dish inside the accumulator minus evaporation in a control enclosure, in grams of water per day. The accumulator suppresses evaporation on bright sunny days. Note the anomaly was disrupted when radioactive fallout from a Chinese atmospheric atomic bomb test arrived at the laboratory area. (J. DeMeo: "Water Evaporation Inside the Orgone Accumulator", Journal of Orgonomy, 14:171-175, 1980.)

builds up a charge, the evaporation in the accumulator and control will be nearly identical. Subtract the quantity of water evaporated in the orgone accumulator from the quantity evaporated in the control for each 24 hour period. This quantity, called EVo-EV, will reveal the changing quantity of orgone energy charge in the local atmosphere, and in the accumulator. The evaporative values on any one day are less interesting than the dynamic manner in which the evaporation differential increases and decreases, according to the orgone energy charge at the Earth's surface.

H) <u>Experimental Orgone-Life Energy Field Meter.</u> To run experiments on this question you will have to build your own orgone field meter, using the instructions in Reich's work *The Cancer Biopathy.* You'll need an induction coil or Tesla-type coil, plus some metal plates, insulating panels, and a photographer's light-meter. In many ways, this meter resembles a "Kirlian" type device, except you don't measure energy fields with a photo-plate, but do so with an analog-type readout based upon how brightly your personal energy field causes an excited bulb to glow. Some experimentation with the right kind of light-bulb will be necessary, as I discovered years ago only some kinds will work (a low-voltage appliance bulb seemed best). Or, you can purchase the ready made *Experimental Life-Energy Field Meter* shown previously in a photo at the end of Chapter 4 (page 45). This unit relies upon solid-state technology to reproduce Reich's original invention, and works quite well. It is the only instrument I know which demonstrates the relative strength or charge of the human energy field in a sustained manner. It will reveal variations from one person to the next, and if right-handed (or left), that hand will yield a stronger charge than the other. More alive and vital people give stronger readings than weak or ill persons, much as Reich's blood test also revealed the energetic parameter underlying health and disease. Living water as from natural springs will yield slightly higher readings than devitalized city-pipe water. It is my prediction that, in some far off Century, Reich's discoveries will constitute the core around which a *"Star Trek"* futuristic type of diagnosis and treatment will be developed.

14. Questions and Answers

- *Q: If the orgone energy really exists, why don't we hear about it from scientists working in the universities?*

A: Scientists working in the universities and research institutions have engaged in verifying research on the bions, orgone accumulator, and cloudbuster, and on the bioelectrical aspects of life, which Reich also pioneered. For example, Dr. James DeMeo, author of this *Handbook,* did research on the weather-related aspects of Reich's discoveries while he was a graduate student and Instructor at the University of Kansas. He continued with that research while a professor at Illinois State University and the University of Miami. Müschenich and Gebauer, of the University of Marburg in West Germany, completed a double-blind, controlled study on the physiological effects of the orgone accumulator on humans. Dr. Bernard Grad, one of Reich's associates, continued with pioneering work on the bions, and life-energy, quite openly and for decades at McGill University in Canada. Other scholars with a research or historical interest in the works of Wilhelm Reich have held positions at Harvard University, Temple University, the State University of New York, York University, Rutgers University, the University of Vienna and elsewhere. Workshops and courses devoted to Reich's works are now held at a few colleges and universities in the North America and Europe. Nonetheless, the history of science repeatedly shows that large institutions do not easily accommodate innovative research which may force radical changes in the major theories of science.

- *Q: Can an accumulator be used during wet or cloudy weather?*

A: Use of an accumulator during humid, wet weather conditions will *not* be harmful, but it will be less effective, as the charge is significantly lower or absent at those times. It is best to use it during clear and sunny weather, when the atmospheric orgone energy continuum is strong and expansive, and the charge at the Earth's surface is greater.

- Q: These accumulating devices are quite simple to construct. Aren't a lot of them accidentally constructed?

A: A lot of "accumulators" are being constructed, without knowledge of the people involved. Every mobile home or house with a metal skin or side paneling will accumulate a charge, and a toxic charge if aluminum is used. Oranur, and other toxic effects appear to easily develop in such houses, which are filled with all the modern orgone disturbing EMF/RF devices, as discussed in prior chapters. Epidemiological studies that would address these general observations have rarely been performed.

- Q: I have an old styrofoam beverage cooler. Can I line it with aluminum foil and make an accumulator?

A: Not with any good result. You can try this, but don't expect any firm results unless you comprehend and take into consideration virtually all of the procedures and warnings given in this *Handbook*. Styrofoam and aluminum are life-negative accumulating materials. If you run a biological experiment, you may wind up demonstrating only a life negative effect. For the scientist interested in orgone energy, these considerations are even more crucial and cannot be ignored.

- Q: My accumulator gave very good charge the first months when it was in use, but now does not yield a good charge any more. Why is this?

A: It is likely that the accumulator has been contaminated with dor. Some researchers have noted this effect, where the accumulator goes temporarily "dead", and hence keep their accumulators outdoors, sheltered from rain, but in the fresh air, with the lids or doors open so that air can circulate inside quite freely. A "dead" accumulator can be refreshed by wiping it inside and out with a damp cloth. Also, keep a bowl of water inside it when not in use. Change the water in this bucket every day or two. Also, be certain that the accumulator is not near any of the oranur-producing devices previously identified, and that your neighborhood is as oranur-free as possible. The accumulator or orgone blanket can also be sun-charged, by exposing it to fresh air and direct sunlight for a few days. These steps should eliminate any dorish tendencies, and "rekindle" the charge.

- *Q: I have heard that sitting inside an accumulator will make a person more sexually potent. Is this true? I once also saw a film which made Reich out to be a pornographer.*

A: There are many lies and ugly rumors propagated by Reich's enemies in smear articles from the 1940s and 1950s. He was attacked as a lunatic, the accumulator a "sex box", and putting false words into his mouth about the ability of the accumulator to restore lost sexual potency. However, Reich never made such claims; in fact, he continually stressed the emotional and psychological foundations of sexual dysfunction, which could not be touched by treatment in an accumulator. Reich also was against pornography, and considered it to be attractive only to sexually-repressed people. The film you reference probably is *WR Mysteries of the Organism*, which was directed by a communist pornographer who hated Reich and made a deliberate mockery of his work. More information on that film is posted here: www.orgonelab.org/makavejev.htm

- *Q: What are orgonite pyramids, orgone generators and chembusters? Can they really bring me more "money, sex and power" as seen on internet advertisements? Do they really protect us against cell-tower radiation?*

A: Unfortunately not. These are ineffective or hoax devices, developed by mystic or unethical individuals since around 1995, and sold widely on internet sites. They were not developed by Dr. Reich or by any of his professional associates. The people making and selling these things knowingly steal and abuse his name and terms, without justifications, making very large and unsupportable claims about the supposed "powers" of their gadgets. Today, most are made in Chinese sweat-shops. See here: www.orgonelab.org/orgonenonsense.htm
www.orgonelab.org/chemtrails.htm

- *Q: Is it true that Dr. Reich was attacked by right-wing "McCarthy-ite" conservatives in the USA?*

A: Not significantly. As detailed in the Introduction, the original smear-articles attacking Dr. Reich were by communist writers such as Mildred Brady, and published in the radical-left *New Republic* magazine, which was edited by the Soviet agent Michael Straight. The leftist Martin Gardner also wrote an influential book which assaulted Reich. Their smear-articles were republished widely and eventually came to the attention of the liberal-left oriented "consumer activist" FDA. One of Reich's lawyers also was a cloaked Soviet sympathizer. In more recent years, the left-wing "skeptic" organizations have assaulted many different natural healing methods and unorthodox scientific discoveries, including scientists and physicians who dare to seriously investigate Reich's findings. While Reich and his supporters included both old-fashioned liberals and moderate conservatives, his major detractors were decidedly left-wing "activists", Comintern hacks and Soviet spys. They tried to kill Reich in Europe, and in the USA they deceptively manipulated American social institutions to achieve their goals.

- Q: Isn't orgone energy the exact same thing as Chi or Prana? And don't psychic healers working with conscious intention do basically the same thing?

A. Orgone energy is a physical and tangible *life-energy*, and as such has been seen, felt and used by different cultures around the world. This is true also in China and India, where *Chi* and *Prana* are a part of their healing and mystic traditions. However, in those mystic traditions, it is often claimed the energy is not something tangibly real, in the "here and now". Consequently, one is forced to approach it through lengthy spiritual exercises, or to study at the foot of a guru before a deeper understanding is claimed possible. Reich is unique in having made clear scientific demonstrations of the life-energy, as a real thing, not cut-off into some nether-world of spirits, demons or angels. He made the life-energy available to ordinary people. Anyone can make and use an orgone blanket or accumulator, even or especially "spiritually mundane" people, and certainly without worshiping at the foot of living or stone idols.

The experiments with conscious intention, as undertaken and published in the parapsychological literature, are fascinating and may in fact work by virtue of direct human influences upon the life-energy. At the Princeton PEAR Laboratory, for example, work with Random Event Generators shows ordinary people can mentally influence these devices to produce non-random variations in their output, which otherwise typically produce streams of purely random numbers. However, it has also been demonstrated that people expressing strong emotion, such as crying or anger, produce even stronger effects than brain-power alone. This suggests, spontaneous emotion – composed as we know from Reich as direct expressions of orgone energy in the body – has a greater influence than intention or meditation.

Among psychic healers, the life-energy is often acknowledged openly as "subtle energy", particularly those who use the *laying of hands* or *hand passing* methods, which date back to Franz Mesmer's work with animal magnetism. Today there are schools which try to teach these methods, and many ordinary people can use them to produce health-benefits to others. Psychic or not, we are all charged with life-energy within our bodies, and by simple and very old methods can learn to transfer this charge to others. Some of the nurse's groups which have started applying simple hand-laying or hand-passing healing methods for patients also sometimes surreptitiously will bring an orgone blanket into the hospital room, without telling the doctors. This can produce an even greater magnitude of effects. More will be clarified when science and medicine tolerate open investigations.

While psychic healing using hand-laying seems obviously an influence of bioenergy transfer, long-distance psychic healing is less clear and so the theory of *conscious intention* has been argued. But the biological effects of such long-distance healing have not been scientifically demonstrated in controlled-blinded experiments, so as to separate them from psychosomatic or placebo effects, which by themselves can be quite powerful. Experiments directed towards increasing the growth of plants have therefore been developed. These studies also document some long-distance psychic effects, but it takes from 100 to 1000 professional healers, engaged in deep intensive thought or meditations with "sweating brains", to produce slight increases in seed sprouting. Those results have been regularly exceeded at the OBRL institute within *one strong orgone energy accumulator, and without any meditation or intention exercises whatsoever* (see page 153). In some "psychic" studies, toxic copper shields were put around the control group, on the premise psychic intent is EMF based, thereby stunting them and yielding a false positive within the tested group. The orgone accumulator – which is the product of Reich's functional natural scientific investigations of bioenergy – influences life and non-living materials in a more direct manner and without the necessity of human mental engagement. As such, the orgone energy accumulator is closer to, and yet superior to other functional methods of natural energy-medicine healing, such as acupuncture, herbalism or homeopathy.

- Q: Is the orgone energy accumulator legal? Can I get in trouble with the law for building or using one?

A: There is no law against orgone energy, or the orgone energy accumulator. You may openly build, own, and use the blanket or accumulator in your own home, or elsewhere, as you choose. It can also be legally used for the self-treatment of any health-related condition, just as you can make very beneficial soups, purchase vitamins, or take soaking baths, without asking a doctor or the police. Additionally, at the time when Reich's conviction was being appealed to the US Supreme Court, a group of physicians filed a *Certiorari Petition* to intervene in his case, stating that any prohibition of the orgone accumulator would negatively affect their medical practice and the health of their patients. The court ruled, under advisement from the US Food and Drug Administration, that they did not care what other people did with the orgone accumulator, only what Dr. Reich did. This ruling firstly clarified that the FDA was really out to "get Reich" and did not care if the orgone energy and accumulator worked or not, nor about government-approved book-burning. But it also cleared the way for everyone to use it freely and openly.

Understand, however, that forces within Big Medicine, Big Pharmaceuticals, and Big Government are hard at work to make it illegal for you to do these things. When the FDA raids a natural healing clinic today, they typically have no interest in whether or not a new product or treatment method is beneficial, but are instead abusing the legal system as a club, to pound people down into submission to medical authoritarianism. If you are concerned about protecting your health freedoms, you should join forces with those social organizations that are working to preserve or extend those freedoms. The price of liberty is eternal vigilance! For more information, see my article *Anti-Constitutional Activities and Abuse of Police Power by the U.S. Food and Drug Administration and other Federal Agencies,* here: www.orgonelab.org/fda.htm

Part III:
Construction
Plans for
Orgone
Accumulating
Devices

15. Construction of a 2-Ply Orgone Energy Blanket

The orgone energy blanket is the most simple to construct of all the orgone charging and accumulating devices. They can be made at any size, and can be easily transported. You can use small ones while resting, or place large ones under and over a person who is laying in a bed. Like a standard accumulator, orgone blankets are not meant to be used for any prolonged period, though one can rest or nap with one if there is a need. In my experience, people will, even when sleeping, push off an uncomfortable orgone blanket just as they would a regular blanket. The following steps tell how to make an orgone energy blanket with final dimensions of 2' by 2'.

A) Obtain enough 100% wool fabric or wool felt, to make three 2' x 2' squares. The fabric should not be highly finished wool, but have some rough texture, as with a comfortable camping blanket. Also obtain several packages of very fine ("000" or "0000") steel wool pads (the kind without any soap) or a reel of steel wool.

B) Lay a 2' x 2' piece of fabric on a flat surface. Cover the exposed top surface of this fabric with a layer of steel wool, from the steel wool reel or unwrapped pads. Spread the steel wool out, so that it is not too thick. You should be able to see parts of the underlying fabric here and there.

C) On top of the steel wool, lay another 2' x 2' piece of fabric.

D) Cover the exposed top surface of this second fabric piece with another layer of steel wool.

E) Finish with another 2' x 2' piece of fabric, placed on top of the last steel wool layer. You now should have three pieces of fabric, with two layers of steel wool sandwiched in between.

Assembly of an orgone blanket. Spread out wool cloth, then layer steel wool loosely in a thin layer on top. Spread it out and allow for trim edges as shown.

F) Trim, stitch, and finish the borders, according to your own tastes and sewing skills.

G) Keep and use the blanket in an environment similar to that advised for a regular accumulator, away from any TV sets, microwave ovens, fluorescent lights, or other electromagnetic or radioactive gadgets. Never use an orgone blanket with an electric blanket. It can be stored on a hangar in the open air, or even inside a larger accumulator for greater charging.

H) Do not wash or dry clean your orgone blanket, as the steel wool will rust! Spot clean only with a slightly damp sponge.

I) Reich once made very heavy orgone blankets, composed of galvanized steel wire mesh, and alternating layers of wool and steel wool. While these work quite well, I find them to be uncomfortable and difficult to use. They do not appear to be any more effective than the simple design given here.

Before constructing anything, be sure to review Part II, on the Safe and Effective Use of Orgone Accumulating Devices.

Rolls of steel wool can be purchased from www.naturalenergyworks.net, or from larger hardware or paint stores. Spread the steel wool out two or three times the width it comes in. Use "000" or "0000" grade, and allow residual oils to dry by unrolling out in the hot sunlight for a day or two. Particle masks should be worn during construction to avoid breathing of fine steel dust. This is also true when making orgone accumulator panels with fiberglass.

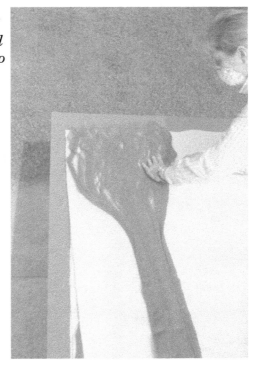

Right:
A functional orgone accumulating blanket showing the alternating layers of steel wool and wool felt.

Below:
Finish off your blanket with a trim to keep everything together. Several quilt-stitches should be added to keep the insides from shifting around.

16. Construction of a 5-Ply Garden Seed Charger – "Coffee Can" Accumulator

One can make a simple garden seed charger from a cleaned tin or galvanized steel food or coffee can, using additional steel wool and fabric materials as described below.

A) Empty a large coffee can or other steel or steel/tin food container (use a magnet to make sure! no aluminum!), clean it, remove all labels, and dry thoroughly. Make sure you save the cut-out metal lid, or make a replacement from another can, or from galvanized steel sheet metal. Use a can large enough to hold all the seeds you will be charging.

B) Obtain several yards of good 100% wool camp-blanket or wool felt. You will need enough fabric to go around the can about 5 times, plus enough for 5 round top pieces, and 5 similar bottom pieces.

C) Purchase several packages of fine grade ("000" or "0000") steel wool pads, or a large reel of steel wool. You will need enough steel wool to cover an area equal to that of the fabric. Again, unwrap the steel wool as you need it, and spread it out.

D) Cut the fabric into a very long strip which is as wide as the can is tall. The length of this long strip should be about 6 times the circumference of the can. As you may not have a single strip of fabric this long, you can splice several pieces together using masking tape to hold the strips in pace. The tape can be left in place and covered over, as it will not interfere with the function of the orgone accumulator.

E) Lay the long fabric strip out flat, and spread a thin layer of steel wool on top of it. Lay the empty can on one end of the steel wool/fabric strip and roll the can up inside the strip. Stop when the strip has been wrapped around the can about five times or more. Add one or two final layers of wool fabric to the outside, and stitch or tape it in place so that it will not unravel.

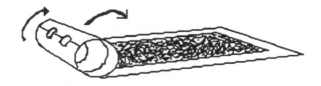

F) Measure the diameter across the top of the can, including the wrappings of fabric and steel wool. Cut out 10 circles of fabric material of this same diameter, 5 for the top, 5 for the bottom.

G) Sandwich steel wool between the fabric circles such that you have 4 layers of steel wool between 5 layers of fabric. Make two of these fabric/steel wool sandwiches, one of which will be used to cover the bottom of the can, and the other for the top.

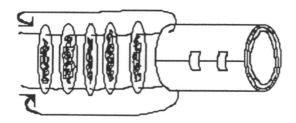

H) Take the metal disk cut from the top of the can and file smooth any jagged edges. Punch two small nail holes near the center, about 1/4" apart. Using a heavy upholstery or knitting needle, thread some heavy twine, wire, or yarn through the center of one of the steel wool/fabric sandwiches, and bring the twine through the holes in the metal can lid. Secure the can lid to the center of the steel wool/fabric sandwich. The steel wool/fabric sandwich should be about 2" wider in diameter than the metal can lid.

I) Using heavy thread, loosely stitch together the edges of the top steel wool/fabric sandwich (the one sewn to the metal can lid). Also loosely stitch the edges of the bottom steel wool/fabric sandwich together, and sew it to the bottom edge of the steel wool/fabric strip, wound around the can. Except for the top opening, the metal can should now be encased in the steel wool/fabric material.

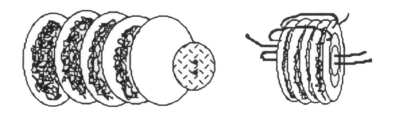

J) Find a heavy pillowcase, laundry bag, or other larger cylindrical non-metallic container in which to keep the entire charger. Or, if you are good with a needle and thread, stitch together your own fabric cover for the charger. The main thing is that the outer layer of fabric, and any open ends of fabric showing pieces of steel wool, should not be subject to "knocking about" or moisture, such that it starts to fall apart or rust.

K) Review the section on seed charging, in the "Simple Experiments" chapter for instructions and additional ideas on the use of your charger. Or, as an alternative to constructing this accumulator, you could store your seeds inside a large metal cookie tin which would then be wrapped up inside the multiple folds of a very large orgone blanket, or be stashed inside one of the other, larger accumulators. Just realize that the greater the number of plys, and the greater the absolute quantity of materials going into the construction of the accumulator "pile", the stronger will be the charge. At the author's laboratory, for instance, the small 5- ply coffee can charger is stored inside the 10-ply, one-cubic foot accumulator, which in turn is stored inside the 3-ply large accumulator. This is a total of 18 plys, and yields a charge which is readily sensible and quite strong.

Before constructing anything, be sure to review Part II, on the Safe and Effective Use of Orgone Accumulating Devices.

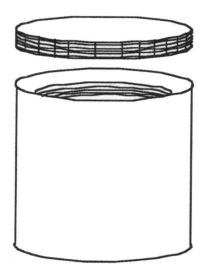

17. Construction of a 10-Ply Orgone Energy Accumulator Charger-Box

A very powerful, one-cubic foot, 10-ply accumulator can be made following the instructions below.

A) Cut six galvanized steel, 27 gauge sheet metal squares, measuring 1' x 1'. Use heavy tape, on the outer metal walls only, to construct a metal cube. Leave the top of the cube open, and do not tape it into place. The interior of the cube should remain bare metal, without any tape showing.

B) Use very fine ("000" or "0000") steel wool, and heavy clear plastic acrylic carpet protector (or sheep's wool or fiberglass materials) for construction of the plys. The clear plastic carpet protector is the same material used to protect carpets from wear, and is often sold on rolls in hardware and department stores. It is not cheap, but it works well and has rows of small tips on the side which normally faces down on the carpet; these tips work very nicely for holding the steel wool in place. Fiberboard, insulation-board ("soundboard") or masonboard should be used for the final outer layer, with wood corner strips. The fiberboard exterior may additionally be coated with natural shellac to increase charging.

C) Ten alternating layers of plastic or wool/fiberglass and steel wool roughly measure 2" in thickness. This being the case, you should construct the fiberboard outer casing in the shape of a cube, 4" larger than the interior metal cube. The interior dimensions of the fiberboard outer casing will be 16" x 16" x 16". Cut six of these fiberboard panels with the following dimensions, assuming the board is 1/2" thick:

Fiberboard Panels:

top:	17" x 17"
bottom:	17" x 17"
2 sides:	17" x 16"
2 sides:	16" x 16"

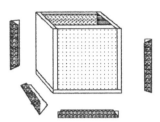

D) Use small nails and wood-glue to fasten five of the six fiberboard panels together, to make a cube shape. Again, as with the metal box, do not attach the top. Add extra glue to the interior and exterior edges of the assembled fiberboard box, and allow it to fully dry before proceeding.

E) Using a miter-box, cut wood corner strips for the outside edges of the fiberboard box. Nail or screw and glue these wood corner strips to the fiberboard box for added strength. You should drill holes for the nails or screws, as otherwise the corner strips will split.

F) Cut 20 square pieces of plastic or wool/fiberglass, 16" x 16". Put ten of these squares aside for later use. Lay the other ten squares one at a time inside the bottom of the fiberboard box. In between each plastic/fiber/wool square place a layer of steel wool. When finished, the top of the last steel wool layer will face upward in the bottom of the fiberboard box

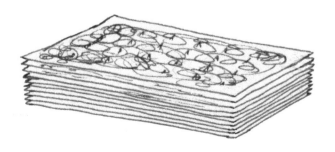

G) Place the galvanized steel sheet metal cube inside the fiberboard box, on top of the ten plys of plastic/fiber/wool and steel wool. If you have constructed the fiberboard box correctly, the top of the metal cube should be about 2" below the top edge of the fiberboard box, and a space of about 2" should exist between the sides of the metal cube and the interior sides of the fiberboard box.

H) Cut 20 pieces of plastic/fiber/wool of 12" x 16", and 20 more pieces, 12" x 12". These will be used to fill the side spaces between the metal cube and the fiberboard. Layer each plastic/fiber/wool piece with steel wool, and stack into bunches of ten layers each. Do this on a flat surface before attempting to place them into a vertical position, in between the fiberboard and metal boxes.

I) When finished with the above steps, place the two stacks of 16" x 12" plastic/steel wool between the fiberboard and metal cubes, on opposite sides of the metal cube. An outer layer of plastic should lay against the inner wall of the fiberboard box, while an inner layer of steel wool should rest against the outside of the metal box. The upper edge of the plastic should be nearly flush with the upper edge of the metal cube, both of which should remain about 2" below the upper edge of the fiberboard box.

J) Next, place the two stacks of 12" x 12" plastic/steel wool in the two remaining spaces between the fiberboard and metal cube, as given in the previous step.

K) Take the 10 remaining pieces of 16" x 16" plastic carpet runner (or the fiberglass or sheeps wool alternative) previously put aside, and layer them with steel wool. Stack them up and set them aside. Unlike prior stacks, however, do not finish the final plastic/fiber/wool layer with steel wool.

L) Take the remaining square of galvanized sheet metal, and drill a small hole in each corner, about 1/2" from the edges. The holes should be large enough to accommodate a long narrow screw of around 2.5" length.

M) Find a firm surface to work on, which won't be bothered by screw or drill marks. Lay the stack of plastic/steel wool squares on the last piece of fiberboard. Center it on the fiberboard; there should be about 1/2" of fiberboard appearing all around the stack. Now place the sheet metal square (with the holes) on top of the plastic/steel-wool/fiberboard stack, and center it also. There should be about 2" of plastic extending beyond the edge of the metal square on each side. Use some masking tape to temporarily hold the fiberboard/plastic/steel stack together.

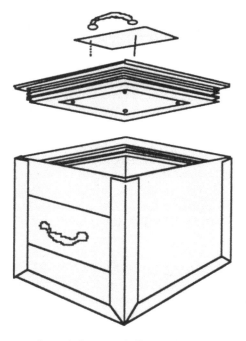

N) Using an ice pick, carefully make four vertical holes through the plastic/steel wool stack, and through the fiberboard, using the corner holes in the sheet metal square as a guide. use a drill only on the external fiberboard, as the steel wool in the layer-stack might spindle around the drill bit.

O) Using four skinny bolts, along with nuts and LARGE washers, secure the metal square and plastic/steel wool stack against the fiberboard square. Use a bolt no longer than necessary, such that the bolt ends will not protrude significantly. When completed, this whole lid assembly should fit snugly on top of the fiberboard box. The metal plate attached to the lid should closely, but not perfectly, align with the metal cube interior. With the lid in place, only bare metal should face to the interior of the accumulator.

P) For handles, first firmly glue a flat, wide and long wood strip to two opposing outer sides of the fiberboard cube, near to the top. When completely dry, screw wood or metal handles to these wood strips. A handle should also be attached to the upper, outer side of the lid assembly, using a similar support mechanism. The fiberboard is simply too lightweight to accept screws or nails alone. You may likewise install a hinge between the lid assembly and the box, or coaster wheels to the bottom, but these are not necessary.

A one-cubic foot, 10-ply orgone accumulator charger-box, with attached shooter funnel.

Q) For additional charging strength, the outer fiberboard walls may be given several coats of protective natural shellac.

R) For additional charging strength, store this cubical accumulator in the bottom part of a larger, human-sized accumulator, under the bench that you normally sit upon. The charge box alone is probably not sufficiently strong to hold your weight, so you don't want to be sitting on that. Be sure to maintain a clean and uncontaminated environment for your accumulator, as per the points given in the previous chapters. Prop the lid open when not in use, and store in a clean, dry place, without electromagnetic or nuclear contamination.

Before constructing anything, be sure to review Part II, on the Safe and Effective Use of Orgone Accumulating Devices.

18. Construction of an Orgone Shooter Funnel and Bowl

The shooter funnel is similar to other accumulating devices, but has an open face allowing for external irradiation of objects. It is often connected to a larger box accumulator, as shown on the facing page, but this is not absolutely necessary.

A) Obtain a galvanized steel funnel with about 6" diameter at the large end, from a hardware, farm supply, or auto supply store. Auto supply stores sometimes sell these with a flexible metal hose already attached, for dispensing oil into a car engine, and this may help in the later attachment to a box accumulator. Test with a magnet to be sure it is not aluminum.

B) Coat the outer metal surface of the funnel with a layer of melted beeswax (caution: only do this outdoors over a hot-plate due to fire danger) or black-plastic electrical insulation tape, leaving exposed the bare metal surface of the funnel interior.

C) If desired, the small "draining" end of the funnel can be attached to a 3/4" or 1" diameter length of hollow, flexible galvanized steel conduit. (No aluminum!) The other end of the cable is then run into the interior of a small box accumulator, through a hole in its side or lid. (See page 41 & 182) Wrap the outer surface of the flexible metal cable with black-plastic electrical insulation tape. Your shooter funnel will then draw orgone down the cable to the funnel opening, increasing its radiating strength. Or, simply store the shooter funnel inside a box-type accumulator, to keep it charged up.

Eva Reich's Orgone Accumulator Bowl Design

D) As an alternative to a galvanized funnel, Eva Reich advocated to make a stand-alone *orgone shooter bowl*, made using a stainless steel kitchen-type mixing bowl. The size should be large and shallow, able to cover a woman's breast or the solar plexus region, about 6" to 8" in diameter at the opening. A magnet should be used to test such a bowl, that it would stick to it, as some kinds of stainless steel are non-magnetic and consequently not good for orgone accumulator devices.

E) Once the bowl has been procured, a flexible sheep's wool felt or fluffy blanket material should be cut, sufficient to cover the full exterior of the bowl. For a 6" bowl which forms about half of a sphere, this requires about 10" square of wool fabric material. When laid across the bowl exterior, the loose extra fabric must be cut away. Before cutting, snugly secure the fabric square to the bowl with masking tape, along the mid-length sides of the fabric square. The four corners of the square will then protrude. They must be cut away, using scissors, in a manner that leaves the bowl completely covered once the corner sections are laid down. Some wrinkles will exist and this does not harm the function. Once the fabric corner cuts have been made, secure the fabric into place with additional masking tape.

F) Place a layer of steel wool on top of the fabric-covered bowl. Then lay down another layer of fabric -- which now should measure slightly larger than the first fabric layer. Proceed to cut and layer it as was done in step E above. Then lay down another layer of steel wool, and then a final fabric layer, to complete a 3-ply orgone shooter bowl.

G) The final exterior layer of the shooter bowl should be fully secured into shape, and also secured to the bowl and all around the bowl's edge, using masking tape. The entire exterior layer of fabric can be fully covered by masking tape, to insure that all of the materials are secure. The masking tape should not significantly intrude into the interior of the mixing bowl, however, just enough around the interior edge of the bowl to secure everything. Holding your hand inside the bowl, or the shooter funnel describe previously, should give a strong radiant feeling.

19. Construction of an Orgone Shooter Tube

The shooter tube is a very simple means for demonstrating the subjective sensations of the orgone radiation, and also for irradiation of orgone energy into body cavities. Simply store the completed shooter tube inside a well maintained accumulator, and remove it for use when necessary. Under relaxed conditions, most people can hold this tube in the hand, or place it on the solar plexus or upper lip, and readily feel the soft radiant glow of the orgone energy.

A) Obtain a Pyrex or similar sturdy test tube of about 3/4" to 1" diameter, and 6" to 9" long, from a laboratory or medical supply company.

B) Fill the test tube full of fine grade ("000" or "0000") steel wool. Compress to firmness.

C) Seal the open end of the test tube with plastic electrical tape.

D) Place the completed shooter tube inside a small orgone accumulator or blanket, to charge it up. Keep it stored inside the accumulator in between uses.

E) If you use the shooter tube to irradiate the throat or other body cavities, or if the Pyrex glass otherwise becomes soiled, wipe both the glass tube and the interior of the accumulator clean with isopropyl alcohol and allow to air out, prior to storing it back inside the accumulator. When a fully-sanitary condition is required, the shooter tube should always be alcohol cleaned and air dried prior to being replaced into the accumulator for charging.

20. Construction of a Large 3-Ply Human-Sized Orgone Energy Accumulator

This accumulator is large enough to sit in, and is composed of 6 large rectangular panels. Each panel is made from a wood frame, galvanized steel sheet metal (27 gauge), steel wool, fiberglass, and fiberboard. One side of each wood frame is faced with galvanized steel, the other with fiberboard, insulation-board ("soundboard") or masonboard, and the three alternating layers of fiberglass and steel wool are sandwiched in between.

A) First compute the size of the panels for an accumulator that will fit your personal needs, adding the necessary dimensions for overlap between the various panels. The side panels and back panel should physically sit on the edges of the bottom panel. The back panel should snuggle between the two side panels. The top panel should overlap and rest upon both side panels and the back panel, covering them. The door panel should, like the back panel, snuggle between the side panels when it is shut. I believe this arrangement is the simplest possible, and most efficient to build. Dimensions are given below for accumulators to accommodate people of varying sitting heights, but of average weight. As the distance of the body surface from the metal walls increases, there will be a reduction in effectiveness of the accumulator. The dimensions of the accumulator should be selected to meet your needs. An additional 1/2" clearance is provided in the width dimension (1/4" each side), such that the door will open and shut freely.

Panel Dimensions:	*Large Size*	*Medium Size*	*Small Size*
Top:	29.5" x 35"	26.5" x 32"	23.5" x 28"
Bottom:	29.5" x 35"	26.5" x 32"	23.5" x 28"
Left side:	35" x 58"	32" x 54"	28" x 50"
Right side:	35" x 58"	32" x 54"	28" x 50"
Back:	25" x 58"	22" x 54"	19" x 50"
Door:	25" x 52"	22" x 48"	19" x 44"

Interior Dimensions:

Height:	58"	54"	50"
Width:	25"	22"	19"
Depth:	31"	28"	24"

You will need:
Height = height sitting erect in a chair + about 3"
Width = shoulder width + about 4" (2" each side)
Breadth = sitting, knee to back distance + about 3"

B) Make wood frames of 3/4" x 1-1/2" pine (called "one by two" in lumber yards), like picture frames, such that the outer edges conform to the computed dimensions for your accumulator panels. Nail and glue all joints.

C) Arrange the open wood frames together, as they will be when the accumulator is complete, to make sure that all dimensions have been properly calculated and cut. If there is an error in your calculations, now is the time to find out, before the more expensive fiberboard and galvanized sheet metal have been cut.

D) Cut the fiberboard or masonboard panels to size, from 1/2" or 3/4" thick fiberboard sheet, to cover fully one side of each wood frame. Nail and glue the fiberboard panels to each wood frame. Wait until step J for the sheet metal. Use 1/4" plywood instead of fiberboard for the bottom panel (and only the bottom panel).

Once the six individual wood frames are nailed or screwed together, temporarily assemble them with tape, to insure a good fit. If your measurements are off, here is where you will discover and correct it, before cutting the expensive galvanized steel or fiberboard/masonboard sheets.

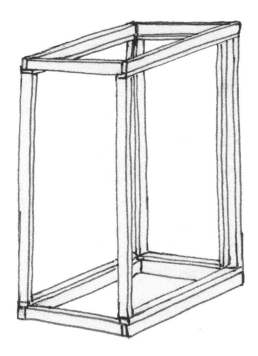

E) Cut batts of 1/4" thick fiberglass material to size and place a layer inside each of the open panel frames. Use gloves and a mask to protect yourself. Do not compress. Avoid lumps and holes. You can use wool fluff, wool batting, wool camp-blankets or cotton fluff instead, if you wish, but for a large accumulator like this, the costs will be higher, and the accumulation will not be significantly stronger. These other materials may yield a slightly different energetic feeling to the orgone charge, and if that is important to you, the cost may be justified.

End Cross-Section of Side, Top, Back and Door Accumulator Panels

This side to inside of accumulator

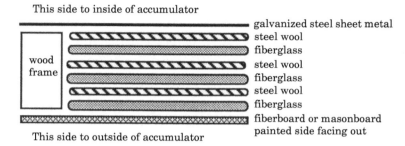

galvanized steel sheet metal
steel wool
fiberglass
steel wool
fiberglass
steel wool
fiberglass
fiberboard or masonboard
painted side facing out

wood frame

This side to outside of accumulator

End Cross-Section of Bottom Accumulator Panel

This side to inside of accumulator

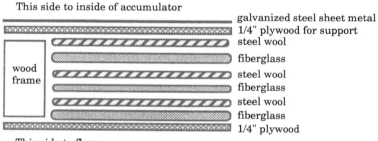

galvanized steel sheet metal
1/4" plywood for support
steel wool
fiberglass
steel wool
fiberglass
steel wool
fiberglass
1/4" plywood

wood frame

This side to floor

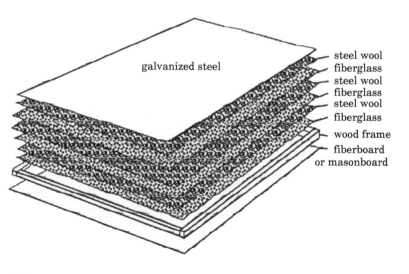

galvanized steel

steel wool
fiberglass
steel wool
fiberglass
steel wool
fiberglass
wood frame
fiberboard or masonboard

F) Unroll very fine ("000" or "0000") steel wool pads, and place a layer inside each of the open panel frames, on top of the fiberglass. Leave it fluffy, but not excessively thick, in as uniform a layer as possible. Steel wool also comes in large reels or rolls which will speed up construction for large accumulators. The layerings are similar to how an orgone blanket is prepared.

G) Repeat steps E and F, placing a new layer of fiberglass on top of the previous steel wool layer, and another layer of steel wool on top of that.

H) Again repeat steps E and F, placing another new layer of fiberglass on top of the previous steel wool layer, and another layer of steel wool on top of that. Note that in my instructions, I advise to place a fiberglass layer next to the exterior fiberboard or masonboard, effectively doubling up the exterior organic high-dielectric layering. I also place one steel wool layer next to the galvanized steel, doubling up the interior metallic layers. I find this adds to the overall accumulator strength.

I) You should now have three alternating layers of fiberglass and steel wool contained in the open frame of each panel. The final layer facing you should be composed of steel wool. The panels should also be filling up, and may need to be slightly compressed before the final layer of galvanized steel sheet metal can be added. If you have used some other type of non-metallic material than fiberglass, and if the material lies loosely in the frame, you may have problems with slumping of the plys when the panels are finally sealed and placed in upright position. If this is the case, now is the time to do something to prevent slumping. Typically this can be prevented by using a staple-gun to secure the fabric and steel wool to the top inside of the panel.

J) Cut the galvanized steel sheet metal to size such that it fits over the open part of each panel, overlapping and covering the wood frames. Use the lightest sheet metal available, such as 27 gauge, which can be cut with hand shears for trimming, and still add to structural strength of the panels. For the bottom (floor) panel, add a layer of 1/2" plywood just under the sheet metal, for additional weight support. Nail it securely onto the

Front View, full-size 3-ply accumulator

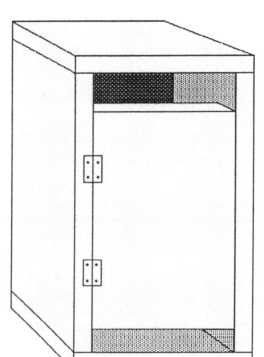

For Warmer, Tropical Climates: *Use door with 3"
convection gaps at top and bottom. If needed, tack screen strips
to door top and bottom, across gaps, to keep out insects.*

For Cooler or Cold Climates: *Use full height door with
small window. Door can swing inside the ORAC, as shown here,
or be secured to exterior and close flush to the ouside. Before
assembling door, cut matching 6" square openings in door sheet
metal and fiberboard, centered at face height. Then frame
opening with 1x2" wood strips. Complete assembly as per
instructions.*

*Use hinges with removable hinge pins for easier assembly and
take-down. Secure inside of door with hook and eye.*

See comparison photos on pages 41, 44 & 195.

wood frames, using a small hole punch if necessary. Small steel tacks should easily penetrate through the sheet metal. After nailing, use file or shears to trim all sharp metal corners.

K) Assemble and secure the panels together. Start by securing one side panel to the bottom panel, by using an "L" shaped metal brace at the front and rear of the side panel, near the bottom. Use screws, such that the accumulator can be taken apart later for easy moving. Secure the other side panel in a similar fashion, followed by the back panel. The back panel must be secured independently by additional small metal braces, placed between the wood frames of the bottom and back. Add the top panel, and secure it to the sides and back in a similar 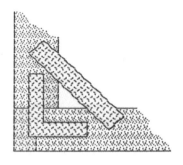 manner. The accumulator should now be quite sturdy, and is almost complete.

L) Carefully mark and drill holes for door hinges and attach them to the door panel and side panel. Make sure you center the door in a way that leaves equal space at the top and bottom, either for convection gaps (for the vented door style), or as clearance to allow the door to freely swing open and shut (for the full-height windowed door style). Use hinges with removable pins so that you can easily take the door off when moving the accumulator. After fixing the door to the side panel, it should open fully and close snugly, without binding.

M) Attach a hook and eye to the inside of the door and side panel interior opposite the hinge, such that the person sitting inside can secure it shut. Finally, add several coats of natural shellac to the outer exposed sides of the panels, to protect them from humidity and add to the accumulating strength.

N) Your accumulator is now complete, except for a seat. You should have a seat which will allow you to place other accumulator chargers underneath. For this purpose, you might wish to specially construct a wooden bench. Wood is a good material to use, as it does not absorb the orgone energy significantly, and is not cold to the touch. Do not use woods that have been soaked in preservative or formaldehyde, however. Metal chairs are OK, but will be quite cold to sit on unless covered with a light fabric.

O) You may also wish to construct a chest board, or orgone pillow, for use inside the accumulator. As you sit inside, notice that there is a great distance from your chest to the front metal wall. This large distance inhibits orgone irradiation to your chest. An additional, small accumulator panel, similar to those used for the wall panels, could be constructed for use inside the larger box, to bring the radiation closer to the chest. However, a simpler way is to use a bundle of cotton, wool, or acrylic felt, rolled into a large pillow shape with equal layers of steel wool. The final outer layer should be composed of steel wool, and the entire bundle is then placed inside a thin cotton pillowcase. It should be large enough that it fits very snugly into the pillowcase. By holding this orgone pillow close to the chest, while you are in the accumulator, it will irradiate those frontal areas of your body that are not so well irradiated by the accumulator walls. Leave the orgone pillow inside the accumulator when not in use, to keep it charged up. You can also use this pillow outside of the accumulator, in a manner similar to the orgone blanket, with equally good results.

P) Do not connect electrical appliances to the accumulator. Follow the cautions given in the previous chapters. You can read a book while inside the accumulator, but should use either a strong external light source (to shine a beam of incandescent light into the accumulator), or you can use a battery-powered reading light inside. Again: no fluorescent lights, television sets, heating blankets, computers, pads, cell phones or other electrical or electromagnetic devices!!

Again: Before constructing anything, be sure to review Part II, on the Safe and Effective Use of Orgone Accumulating Devices.

A twenty-ply orgone accumulator at OBRL, made by the orgonics.com company. Try this one only after having considerable experience with all the others.

SELECTED REFERENCES

Also see the on-line *Bibliography On Orgonomy:*
www.orgonelab.org/bibliog.htm
and the Addendum on page 206.

Books By Wilhelm Reich as republished by Farrar Straus & Giroux, NY.

American Odyssey: Letters & Journals 1940-1947
Beyond Psychology: Letters & Journals 1934-1939
The Bioelectrical Investigation of Sexuality and Anxiety
The Bion Experiments
The Cancer Biopathy (Discovery of the Orgone, Vol. 2)
Character Analysis
Children of the Future: On the Prevention of Sexual Pathology
Cosmic Superimposition: Man's Orgonotic Roots in Nature
The Early Writings of Wilhelm Reich
Ether, God and Devil
The Function of the Orgasm (Discovery of the Orgone, Vol. 1)
Genitality in the Theory and Therapy of Neurosis
The Invasion of Compulsory Sex-Morality
Listen, Little Man!
The Mass Psychology of Fascism
The Murder of Christ (Emotional Plague of Mankind, Vol. 2)
Passion of Youth: Wilhelm Reich, an Autobiography 1897-1922
People in Trouble (Emotional Plague of Mankind, Vol. 1)
Record of a Friendship, Correspondence, Wilhelm Reich & A.S. Neill
Reich Speaks of Freud
Selected Writings: An Introduction to Orgonomy
The Sexual Revolution
Where's The Truth? Letters & Journals 1948-1957

Relevant Special Reports by Wilhelm Reich available from the Wilhelm Reich Museum

The Orgone Energy Accumulator, Its Scientific and Medical Use, Orgone Institute Press, Maine, 1951.

The Oranur Experiment, First Report (1947-1951), Wilhelm Reich Foundation, Maine, 1951.

The Einstein Affair, 1939-1952, Wilhelm Reich Biographical Material, History of the Discovery of the Life Energy, Doc. Vol. A-IX-E, Orgone Institute Press, Rangeley, Maine, 1953.

Contact With Space: Oranur 2nd Report, CORE Pilot Press, NY 1957.

Relevant Research Articles by Wilhelm Reich:

"Orgonotic Pulsation: The Differentiation of Orgone Energy from Electromagnetism", *Int. J. Sex-Economy & Orgone Research,* III:74-79, 1944.

"Orgone Biophysics, Mechanistic Science and 'Atomic Energy'", *Int. J. Sex-Economy & Orgone Research,* IV:200-201, 1945.

"Orgonotic Light Functions 1: Searchlight Phenomena in the Orgone Energy Envelope of the Earth", *Orgone Energy Bulletin,* I(1):3-6, 1949.

"Orgonotic Light Functions 2: An X-Ray Photograph of the Excited Orgone Energy Field of the Palms", *Orgone Energy Bulletin,* I(2):49-51, 1949.

"Orgonotic Light Functions 3: Further Characteristics of Vacor Lumination", *Orgone Energy Bulletin,* I(3):97-99, 1949.

"Meteorological Functions in Orgone-Charged Vacuum Tubes", *Orgone Energy Bulletin,* II(4):184-193, 1950.

"The Storm of November 25th and 26th, 1950", *Orgone Energy Bull.,* III(2):76-80, 1951.

"Three Experiments with Rubber at the Electroscope", *Orgone Energy Bulletin,* III(3):144-145, 1951.

"The Anti-Nuclear Radiation Effect of Cosmic Orgone Energy", *Orgone Energy Bulletin,* III(1):61-63, 1951.

"'Cancer Cells' in Experiment XX", Orgone *Energy Bulletin,* III(1):1-3, 1951.

"The Leukemia Problem: Approach", *Orgone Energy Bulletin,* III(2):139-144, 1951.

Books on Orgonomy and Wilhelm Reich, by Others:

Baker, E.F.: *Man in the Trap,* Macmillan, NY, 1967.

Bean, O.: *Me and the Orgone,* St. Martin's Press, NY, 1971.

DeMeo, J.: In Defense of Wilhelm Reich: Opposing the 80-Years' War of Mainstream Defamatory Slander Against One of the 20th Century's Most Brilliant Physicians and Natural Scientists, Natural Energy Works, Ashland, Oregon 2013.

DeMeo, J. (Editor): On Wilhelm Reich and Orgonomy (Pulse *of the Planet #4),* Natural Energy Works, Ashland, Oregon 1993.

DeMeo, James (Ed.): *Heretic's Notebook: Emotions, Protocells, Ether-Drift and Cosmic Life Energy, With New Research Supporting Wilhelm Reich (Pulse of the Planet #5)* Natural Energy Works, Ashland, Oregon 2002.

DeMeo, J. & Senf, B.(Editors), *Nach Reich: Neue Forschungen zur Orgonomie: Sexualökonomie, Die Entdeckung Der Orgonenergie* Zweitausendeins Verlag, Frankfurt, 1998.

Herskowitz, M.: *Emotional Armoring*, Transactions Press, NY, 1998.

Kavouras, J.: *Heilen mit Orgonenergie, Die medizinische Orgonomie,* Turm Verlag, 74321 Bietigheim, Germany, 2005.

Müschenich, S.: *Der Gesundheitsbegriff im Werk des Arztes Wilhelm Reich (The Concept of Health in the Works of Dr. Wilhelm Reich)*, Verlag Görich & Weiershäuser, Marburg 1995.

Ollendorff, I.: *Wilhelm Reich, A Personal Biography,* St. Martin's Press, NY, 1969.

Raknes, O.: *Wilhelm Reich and Orgonomy,* St. Martin's, NY, 1970.

Reich, P.: *A Book of Dreams,* Harper & Row, NY, 1973.

Sharaf, M.: *Fury on Earth,* St. Martin's-Marek, NY, 1983.

Wyckoff, J.: *Wilhelm Reich, Life Force Explorer,* Fawcett, Greenwich, CT, 1973.

Works Addressing the 1950s Smear Campaign and FDA Attacks Against Wilhelm Reich

Baker, C.F.: "An Analysis of the United States Food & Drug Admini-stration's Scientific Evidence Against Wilhelm Reich, Part II, the Physical Concepts", *Journal of Orgonomy,* 6(2):222-231, 1972; "...Part III, Physical Evidence", *Journal of Orgonomy,* 7(2):234-245, 1973.

Blasband, D.: "United States of America v. Wilhelm Reich, Part I", *Journal of Orgonomy,* 1(1-2):56-130, 1967; "...Part II, the Appeal", *Journal of Orgonomy,* 2(1):24-67, 1968.

Blasband, R.A.: "An Analysis of the United States Food and Drug Administration's Scientific Evidence Against Wilhelm Reich, Part I, the Biomedical Evidence", *Journal of Orgonomy,* 6(2):207-222, 1972.

DeMeo, J.: "Postscript on the F.D.A.'s. Experimental Evidence Against Wilhelm Reich", *Pulse of the Planet,* 1(1):18-23, 1989.

DeMeo, J.: *In Defense of Wilhelm Reich: Opposing the 80-Years' War of Mainstream Defamatory Slander Against One of the 20th Century's Most Brilliant Physicians and Natural Scientists,* Natural Energy Works, Ashland 2013.

Greenfield, J.: *Wilhelm Reich Versus the USA,* W.W. Norton, NY, 1974.

Martin, J.: *Wilhelm Reich and the Cold War*, Natural Energy Works, Ashland, OR 2014.

Reich, W.: *Conspiracy: An Emotional Chain Reaction*, Wilhelm Reich Biographical Material, History of the Discovery of the Life Energy (American Period, 1942-54), documentary volume A-XII-EP, Orgone Institute Press, Maine, 1954.

Wilder, J.: "CSICOP, Time Magazine and Wilhelm Reich", in *Heretic's Notebook*, J.DeMeo, Ed., OBRL, p.55-66, 2002.

Wolfe, T.: *Emotional Plague Versus Orgone Biophysics: The 1947 Campaign,* Orgone Institute Press, NY, 1948.

Selected Research Articles on the Orgone Energy:

Anderson, W.A.: "Orgone Therapy in Rheumatic Fever", *Orgone Energy Bulletin,* II(2):71-73, 1950.

Atkin, R.H.: "The Second Law of Thermodynamics and the Orgone Accumulator", *Orgone Energy Bulletin,* I(2):52-60, 1949.

Baker, C.F.: "The Orgone Energy Continuum", *Journal of Orgonomy,* 14(1):37-60, 1980.

Baker, C.F.: "The Orgone Energy Continuum: the Ether and Relativity", *Journal of Orgonomy,* 16(1):41-67, 1982.

Baker, C.F., et al: "The Reich Blood Test", *Journal of Orgonomy,* 15(2):184-218, 1981.

Baker, C.F., et al: "The Reich Blood Test: 105 Cases", *Annals, Institute for Orgonomic Science,* 1(1):1-11, 1984.

Baker, C.F., et al.: "Wound Healing in Mice, Part I", "...Part II", *Annals, Institute for Orgonomic Science,* 1(1):12-32, 1984; 2(1):7-24, 1985.

Baker, C.F., et al.: "The Reich Blood Test: Clinical Correlation", *Annals, Institute for Orgonomic Science,* 2(1):1-6, 1985.

Baker, C.F. (pseud: Rosenblum, C.F.): "The Red Shift", *J. Orgonomy,* 4:183-191, 1970.

Baker, C.F. (pseud: Rosenblum, C.F.): "The Electroscope - Parts I - IV", *Journal of Orgonomy,* 3(2):188-197, 1969; 4(1):79-90, 1970; 10(1):57-80, 1976; 11(1):102-109, 1977.

Baker, C.F. (pseud: Rosenblum, C.F.): "The Temperature Difference: An Experimental Protocol", *Journal of Orgonomy,* 6(1):61-71, 1972.

Blasband, R.A.: "Thermal Orgonometry", *Journal of Orgonomy,* 5(2):175-188, 1971.

Blasband, R.A.: "The Orgone Energy Accumulator in the Treatment of Cancer Mice", *Journal of Orgonomy,* 7(1):81-85, 1973.

Blasband, R.A.: "Effects of the ORAC on Cancer in Mice: Three Experiments", *Journal of Orgonomy,* 18(2):202-211, 1985.

Blasband, R.A.: "The Medical DOR-Buster in the Treatment of Cancer Mice", *Journal of Orgonomy*, 8(2):173-180, 1974.

Bremmer, K.M.: "Medical Effects of Orgone Energy", *Orgone Energy Bulletin,* V(1-2):71-83, 1953.

Brenner, M.: "Bions and Cancer, A Review of Reich's Work", *Journal of Orgonomy,* 18(2):212-220, 1984.

Cott, A.A.: "Orgonomic Treatment of Ichthyosis", *Orgone Energy Bulletin,* III(3):163-166, 1951.

DeMeo, J.: "Effect of Fluorescent Lights and Metal Boxes on Growing Plants", *Journal of Orgonomy,* 9(1):95-99, 1975.

DeMeo, J.: "Seed Sprouting Inside the Orgone Accumulator", *Journal of Orgonomy,* 12(2):253-258, 1978.

DeMeo, J.: "Orgone Accumulator Stimulation of Sprouting Mung Beans", in *Heretic's Notebook*, J.DeMeo, Ed., p.168-176, 2002.

DeMeo, J.: "Water Evaporation Inside the Orgone Accumulator", *Journal of Orgonomy,* 14(2):171-175, 1980.

DeMeo, J.: "Bion-Biogenesis Research and Seminars at OBRL: Progress Report", in *Heretic's Notebook*, J.DeMeo, Ed., OBRL, p.100-113, 2002.

Dew, R.A.: "Wilhelm Reich's Cancer Biopathy", in *Psychotherapeutic Treatment of Cancer Patients,* J.G. Goldberg, ed., Free Press, NY, 1980.

Espanca, J.: "The Effect of Orgone on Plant Life, Parts I - VII", *Offshoots of Orgonomy,* 3:23-28, Autumn 1981; 4:35-38, Spring 1982; 6:20-23, Spring 1983; 7:36-37, Autumn 1983; 8:35-43, Spring 1984; 11:30-32, Fall 1985; 12:45-48, Spring 1986.

Espanca, J.: "Orgone Energy Devices for the Irradiation of Plants", *Offshoots of Orgonomy,* 9:25-31, Fall 1984.

Grad, B.: "Wilhelm Reich's Experiment XX", *Cosmic Orgone Engineering,* VII(3-4):203-204, 1955.

Grad, Bernard: "The Accumulator Effect on Leukemia Mice", *Journal of Orgonomy,* 26(2):199-218, 1992.

Hamilton, A.E.: "Child's-Eye View of the Orgone Flow", *Orgone Energy Bulletin,* IV(4):215-216, 1952.

Harman, R.A.: "Further Experiments with Negative To Minus T", *Journal of Orgonomy,* 20(1):67-74, 1986.

Hebenstreit, Günter: *"Der Orgonakkumulator Nach Wilhelm Reich. Eine Experimentelle Untersuchung zur Spannungs-Ladungs-Formel",* Diplomarbeit zur Erlangung des Magistergrades der Philosophie an der Grung- und Integrativ-wissenschaftlichen Fakultat der Universitat Wien, 1995.

Hoppe, W.: "My First Experiences With the Orgone Accumulator", *International Journal for Sex-Economy & Orgone Research,* IV:200-201, 1945.

Hoppe, W.: "My Experiences With the Orgone Accumulator", *Orgone Energy Bulletin,* I(1):12-22, 1949.

Hoppe, W.: "Further Experiences with the Orgone Accumulator", *Orgone Energy Bulletin,* II(1):16-21, 1950.

Hoppe, W.: "Orgone Versus Radium Therapy in Skin Cancer, Report of a Case", *Orgonomic Medicine,* I(2):133-138, 1955.

Hoppe, W.: "The Treatment of a Malignant Melanoma with Orgone Energy", contained in *In the Wake of Reich,* D. Boadella, ed., Coventure Press, London, 1976.

Hughes, D.C.: "Some Geiger-Muller Counter Observations After Reich", *Journal of Orgonomy,* 16(1):68-73, 1982.

Konia, C.: "An Investigation of the Thermal Properties of the ORAC, Part I & II", *J. Orgonomy,* 8(1):47-64, 1974; 12(2):244-252, 1978.

Lance, L.: "Effects of the Orgone Accumulator on Growing Plants", *Journal of Orgonomy,* 11(1):68-71, 1977.

Lassek, H.: "Orgone Accumulator Therapy of Severely Diseased Persons", *Pulse of the Planet,* 3:39-47, 1991.

Lappert, P.: "Primary Bions Through Superimposition at Elevated Temperature and Pressure", *J. Orgonomy,* 19(1):92-112, 1985.

Levine, E.: "Treatment of a Hypertensive Biopathy with the Orgone Accumulator", *Orgone Energy Bulletin,* III(1):53-58, 1951.

Mannion, M.: "Wilhelm Reich, 1897-1957: A Reevaluation for a New Generation", *Alternative & Complementary Therapies,* 3(3):194-199, June 1997.

Müschenich, S. & Gebauer, R.: "The (Psycho-) Physiological Effects of the Reich Orgone Accumulator", Dissertation, University of Marburg, West Germany, 1985.

Opfermann-Fuckert, D.: "Reports on Treatments With Orgone Energy: Ten Selected Cases", *Annals, Institute for Orgonomic Science,* 6(1):33-52, September 1989.

Raphael, C.M.: "Confirmation of Orgonomic (Reich) Tests for the Diagnosis of Uterine Cancer", *Orgonomic Med.* II(1):36-41, 1956.

Raphael, C.M. & MacDonald, H.E.: *Orgonomic Diagnosis of Cancer Biopathy,* Wilhelm Reich Foundation, Maine, 1952.

Sharaf, M.: "Priority of Wilhelm Reich's Cancer Findings", *Orgonomic Medicine,* I(2):145-150, 1955.

Seiler, H.: "New Experiments in Thermal Orgonometry", *Journal of Orgonomy,* 16(2):197-206, 1982.

Silvert, M.: "On the Medical Use of Orgone Energy", *Orgone Energy Bulletin,* IV(1):51-54, 1952.

Sobey, V.M.: "Treatment of Pulmonary Tuberculosis with Orgone Energy", *Orgonomic Medicine,* I(2):121-132, 1955.

Sobey, V.M.: "A Case of Rheumatoid Arthritis Treated with Orgone Energy", *Orgonomic Medicine,* II(1):64-69, 1956.

Southgate, L.: "Chinese Medicine and Wilhelm Reich", *European Journal of Chinese Medicine,* Vol 4(4): 31-41, 2003. Also by Lambert Academic Publishing, London 2009.

Tropp, S.J.: "The Treatment of a Mediastinal Malignancy with the Orgone Accumulator", *Orgone Energy Bull.,* I(3):100-109, 1949.

Tropp, S.J.: "Orgone Therapy of an Early Breast Cancer", *Orgone Energy Bulletin,* II(3):131-138, 1950.

Trotta, E.E. & Marer, E.: "The Orgonotic Treatment of Transplanted Tumors and Associated Immune Functions", *Journal of Orgonomy,* 24(1):39-44, 1990.

Wevrick, N.: "Physical Orgone Therapy of Diabetes", *Orgone Energy Bulletin,* III(2):110-112, 1951.

Research on Natural Forces Similar to Orgone:

Alfven, H.: *Cosmic Plasmas,* Kluwer, Boston, 1981.

Arp, H., et al: *The Redshift Controversy,* W.A. Benjamin, Reading, MA, 1973.

Arp, H.: *Quasars, Red Shifts, and Controversies,* Interstellar Media, Berkeley, CA, 1987.

Becker, R.O. & Selden, G.: *The Body Electric: Electromagnetism and the Foundation of Life,* Wm. Morrow, NY, 1985.

Bortels, V.H.: "Die hypothetische Wetterstrahlung als vermutliches Agens kosmo-meteoro-biologischer Reaktionen", *Wissenschaftliche Zeitschrift der Humboldt-Universität zu Berlin,* VI:115-124, 1956.

Brown, F.A.: "Evidence for External Timing in Biological Clocks", contained in *An Introduction to Biological Rhythms,* J. Palmer, ed., Academic Press, NY, 1975.

Burr, H.S.: *Blueprint For Immortality,* Neville Spearman, London, 1971; *The Fields of Life,* Ballantine Books, NY, 1972.

Cope, F.W.: "Magnetic Monopole Currents in Flowing Water Detected Experimentally...", *Physiological Chemistry & Physics,* 12:21-29, 1980.

DeMeo, J.: "Dayton Miller's Ether Drift Research: A Fresh Look", in *Heretic's Notebook,* J.DeMeo, Ed., OBRL, p.114-130, 2002.

DeMeo, J.: "A Dynamic and Substantive Cosmological Ether", in *Proceedings of the Natural Philosophy Alliance,* Cynthia Whitney, Ed., 1(1):15-20, Spring 2004.

Dewey, E.R., ed.: *Cycles, Mysterious Forces that Trigger Events,* Hawthorn Books, NY, 1971.

Dudley, H.C.: *Morality of Nuclear Planning,* Kronos Press, Glassboro, NJ, 1976.

Eden, J.: *Animal Magnetism and the Life Energy,* Exposition Press, NY, 1974.

Kervran, L.C.: *Biological Transmutations,* Beekman Press, Woodstock, NY, 1980.

Miller, D.: "The Ether-Drift Experiment and the Determination of the Absolute Motion of the Earth", *Reviews of Modern Physics,* 5:203-242, July, 1933.

Moss, T.: *The Body Electric, A Personal Journey into the Mysteries of Parapsychological Research,* J. P. Tarcher, Los Angeles, 1979.

Nordenstrom, B.: *Biologically Closed Electric Circuits:,* Nordic Medical Press, Stockholm, 1983.

Ott, J.: *Health and Light,* Devin Adair, Old Greenwich, CT, 1973.

Piccardi, G.: *Chemical Basis of Medical Climatology,* Charles Thomas Publishers, Springfield, IL, 1962.

Ravitz, L.J.: "History, Measurement, and Applicability of Periodic Changes in the Electromagnetic Field in Health and Disease", *Annals, NY Acad. Sciences,* 98:1144-1201, 1962.

Sheldrake, R.: *A New Science of Life: The Hypothesis of Causative Formation,* J.P. Tarcher, Los Angeles, 1981.

On *Oranur Effects* from A-bomb Tests & Atomic Radiation

DeMeo, J.: "Oranur Effects from the Three Mile Island Nuclear Power Plant Accident", *Pulse of the Planet,* 3:26, 1991; and "Weather Anomalies and Nuclear Testing", in *On Wilhelm Reich and Orgonomy,* J.DeMeo, Ed., 1993, p.117-120.

DeMeo, J.: "Oranur Report: Drought Crisis Following Underground Nuclear Bomb Tests in India and Pakistan, May 1998. www.orgonelab.org/oranur.htm

Eden, J.: "Personal Experiences with Oranur", *Journal of Orgonomy,* 5(1):88-95, 1971.

Gould, J.M.: *The Enemy Within: The High Cost of Living Near Nuclear Reactors,* Four Walls Eight Windows, NY, 1996; and *Deadly Deceit: Low-Level Radiation, High Level Cover-Up,* Four Walls Eight Windows, NY 1991.

Graeub, R.: *The Petkau Effect: Nuclear Radiation, People and Trees,* Four Walls Eight Windows, NY, 1992.

Katagiri, M.: "Three Mile Island: The Language of Science versus the People's Reality", *Pulse of the Planet,* 3:27-38, 1991. and: "Three Mile Island Revisited", in *On Wilhelm Reich and Orgonomy,* J.DeMeo, Ed., 1993, p.84-91.

Kato, Y.: "Recent Abnormal Phenomena on Earth and Atomic Bomb Tests", *Pulse of the Planet* 1:5-9, 1989.

Milian, V.: "Confirmation of an Oranur Anomaly", *Pulse of the Planet* 5:182, 2002.

Sternglass, E.: *Secret Fallout,* McGraw Hill, NY, 1986; and *Low Level Radiation,* Ballentine Books, NY, 1972.

Wassermann, H.: *Killing Our Own,* Doubleday, NY, 1985.

Whiteford, G.: "Earthquakes and Nuclear Testing: Dangerous Patterns and Trends", *Pulse of the Planet,* 2:10-21, 1989.

Addendum: Newest Publications

DeMeo, J., et al.: "In Defense of Wilhelm Reich: An Open Response to *Nature* and the Scientific /Medical Community", *Water: A Multidisciplinary Research Journal*, V.4, p.72-81, 2012. www.waterjournal.org/volume-4

DeMeo, J.: "Water as a Resonant Medium for Unusual External Environmental Factors", *Water: A Multidisciplinary Research Journal*, V.3, p.1-47, 2011. www.waterjournal.org/volume-3

DeMeo, J.: "Anomalous 'Living' Spectrographic Changes in Water Structures: Explorations in New Territory", *Water: A Multidisciplinary Research Journal*, V.10, p.41-81, 2018. www.waterjournal.org/volume-10

DeMeo, J.: *The Dynamic Ether of Cosmic Space: Correcting a Major Error in Modern Science*, Natural Energy Works, 2019.

DeMeo, J.: "Report on Orgone Accumulator Stimulation of Sprouting Mung Beans", *Subtle Energies and Energy Medicine,* 21(2):51-62, 2010.

DeMeo, J.: "Following the Red Thread of Wilhelm Reich: A Personal Adventure", *Edge Science,* p.11-16, October-December 2010.

DeMeo, J.: "Experimental Confirmation of the Reich Orgone Accumulator Thermal Anomaly", *Subtle Energies and Energy Medicine,* 20(3):17-32, 2009.

DeMeo, J.: *Saharasia: The 4000 BCE Origins of Child Abuse, Sex-Repression, Warfare and Social Violence, In the Deserts of the Old World*, Revised 2nd Edition, Natural Energy Works, 2006.

DeMeo, J.: *In Defense of Wilhelm Reich: Opposing the 80-Years' War of Mainstream Defamatory Slander Against One of the 20th Century's Most Brilliant Physicians and Natural Scientists,* Natural Energy Works, Ashland 2013.

Jones, P.: *Artificers of Fraud: The Origin of Life and Scientific Deception*, Orgonomy UK,Preston 2013.

Maglione, R.: *Methods and Procedures in Biophysical Orgonometry*, Gruppo Editoriale L'Espresso, Milano, 2012.

Martin, J.: *Wilhelm Reich and the Cold War*, Natural Energy, Works, Ashland, Oregon 2014.

INFORMATION SOURCES
On Wilhelm Reich and Orgonomy
For additional listings, see: www.orgonelab.org/resources.htm

Orgone Biophysical Research Lab, *Research and Educational Center*: PO Box 1148, Ashland, Oregon 97520 USA. Websites: www.orgonelab.org www.saharasia.org
Email: info@orgonelab.org
– Publishes *Pulse of the Planet* journal, books and *Special Reports*. Public educational lectures & seminars focused on Wilhelm Reich & orgonomy. Active program of orgonomic atmospheric & environmental laboratory research.

Natural Energy Works: PO Box 1148, Ashland, Oregon 97520 USA   Email: info@naturalenergyworks.net
Website: http://www.naturalenergyworks.net
– Mail-order sales of books, products, accumulator construction supplies, research instruments, radiation detection meters.

The Wilhelm Reich Museum: PO Box 687, Rangeley, Maine 04970 USA.   Email: wreich@rangeley.org
Website: www.wilhelmreichmuseum.org
– Preserves Wilhelm Reich's home and laboratory (called Orgonon) for public viewing and tours. Publishes a *Newsletter*, and *Orgonomic Functionalism*. Sells xerox copies of various out-of-print books, journals, and pamphlets by Wilhelm Reich. Occasional seminars and symposia.

Orgonics: Website: www.orgonics.com   Email: Orgonics@aol.com
– Sells quality experimental orgone blankets, seed-chargers & full-size accumulators.

Appendix
A Dynamic and Substantive Cosmological Ether*
by James DeMeo, PhD.

Abstract: The ether-drift experiments of Dayton Miller (c.1906-1929) using a highly sensitive Michelson light-beam interferometer, demonstrated systematic positive effects. Subsequent work by Michelson-Pease-Pearson (1929), Galaev (2001-2002) and others have experimentally confirmed Miller's result, which suggests: 1) the cosmological ether is substantive with a slight mass, and may be blocked or reflected by dense material surroundings, 2) Earth-entrainment occurs, and the best detections are made at high-altitude locations. 3) Miller's computed axis of Earth's net motion of ether-drift is in close agreement with findings from diverse disciplines, including from biology and physics, regarding ether-like phenomena with similar sidereal-day and seasonal-sidereal fluctuations. Neither an intangible static, or even a tangible entrainable but stagnant ether appear reconcilable with such results. A dynamic ether acting as cosmic "prime mover" is the alternative solution, but requires the ether to have both slight mass and specific motions in space. A solution is found in the bioenergetic research of Wilhelm Reich (1934-1957) who demonstrated an energy continuum with distinct biological and meteorological properties, existing in high vacuum, interactive with matter, reflected by metals, and with self-attracting (ie., gravitational) spiral-form streaming motions. Giorgio Piccardi (c.1950-1970) and his followers also demonstrated a metal-reflectible solar-modulated energy affecting the physical chemistry of water, chemical reactions and radioactive decay rates, correlated to Earth's spiral-form motion through cosmic space. More recent research on the annual variation in "dark matter wind" also shows very similar velocity shifts associated with Earth's spiral-form motion around the moving Sun, suggesting "dark matter" is a misunderstood substitute for a dynamic and substantive cosmological ether.

---

* For more details, see J. DeMeo: *The Dynamic Ether of Cosmic Space: Correcting a Major Error in Modern Science*. Natural Energy, 2019.

Positive Ether-Drift Experiments in the 1900s

The work of Dayton Miller stands out as the most remarkable of all ether-drift experiments,[1] with clearly positive results from over 12,000 turns of a Michelson-type light-beam interferometer, with over 200,000 individual readings undertaken at different months of the year starting in 1902 with Edward Morley at Case School in Cleveland (now Case-Western Reserve University) and ending in 1926 with his Mt. Wilson experiments. Miller also undertook rigorous control experiments at Case School Physics Department, from 1922 to 1924. More than half of Miller's readings were made at Mt. Wilson in 1925-1926, with the most telling positive results. Miller's interferometer was the largest and most sensitive ever constructed, with iron cross-arms 4.3 meters across, and standing 1.5 meters high, floated in a tank of mercury for easy and smooth rotation. Four sets of mirrors were mounted on the ends of each cross-arm to reflect light beams 16 times horizontally, for a total light path of 64 meters, round-trip.[2] Miller also became convinced, during the course of his experiments and given the small (but never "null") result previously observed by Michelson-Morley (M-M),[3] of an Earth-entrainment effect which necessitated using the apparatus at higher altitudes, and only within structures where the walls at the level of the light-path were open to the air, covered only with light materials. Only canvas, glass, or light paper covers were used along the light-beam paths of Miller's interferometer, with all wood, stone or metal shielding eliminated. His Mt. Wilson experiments transpired in a special shelter constructed accordingly, at 1800m (6000') elevation, without nearby geographical obstructions.[1,2]

By comparison, the original M-M interferometer had a round-trip light path of only 22 meters [3, p.153], and the experiments were undertaken with an opaque wooden cover over the instrument, situated in the below-ground basement of one of the large stone buildings at Case School in Cleveland (~300' elevation). The published results of the widely misquoted M-M experiment reflected only six hours of data collection, over four days (July 8, 9, 11 & 12) in 1887, with a grand total of only 36 turns of their interferometer. Even so, M-M originally obtained a slight positive result, and they expressed the need for more experimental work at different times of the year to avoid "uncertainty". Miller used an interferometer with nearly 3 times the light-path sensitivity as M-M, with 333 times as many turns of the interferometer.[2]

By 1928 and from his measured interferometer results of ~10 km/sec displacement, Miller computed the Earth was moving at a speed of 208 km/sec towards an apex in the Northern Celestial Hemisphere, towards the constellation Draco, right ascension of 17 hrs (255°), declination of +68°, within 6° of the pole of the ecliptic, and 12° of the Sun's apex of rotation.[4]

Dayton Miller's Light-Beam Interferometer, *the largest and most sensitive instrument of its type ever constructed, situated inside a special hut on top of Mt. Wilson. During Miller's experiments of 1925-1926, he detected a clear ether-drift signal and published his findings widely in mainstream science journals. He was ignored by most physicists, however, who at that time were captivated by the theories of Albert Einstein, which demanded that no tangible cosmic ether, or ether-drift exist. Never refuted, Miller died largely ignored except by Michelson, who confirmed a similar ether-drift signal in separate experiments (with Pease-Pearson) atop Mt. Wilson shortly after Miller.*

Miller believed the Earth was pushing "northward" through a stationary but Earth-entrained ether in that particular direction. By 1933, for reasons discussed below, he changed his view and argued that, while his speed and axis-of-drift calculations were correct, the *direction of motion along the axis* was towards an apex in the Southern Celestial Hemisphere, towards Dorado, the swordfish, right ascension 4 hrs 54 min., declination of -70° 33' (south), in the middle of the great Magellanic Cloud and 7° from the southern pole of the ecliptic.[1, p.234]

While he was alive, Miller's work was given serious considerations, including by Einstein, who correctly understood his relativity theory was threatened.(2, p.114) Subsequent work by others, including by Michelson, generally corroborated Miller's findings. For example:

1. In the late 1920s, Michelson-Pease-Pearson[5] (M-P-P) used Michelson-type turning cross-beam interferometers; the first two of their tests, using interferometers of 22 and 32 meters round-trip light-path length, but at low altitudes, got *"no displacement of the order anticipated"*, third trial atop Mt. Wilson using a 52-meter light-path interferometer and therefore more in keeping with Miller, got a positive result, a measured displacement of "no greater than" ~20 km/sec. However, this result was dismissed by M-P-P apparently due to their *a-priori* and unwarranted rejection of a substantive and Earth-entrainable ether, which led them to expect a much larger result.

2. Kennedy-Thorndike in 1932 reported a ~24 km/sec result, but they also *a-priori* dismissed a substantive and Earth-entrained ether, prejudicially claiming their result to be "null".[6]

3. M-P-P in 1933 pursued standard "speed of light" measurements in a one-mile long partially evacuated steel tube,[7] lying flat on the ground, but even in these inhospitable conditions for detection of ether-drift they observed — but admitted only to a newspaper reporter — variations of ~20 km/sec.[8]

After the death of Michelson in 1931, and Miller in 1941, there was a near silence on the question of the ether-drift and an entrainable, substantive cosmological ether in space. The world of science followed the lead of Einstein and his relativity theory which demanded space to be free of any ether with tangible properties[9] much less of variations in light-speed.

> *"According to the general theory of relativity space is endowed with physical qualities; in this sense, therefore, an ether exists... But this ether must not be thought of as endowed with the properties characteristic of ponderable media, as composed of particles the motion of which can be followed; nor may the concept of motion be applied to it."*
> – Albert Einstein, *Meine Weltbild* [9: p.111]

By Einstein's theoretical requirements, ether-drift experiments yielding positive results were simply ignored or never mentioned, as if they had never been undertaken. Finally, in 1955, with the cooperative encouragement of Einstein, a team led by one of Miller's former students, Robert Shankland, undertook a reanalysis of Miller's ether-drift data, in what can only be called a highly prejudiced and incompetent post-mortem.[10] The overriding consideration ignored by the Shankland team was the highly structured nature of Miller's data, which for all four seasonal epochs pointed to the same set of sidereal coordinates for ether-drift — which vanished if the same data were organized by civil clock-time — demonstrating a very real cosmical influence.[4, pp.362-363] I have already discussed the severe problems in the Shankland, et al critique of Miller,[2] and so will not repeat those issues here, except to emphasize their claim to have "refuted" Miller is *bogus,* based upon biased data selection, with negative presumptions Miller had already rebutted years earlier, and misunderstandings of basic ether-drift interferometry.

By the late 1990s, Maurice Allais had also made a reinvestigation of Miller's ether-drift research, finding additional non-random patterns in the Miller data which he related to his own work on anomalous pendulum behavior during solar eclipses.[11]

The most significant development since Miller has been the experiments of Yuri Galaev of the Institute of Radiophysics and Electronics in the Ukraine. Galaev made independent measurements of ether-drift using radiofrequency[12] and optical wave bands.[13] His research not only *"confirmed Miller's results down to the details"*[14] but also allowed computation of the increase of ether-drift with altitude above the Earth's surface (calculated to be 8.6 m/sec per meter of

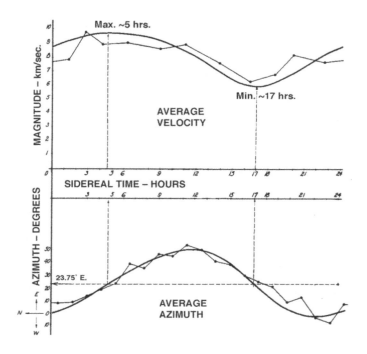

Figure 1: Average Velocity and Azimuth of Ether Drift Data, from Miller's Mt. Wilson Experiments. (1928) *Top Graph:* Average variations in observed magnitude of ether-drift from all four seasonal epochs of measurement, by Sidereal Time. Maximum ether velocity occurred at ~5 hrs sidereal and minimum at ~17 hrs sidereal. *Bottom Graph:* Average azimuthal readings by Sidereal Time, with the baseline as taken from Miller's 1933 revised seasonal averages – see Figure 2 at right.[4, p.365; 1, p.234] The averages for the four seasonal epochs together yield a mean displacement of 23.75° east of north, very close to the Earth's axial tilt of 23.5°. Coincidence?

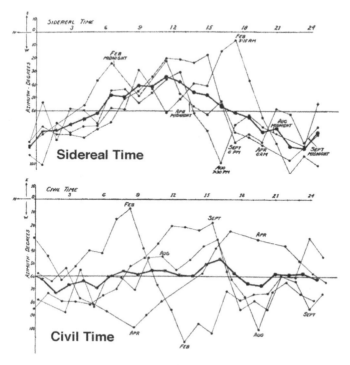

Figure 2: Sidereal Versus Civil Time Display of Ether-Drift Data, from Miller's Mt. Wilson Experiments. (1928) *Top Graph:* Miller's data organized according to sidereal time coordinates, showing an anomalous structured variation in the data. The Azimuth of the signal shifts from a maximum Easterly component at around 12 hours Sidereal and minima Westerly component 22.5 hrs Sidereal (comparable to the lower curve in Figure 1 at left). *Bottom Graph:* The same data organized by Civil Clock Time coordinates, showing no structured pattern to the data. If the signal variations were due to some diurnal factor such as solar heating, the Civil Time graph would also show the anomalous patterned structure.

altitude). Miller's own altitude-dependent results suggest the speed of the ether-drift at Mt. Wilson was ~5.14% of the estimated speed of the "ether-wind" in open space (Miller's reduction factor "k", [1, p.234-235]), though with seasonal and Sidereal-day variations, as discussed below.

These experiments are all suggestive of the older concept of the cosmological ether as a fluidic medium, a tangible "stuff" which can be entrained or slowed down as it moves close to the Earth's surface. This fundamental property of ether, which repeatedly shows up in the experimental results — of being a fluidic substantive medium with a very slight mass and thereby interacting with matter, which can be slowed by matter obstructing its path and which thereby may *impart a slight momentum to obstructing matter* — is of central importance for integrating ether-theory into modern cosmology. We may construct a model directly from these results, which do not require reference to metaphysical constructs such as relativistic curved space-time, nor to Lorentz-type contractions of our measuring rods. To do so, we must reference other researchers who, like Miller, discovered a cosmological phenomena of an "ethereal" quality, but which nevertheless had measurable substance.

Reich's Dynamic Ether-Like *Orgone*

From 1934 to 1957, Reich produced a series of experimental reports documenting the existence of a unique form of energy, called the *orgone*.[15, 16] By his determinations, orgone energy charged the tissues of living organisms and played a fundamental role in life processes. It also was determined to exist in a freely-moving dynamic form within the atmospheric ocean, and inside high-vacuum tubes. From his experiments, Reich postulated the orgone filled the vacuum of cosmic space.[17,18] The properties of Reich's orgone were remarkably similar to Miller's cosmic ether:

A) Mass-free orgone energy filled all space, much like a cosmic ether, but it was in constant *lawful* motion, with flowing or streaming motions but capable of concentrating or building up in one place, while rarifying or diminishing in another. The orgone could penetrate matter easily, but also weakly interacted with it, being attracted to and charging all matter. Metals rapidly discharged, or reflected it, allowing special metallic-dielectrical enclosures (*orgone energy accumulators*) to be constructed, which yielded anomalous stimulation of plant growth, tissue regeneration and healing effects, as well as anomalous physical effects such as spontaneous heat production, decreased rate of electroscopical discharge, and anomalous ionization effects within orgone-charged high-vacuum and Geiger tubes.[16,19,20,21,22] Nearly all of his experimental claims have been independently replicated and confirmed by other scientists.[22]

B) Based upon his observations of the Earth's *orgone energy envelope,* which rotated from West to East *faster* than Earth rotation, and the existence of a discrete energy stream moving SW to NE within the atmosphere, Reich postulated the existence of large spiraling streams of orgone in cosmic space. He noted one streaming motion along the plane of the Milky Way Galaxy (called the *Galactic Stream*), with secondary streams flowing parallel to the plane of the Solar System Ecliptic and to the Earth's equator (the *Equatorial Stream*). Reich further argued, based upon atmospheric and telescopic observations, that the cosmic energy streams would attract each other, superimpose in a spiral form and condense to create new matter out of the cosmic energy substrate.[18] Reich described these spiral waveforms, giving them the German name *Kreiselwelle* (*spinning wave* or, literally, "gyroscopic-wave"), which he believed underlay various biological, atmospheric and cosmic motions.[18,23] By Reich's theory of *Cosmic Superimposition,*[18] The rotation of planets on their axis, and the revolution of planets around their suns, and of moons around planets, were all products of giant superimposing streams of cosmic energy.

C) Reich never cited Miller's work, but he considered the older ether theory to be a "useful concept". Like Miller, he also noted orgone energy moved faster and was more active at higher altitudes, and he identified the Northern Hemisphere Spring Equinox, as well as the peak of the Solar sunspot-abundance to be times of increased orgone energy charge and activity.

Reich's findings and theory of *Cosmic Superimposition* agrees with much of acknowledged astronomy, in that moving stars and orbiting planets describe large open spiral-forms in space. However, no special emphasis is placed upon this fact, given the assumption of "empty space". Only a few textbooks make mention of it. Reich, by contrast, worked out his own special functional equations of gravitation and pendulum behavior,[25] based upon his insights on the spinning wave, and space being filled with an energy-rich substrate. His findings are highly compatible with the concept of a dynamic ether, which would also fulfill the role of being a *cosmic prime mover*, but not with the concept of a *static* or *stagnant and immobile ether*, nor even with Miller's *passive Earth-entrained ether*. Reich's universe was animated by streams of flowing and pulsing cosmic orgone energy, which moved the planets and suns along on their paths in the heavens, much as a ball floating on the water is moved forward by the water waves.[18]

The Ether: Static, Earth-Entrained, or Dynamic?

Ever since Isaac Newton, many physicists considered the ether to be a *static* or *stagnant* phenomenon, something which existed throughout the cosmos, but primarily as a *non-moving and immobilized* background medium. A static ether or "Absolute Space" was a necessity for the elder Newton, who basically eliminated all of its tangible properties save for the ability to transmit light waves.§ This was done in large measure to reconcile his mathematical *laws of motion* with his theology. Newton appeared motivated to "heal the schism" between Science and the Church, which had developed since Galileo, by *ridding the universe of any notion of cosmic prime mover, other than deity*. The ether was henceforth declared dead, static and without tangible properties (by which it might influence celestial motions), and God was rescued from the unemployment lines, his role as the source of all universal motion preserved.[24] This viewpoint is not apparent from his mathematics, but is a part of the underlying philosophy. Consequently, M-M and many others always looked for, but never detected, a static

---

§ The *young* Isaac Newton was a firm believer in the cosmic ether of space. He only dropped this belief later in life, when theological matters more decidedly occupied his time and thoughts. See *Isaac Newton's Letter to Robert Boyle, on the Cosmic Ether of Space*, here: www.orgonelab.org/newtonletter.htm

substance-less ether which would not display any properties or affects, nor be entrained as the Earth swiftly moved through it.

In fact, Miller's view diverged from the concept of a *static* ether only insofar as was necessary to explain an Earth-entrainment phenomenon, and ether-reflecting capabilities of dense matter which his empirical measurements demonstrated. Miller's ether was *stagnant*, though fluidic and with sufficient substance to become entrained at the Earth's surface. Consequently, he never accepted the preliminary results of M-M, and sought to undertake ether-drift measurements at higher altitudes and at different seasons. By 1933 he concluded the Earth was pushing through a stagnant but Earth-entrained ether, towards the constellation Dorado, near the South Pole of the Ecliptic. But this view always contained the seeds of a major contradiction.

If one assumes the ether is stationary or stagnant but has some slight mass, and therefore is a tangible "stuff" which can interact with matter, and become "entrained" along the Earth's surface, then by definition this "entrainable ether" will act as a *braking force against planetary motions over time.* And given enough time, such an entrainable but basically stagnant ether might eventually bring all cosmological motion to a standstill. In order to make the universe function, one is forced to postulate some other independent energizing force to create all cosmic motion, to oppose the "brake" of the stagnant but entrainable ether. Or, one must eliminate all the tangible properties of the ether, and render it into an abstraction. One thereby arrives back at the very same postulate of Newton: *the need for a counter-force in nature, aside from ether, to constantly refresh cosmic motion,* or at the very least to get everything started in one "big bang". One is forced to invoke some metaphysical principle, something more than ordinary gravitational forces, which appear insufficient to fully overcome the long-term "cosmological brake" of an entrainable but stagnant ether. Or, the ether must be made abstract, intangible.

A third solution, which appears to have been steadfastly avoided by Newton, Michelson, Miller, Einstein, and nearly everyone else except for Reich, is *to give the cosmological ether not only substance and tangible properties, but also dynamical properties of spiral-form motion, which reflect observed planetary motions.*

Miller's 1928 Versus 1933 Conclusions

There is an astonishing *empirical* agreement between Miller and Reich. Figure 3 gives a rough approximation of Miller's observed conclusions, which can be interpreted as Miller proposed, or as Reich proposed. The "X" marks on the globe in Figure 3 represent the interferometer at different positions throughout the day, and one can see how the ether-flow would

**Draco - Vega - Hercules
North Pole of the Ecliptic**

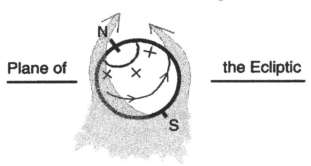

Plane of   the Ecliptic

**Dorado - Great Magellanic Cloud
South Pole of the Ecliptic**

Figure 3: Relative Motion of the Earth and Ether. Is the Earth pushing southward through a passive, stationary ether, or is the ether dynamic, similar to Reich's orgone, streaming northward in a superimposing spiral spinning-wave, and carrying the Earth-Sun system with it? The "X" marks on the Earth diagram represent Miller's interferometer cross-arms at different times of day, showing how the movement of ether would vary according to Solar-civil time, but still remain relatively constant according to galactic sidereal-day coordinates.

intersect the interferometer cross-beams at different angles as the Earth rotated.

As mentioned above, Miller's final conclusions of 1933 were that the Earth was drifting towards a point near the constellation Dorado, close to the South Pole of the Ecliptic.[1, p.234] However, his *earlier conclusion* made in 1928 from the same data, viewed the direction of motion along the *same axis of ether-drift*, but in the *opposite direction*, towards the North Pole of the Ecliptic.[4] Miller's original calculations of this northerly apex are more compatible with a dynamic theory of ether drift, where the ether flowed and moved *from Dorado generally towards the northern pole of the ecliptic (Draco)*, a movement which would carry the Sun-Earth-Moon system along with it as it moved, though only a small portion of the ether's velocity could be detected (~10 km/sec) due to Earth-entrainment. The interferometer alone, as he noted, could determine *"...the line in which the motion of the Earth with respect to the ether takes place, but does not determine the direction of motion in this line."*[1, p.231]

Today, the accepted direction of the Sun's local movement is towards Vega, in the constellation Lyra, which lies in the middle of a small triangle created by the constellations Draco, Hercules and Cygnus. All these constellations are reasonably close to the northern pole of the ecliptic, and to Miller's northern polar axis of ether-drift. They all are found close to the plane of the Milky Way, as if the Solar System is spiraling merrily along, caught in one of the giant sweeping energetic motions of one of the Galactic arm bands. Figures 3 and 4 show these relationships, to which the following structure and patterns can be added.

Miller's data provides velocity calculations which show both hourly variations by sidereal time, and also seasonal variations according to the four monthly epochs of his Mt. Wilson experiments. They are as follows:

<u>Sidereal Hour Variations: Miller 1928 (see Fig.1, Top)</u>
Maximum velocity ~10 km/sec at 5 hrs sidereal
Minimum velocity ~6-7 km/sec at 17 hrs sidereal

The *Sidereal Hour Variations* in ether-drift velocity are most easily explained as being due to the shielding effects of the Earth's mass upon the interferometer at 17 hrs, and the alignment of the interferometer for maximal detection of ether-drift at 5 hrs. One may get a rough approximation of this from Figure 3, where the "X" indicating the interferometer on the far left-side of the Earth diagram is fully exposed to ether-wind, while the "X" on the far right-side is largely shielded by the mass of the Earth. In fact, Miller's measured velocity *and azimuthal* variances over the Sidereal Day follows such a pattern.[25, p.142-143]

Seasonal Variations:	Miller 1933 [1, p.235]
15 September	9.6 km/sec
2 December — calculated velocity minima	
8 February	9.3 km/sec
1 April	10.1 km/sec
2 June — calculated velocity maxima	
1 August	11.2 km/sec

The *Seasonal Variations* in ether-drift velocities are also easily understood as the consequence of the combined motion of the Earth around the Sun, and the Sun's translational motion through the Galaxy. Figures 4 and 5 are derived from a combination of Miller's and Reich's cosmological ideas, in accordance with known astronomy. From April through August, the Earth moves quite a large distance through the heavens, while in December and January, the Earth moves through only a relatively small distance of space. The Figure 4 distances for B-C-D from March 21st through September 21st, for example, are approximately twice those for D-A-B, which cover the period from September 21st through March 21st. There is a period when the Earth accelerates to maximum speed, starting around the time of the Spring Equinox (B towards C) followed by deceleration (C towards D) where the Earth then enters a region where it moves relatively slowly in relationship to the background of space (D-A-B). With the cycle completed, there is rapid acceleration the next March. It gives the impression of a strong energetic wave or pulse, which imparts momentum to the Earth, *accelerating it towards the Galactic Center in the months immediately after March,* and then decelerating when the Earth retreats away from the Galactic Center after September. Similar changes in velocity affect all the other planets.

Reich noted this variation in Earth-speed as well as the 62° angular relationship between the rotating Galactic Plane, and the Earth's Equatorial Plane.[18,25] In a similar fashion, the Plane of the Ecliptic is also inclined to the Sun's path towards Vega by ~60°. And a similar set of angular relationships exist in Miller's ether-drift measurements, which "...*oscillated back and forth through an angle of about 60°...*".[4, p.357] Miller and Reich both emphasized similar translational movements of Earth through cosmic space, as demanded by their respective findings.

Piccardi's Biometeorology and "Dark Matter"

A similar set of observations were made by the Italian chemist, Giorgio Piccardi[26] in cosmic influences upon laboratory phase-change experiments under constant environmental conditions (such as the precipitation of bismuth chloride from solution, or the freezing of supercooled water). Piccardi eventually concluded the helicoidal movement of the Earth around the Sun was the determinant which imparted the anomalous seasonal variations in his experiments, peaking in the Northern Hemisphere Spring-Summer period. Piccardi's anomalous cosmic factor could be influenced by metal enclosures very similar to Reich' orgone energy accumulators or Miller's ether-shielding, and expressed itself globally. That is, the phenomenon affected simultaneous experiments in both the Northern and Southern Hemispheres in an identical manner, indicating the phenomenon affected the entire Earth all at once, and was not related to seasonal environmental factors, such as temperature or humidity. He noted:

> "*If space were empty, empty of fields of matter and inactive, a consideration of this type would be of no importance. But today, we know instead that both matter and fields exist in space.*"[26, pp.97-98]

In a similar manner, the biologist Frank Brown working at Wood's Hole Institute in Massachusetts noted cosmic sidereal-day and seasonal variations in the biological clock of a variety of creatures maintained under constant environmental condi-

Planetary Spiral Motions and Miller's Ether-Drift

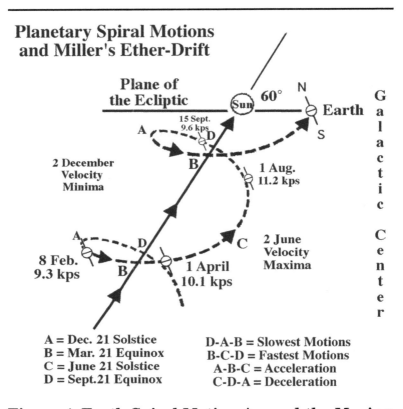

A = Dec. 21 Solstice
B = Mar. 21 Equinox
C = June 21 Solstice
D = Sept.21 Equinox

D-A-B = Slowest Motions
B-C-D = Fastest Motions
A-B-C = Acceleration
C-D-A = Deceleration

Figure 4: Earth Spiral Motion Around the Moving Sun. The Earth moves a greater distance during the period March-September (B-C and C-D) than during the period September-March (D-A and A-B). This acceleration and deceleration over the course of the year appears related to the motion towards or away from the Galactic Center. The graphic includes the measured season variations in ether-drift velocities from Miller's Mt. Wilson experiments, which are in keeping with this spiral-form model. Note: these only reflect measurements at the interferometer, and due to Earth-entrainment should *not be confused with the net speed of the ether-wind or of the Earth itself through open space.*[25]

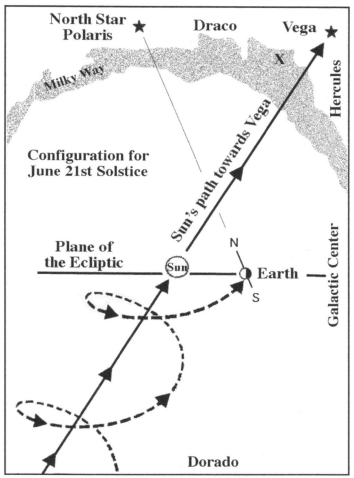

Figure 5: Spiral Motion of Sun-Earth System The Earth (shown here in summer solstice position) moves around the Sun in a spiral, while the Sun moves towards Vega. The constellation Draco marks the approximate location of the northern pole of the Plane of the Ecliptic, which is within around 7° of the north pole of Miller's computed axis of ether-drift (at the "X"). The Plane of the Ecliptic is inclined with the Sun's path by around 60°, giving rise to seasonal variations in the Earth's speed of motion.[25]

tions, most of which are in keeping with the cosmological model presented here.[27] There is a rich interdisciplinary literature documenting similar anomalous sidereal-day and seasonal-cycle variations, suggestive of cosmic ether-influences.[19]

Finally, we may reconsider the many recently measured seasonal variations in "Dark Matter Wind",[28] which are acknowledged as being the consequence of the Earth's spiral-form motion through the cosmos, though without any reference to ether-drift. When combined with the 30 km/sec velocity of the Earth around the Sun, and the 232 km/sec velocity of the Solar System through space, there is a postulated "dark matter wind" velocity maximum on 2 June and velocity minima on 2 December, very much as diagrammed above in *Figures 4, 5 and 6*. "Dark matter" has always remained an elusive entity, suggested by virtue of gravitational anomalies indicating a very slight mass within open space, but essentially transparent to light-waves except as seen in galactic haloes. I suggest, "dark matter" — now shown to have a peak "wind velocity" in agree-

Figure 6: Piccardi's Animated Model of the Helicoidal Motion of the Earth Around the Sun, as presented at the Brussels World-Fair in 1958.[26, p.98] The Earth moves faster through the cosmos in June than during December.

ment with the cosmological ether-motions as determined from the integration of Miller, Reich and Piccardi — is nothing more than the *substantive and dynamic ether of space.*

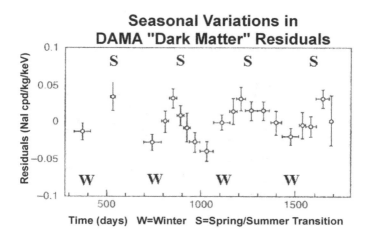

Figure 7: Annual Variations (N. Hem.) in "Dark Matter Wind", from the DAMA Project in Italy (after Bernabei) [28] The cosmic wind, be it ether, dark-matter, or orgone energy, increases in June as the Earth's velocity reaches its maximum, and then declines towards a December minima.

Citations to Ether-Drift Paper

[1] D. Miller, *Rev. Modern Physics,* Vol.5(2), p.203-242, July 1933.
[2] J. DeMeo "Dayton Miller's Ether-Drift Research: A Fresh Look", *Pulse of the Planet,* 5, p.114-130, 2002. http://www.orgonelab.org/miller.htm
[3] A.A. Michelson & E. Morley, *Am. J. Sci.,* 3rd Ser., Vol.XXXIV (203), Nov. 1887.
[4] D. Miller, *Astrophys. J.,* LXVIII (5), p.341-402, Dec. 1928.

[5] A.A. Michelson, F.G. Pease, F. Pearson, "Repetition of the Michelson-Morley Experiment", *Nature*, 123:88, 19 Jan. 1929; also in J. Optical Soc. Am., 18:181, 1929.

[6] J. Kennedy, E.M. Thorndike, *Phys. Rev.* 42 400-418, 1932.

[7] A.A. Michelson, F.G. Pease, F. Pearson, "Measurement of the Velocity of Light in a Partial Vacuum", *Astrophysical J.*, 82:26-61, 1935.

[8] D. Deitz, "Case's Miller Seen Hero of 'Revolution'. New Revelations on Speed of Light Hint Change in Einstein Theory", *Cleveland Press*, 30 Dec. 1933.

[9] A. Einstein, "Relativity and the Ether", *Essays in Science*, 1934, (translated from the German, c.1928?, published in *Meine Weltbilt*, 1933.)

[10] R.S. Shankland, et al., "New Analysis of the Interferometer Observations of Dayton C. Miller", *Rev. Modern Physics*, 27(2):167-178, April 1955.

[11] M. Allais, *L'Anisotropie de L'Espace*, Clément Juglar, Paris, 1997.

[12] Y.M. Galaev, "Ethereal Wind in Experience of Millimetric Radiowaves Propagation", *Spacetime and Substance*, V.2, No.5 (10), 2000, p.211-225. http://www.spacetime.narod.ru/0010-pdf.zip

[13] Y.M. Galaev, "The Measuring of Ether-Drift Velocity and Kinematic Ether Viscosity Within Optical Waves Band", *Spacetime and Substance*, Vol.3, No.5 (15), 2002, p.207-224. http://www.spacetime.narod.ru/0015-pdf.zip

[14] Y.M. Galaev, personal communication to author, 6 April 2004.

[15] W. Reich, *Discovery of the Orgone, Vol.1: Function of the Orgasm*, Farrar, Straus & Giroux, NY, 1973 (reprinted from 1942).

[16] W. Reich, *Discovery of the Orgone, Vol.2: The Cancer Biopathy*, Farrar, Straus & Giroux, NY, 1973 (reprinted from 1948)..

[17] W. Reich, *Ether, God & Devil*, Farrar, Straus & Giroux, NY, 1973 (reprinted from 1951).

[18] W. Reich, *Cosmic Superimposition*, Farrar, Straus & Giroux, NY, 1973 (reprinted from 1951).

[19] J. DeMeo, *"Evidence for... a Principle of Atmospheric Continuity"*, in Press.

[20] J. DeMeo (editor) *Heretic's Notebook*, Natural Energy, 2002.

[21] W. Reich, *The Oranur Experiment*, Wilhelm Reich Foundation, Rangeley, ME, 1951.

[22] The online *Bibliography on Orgonomy* has hundreds of citations organized for keyword search: http://www.orgonelab.org/bibliog.htm

[23] W. Reich, *Contact With Space*, Farrar, Straus & Giroux, NY, 1957, pp.95-110.

[24] L. Stecchini, "The Inconstant Heavens", in *The Velikovsky Affair: Warfare of Science and Scientism*, A. deGrazia, Ed., University Books, 1966.

[25] J. DeMeo, "Reconciling Miller's Ether-Drift With Reich's Dynamic Orgone", *Pulse of the Planet,* 5:137-146, 2002. http://www.orgonelab.org/MillerReich.htm

[26] G. Piccardi, *Chemical Basis of Medical Climatology,* Charles Thomas, Springfield, 1962.

[27] F. Brown, "Evidence for External Timing of Biological Clocks" in *An Introduction to Biological Rhythms*, J. Palmer (Ed.), Academic Press, NY 1975.

[28] R. Bernabei, "DAMA Experiment: Status and Reports", Sept. 2003 & R. Bernabei, "DAMA/NaI results", Feb. 2004.
http://people.roma2.infn.it/~dama/bernabei_alushta_dama.pdf
http://people.roma2.infn.it/~dama/belli_noon04.pdf
http://www.lngs.infn.it/lngs/htexts/dama/

For more information on the subject of cosmic ether, see James DeMeo's latest book: *The Dynamic Ether of Cosmic Space: Correcting a Major Error in Modern Science*. Natural Energy, 2019.

INDEX

About the Author

James DeMeo, PhD is Director of the Orgone Biophysical Research Lab (OBRL), which he founded in 1978. He received his doctorate in Geography from the University of Kansas, where his research corroborated various aspects of Wilhelm Reich's social and biophysical discoveries. He also studied environmental science and chemistry at Florida International University and Florida Atlantic University. Dr. DeMeo was formerly on the faculty of Geography at Illinois State University and the University of Miami. His interdisciplinary research ranges across social/cultural and biophysical subjects such as: Cross-cultural, historical studies on the effects of drought and desertification on the origins of warfare and social violence, laboratory experiments on cosmic cycles and life-energy subjects, and field research and applications of the Wilhelm Reich cloudbuster for drought-abatement and greening of drylands. He has published over 100 journal articles and book-chapters on the issues of energy resources, health, cultural history, environmental problems, and experimental orgone biophysics. He is author of several books including the popular *Orgone Accumulator Handbook*, *Saharasia, The 4000 BCE Origins of Child-Abuse, Sex-Repression, Warfare and Social Violence, In the Deserts of the Old World*, and *The Dynamic Ether of Cosmic Space: Correcting a Major Error in Modern Science*. He is also Editor of *Heretic's Notebook*, and *On Wilhelm Reich and Orgonomy*, and Co-Editor of the German-language work *Nach Reich: Neue Forschungen Zur Orgonomie*. Dr. DeMeo today lives in the mountains of the Southern Oregon Siskiyou Range, where he maintains OBRL as a private high-altitude research laboratory and educational facility.

Additional Publications Available from Natural Energy Works

www.naturalenergyworks.net

The Dynamic Ether of Cosmic Space: Correcting a Major Error in Modern Science,
by James DeMeo

Spiraling, Material,
Motional,
Life-Energetic
Evidence Suppressed,
Misrepresented, Forbidden

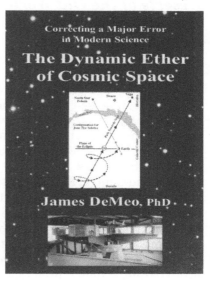

The Cosmic Ether Changes
Everything!

The historical ether-drift experiments of Michelson-Morley, Dayton Miller and others yielded positive results for an ether wind and light-speed variation of 5 to 18 kilometers per second. Academic bias and erasure has misrepresented these facts for over 120 years, to the point that few dare question today. Scientist James DeMeo reviews the original documents and archives, exposing the facts which demolish nearly all of the post-ether astrophysical theories, including Einstein's relativity, the "big bang", "black holes" and quantum magic. Cosmic ether exists and moves in a creative gravitational spiral vortex, as the long-sought prime mover and life-energy. A must-read item for the professional scientist, educated layperson and student, in ordinary language with minimal maths.

SAHARASIA: The 4000 BCE Origins of Child-Abuse, Sex-Repression, Warfare and Social Violence, In the Deserts of the Old World, Revised & Updated 2nd Edition by James DeMeo, PhD

Dr. DeMeo's *magnum opus* on the origins of human violence and biophysical armoring, the first geographical, cross-cultural study of human behavior around the world, using Wilhelm Reich's sex-economic discoveries as a basic starting point, presenting world maps of different behaviors and social institutions. Source-regions (Arabia and Central Asia) for patriarchal authoritarian culture were identified, and migratory-diffusion patterns were traced, back in time, to pinpoint where and how the human tragedy began. Solves the riddle of the origins of human violence and armoring. A breakthrough in the scientific study of human sexuality, psychology and anthropology, and must-reading for every parent, student, professor and clinical worker in the field of human health and behavior. 464 pages, with over 100 maps, photos, and illustrations. A new Appendix document included, "Update on Saharasia". Large format with vivid full-color cover, extensive citations and bibliography and index.

In Defense of Wilhelm Reich: Opposing the 80-Years' War of Mainstream Defamatory Slander Against One of the 20th Century's Most Brilliant Physicians and Natural Scientists,
by James DeMeo, PhD.

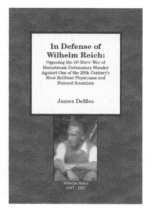

Dr. Wilhelm Reich is the man whom nearly everyone loves to hate. No other figure in 20th Century science and medicine could be named who has been so badly maligned in popular media, scientific and medical circles, nor so shabbily mistreated by power-drunk federal agencies and arrogant judges.

Publicly denounced and slandered in both Europe and America by Nazis, Communists and psychoanalysts, placed on both Hitler's and Stalin's death lists but narrowly escaping to the USA, subjected to new public slanders and attacks by American journalists and psychiatrists who deliberately lied and provoked an "investigation" by the US Food and Drug Administration (FDA), imprisoned by American courts which ignored his legal writs and pleas about prosecutorial and FDA fraud, denied appeals all the way up to the US Supreme Court, which rubber-stamped the FDA's demands for the *banning and burning of his scientific books and research journals,* and finally dying alone in prison – who was this man, Wilhelm Reich, and why today, some 50 years after his death, does he continue to stir up such emotional antipathy? It is a literal *80-Years' War* of continuing misrepresentation, slander and defamation.

Who were and are Reich's attackers? Author and Natural Scientist James DeMeo takes on the book-burners, exposing with clarity and documentation their many slanderous fabrications, half-truths and lies of omission. In so doing, he also summarizes the lesser-known facts about Reich's important clinical and life-energetic experimental findings, now verified by scientists and physicians worldwide, and holding great promise for the future. 269 pages, illustrated, fully cited, index.

Heretic's Notebook: Emotions, Protocells, Ether-Drift and Cosmic Life-Energy, with New Research Supporting Wilhelm Reich, Edited by James DeMeo, PhD

Contains 28 insightful essays and research articles by 17 different authors, on natural childbirth, sexuality, archaeology of early human violence, Reich's orgonomic functionalism, exposés on Reich's detractors, Giordano Bruno's work, bion-biogenesis research, Dayton Miller's ether-drift discoveries, emotional effects in REG (psychokinesis) experiments, new detector for orgone energy, dowsing research, cloudbusting desert-greening experiments in Africa, plant growth stimulation in the orgone accumulator, the orgone energy motor and "free energy", plus UFO research, book reviews, and much more, with color cover photos, text-photos and illustrations.

272 pages, illustrated, fully cited throughout.

*Wilhelm Reich
and The Cold War:
The True Story of How a
Communist Spy Team,
Government Hoodlums and
Sick Psychiatrists
Destroyed Sexual Science
and Cosmic Life Energy
Discoveries.*
by James Edward Martin
Revised and Updated 2nd Edition.

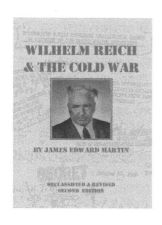

Author and researcher James Edward Martin took on the subject of the controversial psychoanalytic pioneer and natural scientist, Wilhelm Reich, expecting to disprove Reich's suspicions that his detractors were predominantly communists and even Soviet spies. Instead, his research forced him to conclude that Reich was correct in his assertions that the communists were behind the attacks against him, which ultimately led to his incarceration and death in prison, and the burning of his books. Martin's investigations on this and related controversies, including the subject of Reich's research on low-level radiation and rain-making experiments in the deserts near Tucson, Arizona, are detailed, citing interviews with key witnesses to the events of that period, and original sources from private and university archives, including Freedom of Information Act searches of FBI, FDA and CIA files on Reich's detractors. *Wilhelm Reich and the Cold War* is essential reading for anyone who wants the facts about Reich's early flirtation with European Marxism and later anti-Communist sentiments during the period of his persecution and death in the USA. 426 pages, illustrations, fully cited with bibliography, index.

The History of Modern Morals,

By Max Hodann, a central participant in the European Weimar-era sexual reform movement. With a New Introduction by James DeMeo, PhD.

European Emperors, Kings, Kaisers and Tsars, and their Churches, forbade contraception, women's equality and divorce. Baptismal Certificates and class barriers dictated who could legally marry, attend school or the university, advance socially, and who could not. World War I finally swept them from power, but their dictates frequently remained as law, in a turbulent era of struggle for freedom and democracy, versus resurgent fascism and slavery.

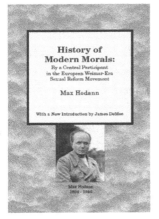

Hodann's *History* contains a clear discussion of these historical developments within the sexual reform and women's rights movements of Weimar Germany and Europe generally, in the early decades of the 1900s. The parallel advance of scientific knowledge on human sexuality is also detailed. Unlike many contemporary works on these subjects, *History of Modern Morals* is authored by a physician who lived the struggle, was a leader in it, got arrested by the Nazis for it, and intimately worked with other professionals who also had personally suffered for their work in the same social-sexual reform movement. His writings are therefore filled with a strong passion and vitality, and with many personal observations, anecdotes, and clarifying information not found elsewhere.

Hodann's *History* is also unique in that he frequently and positively discusses the work of his contemporary and associate, Wilhelm Reich. This is especially important given their life-positive emphasis upon love and emotion in sexuality, and their distinction between natural-healthy *heterosexual genitality* versus neurotic and unhealthy sexual expressions. In the modern era of "politically correct" moral equivalence, this essential distinction has been diminished or erased from public discussion. 364 pages, fully cited, index.

The Orgone Accumulator Handbook